The Death Ride

THE DEATH RIDE

A NOVEL

To Garry
Connect Globette!, 2009

Bo Crane

Bo Crane

To order additional copies of this book, contact:
Xlibris Corporation
1-888-795-4274
www.Xlibris.com
Orders@Xlibris.com
59905

Contents

PART 1 Portola Valley

PART 2 The Death Ride

*"And I saw, and behold a pale horse,
and its rider's name was Death."*

Revelations 6.8

*

Dedicated to Karl Van Deinse, who introduced the author to the Death Ride, 1989.

*

Special thank you to my wife, Kristen, who undertook the Death Ride ordeal in 1992 and 1993, then married me anyway in 1994.

*

Final word of appreciation to Steely Bill Sorich for his inspirational encouragement.

CHARACTERS

Dennis Crowe. Woodworker living on Pomponio Ridge Road with wife Ophelia Harrison, artist.

Carlos Cordova. Born in Spain, living in Cupertino, divorced from wife Gertrude, with three daughters, owns a Home Security Wiring business.

Bert Leunberger. Psychoanalyst, divorced, living in East Palo Alto, adult son and daughter.

Erik Erikksson. Gynecologist, born in Iceland, married to Irina, structural engineer, two sons.

Boston Reed. Civil Engineer, married to Katherine Kirk, architectural designer, living in Palo Alto, one daughter, formerly married to Shannon, living now in Stockton.

Caitlin Carter. San Jose State associate art professor, living in Palo Alto, young daughter Mandy living with her father.

Bethy Kono. Psychoanalyst, married to Henry, living in Palo Alto.

Raymond and Lina Delzio, married, Stanford professor and soils engineer, living in Belmont, one son Zack.

OREGON

NEVADA

LAKE
TAHOE

MARKLEEVILLE

SACRAMENTO

SAN
FRANCISCO

CALIFORNIA

LOS ANGELES

MEXICO

MARKLEEVILLE,
CALIFORNIA near NEVADA stateline

PART 1
Portola Valley

Saturday November 4, 1769, soldiers in service to Spain under the command of Don Gaspar de Portola, Captain of the Spanish Dragoons Regiment, ascended a ridge east of present day Pacifica in hopes of being able to spot a port called San Francisco, north of the present day city named during the previous century by a Spanish sea captain, Sebastian Ceremeño as the location of his shipwreck. Portola's expedition members were sick, tired and hungry. No other people of European ancestry were within 600 miles.

According to the diary of Miguel Costanso: "divisamos el grandioso estero" or "we saw a most grand estuary," which was San Francisco Bay. Worn out, the expedition didn't know where or how the estuary connected to the ocean they had been tracking since leaving San Diego on July 14, but they were ready to explore the peninsula. Hiking downhill, they headed south through a rounded valley which five years later would be named the Cañada de San Andreas, camping at a small pond that today is known as a sag pond, formed where constant earthquake activity both depresses the soil and churns it into impermeable clay.

The next night was spent on the banks of "un arroio de buena agua," or "a creek of good water," now covered by Crystal Springs Reservoir. The following day they reached an "arroio hondo"or "deep creek," also named five years later as the Arroyo de San Francisquito, the "Little Creek of St. Francis." At this creek was a tall redwood tree, washed downstream from the forests to the west. The "palo alto" or "tall stick-like tree" became both the symbol and name of the future adjacent tract, later incorporated into a city.

Rather than venture farther into unknown territory, they turned back north, camping in a long narrow valley, called a cañada, on November 11 near what is now the Pulgas Water Temple on Cañada Road. After spending the next night back at the sag pond, the expedition returned to Pacifica and began the *long journey back, stopping at "un arroio hondo de buen agua," or a "deep creek of good water," later named Tunitas Creek, before reaching San Diego on January 24.*

The cañada traveled by the 1769 expedition became known as Portola's Valley. The redwood trees were most abundant at the southern end of the cañada, which was called the "corte madera," the 'woodcutting area," later identified on a Mexican land grant given to Maximo Martinez. As the northern watershed of the large cañada with its three creeks was acquired by San Francisco, the name of Portola Valley was reduced to a small area of the redwoods to the south and later became the name of town incorporated in 1964.

Portola Valley is traversed by a road biking route known as the Loop. A biking destination in itself, the Loop also serves offshoot roads that lead to the westward ridgecrest of the Sierra Morena Mountains and the rugged Pacific Ocean coast beyond.

The variety of bicycling routes, the ambience of the redwood forest, and the scenic diversity provided by the coast, the shores of San Francisco Bay, several surrounding mountains and the lengthy cañada, plus the generally year-round good climate all make Portola Valley a road biking paradise where motivated bicyclists can readily accumulate two-hundred to five-hundred miles per month, thereby establishing a strong base for tackling long and difficult one-day organized rides, the most extreme of which takes place annually in the indomitable Sierra Nevada mountains, quietly lying in wait to the east, known by the chilling sobriquet "The Death Ride."

Chapter 1

Devils Canyon

Seventeen Devils Canyons are in California, including one in the Santa Cruz Mountains, west of Skyline Ridge, south of Alpine Road, named on the 1863 California Geological Survey Map. Canyons receiving such names are usually rugged and inhospitable places. The canyon off Skyline is such a place, thick with growth bounded by steep slabs of rock forming cliffs that provides updrafts for golden eagles and turkey buzzards alike.

Broken hunks of rock also create small shelters and caves as well as provide waterfall steps for the creek that rushes through the canyon in winter. The nearby long ridge was fully logged in the 1800s and the logging roads became the conduits for isolated properties, occupied by individuals as hearty as the surrounding terrain.

October ride, part 1

Dennis Crowe stood on the balcony of his making staring out over the Santa Cruz Mountains as if he were Ahab looking for the white whale. The nearby trees fell away to a forest which itself descended into valleys peeling off to the ocean's horizon to the west, a thin blue line barely visible. It was all he ever really wanted: this view, his own house and workshop, and Ophelia Harrison, his wife, or rather, his woman because they weren't ever married but had lived together six years on Pomponio Ridge, an isolated road on the ocean side of the range which divided the Pacific Ocean and San Francisco Bay.

Captain of his world, self-employed, he could work when he felt like it, smoke dope, go naked, piss on his driveway, basically do whatever he wanted. His property had solar power, well water and a potbelly stove. Outside of the

13

scratchy phone and a need to fill up his delivery truck, he was pretty much cut off from the world's tentacles, and he'd the first to say so. All he owed society was to be good to his woman, pay his taxes and obey the traffic laws. None of those three items came particularly easy to him and they all made him wince.

The rip-roaring motorcyclists on near-by Skyline Boulevard bugged the hell out of him but it was those bicyclists that got his goat. He couldn't figure out why they persisted in wasting time pedaling their sorry butts around, clinging to that little ribbon of pavement edge while real adults drove by in automobiles for which highways were made in the first place.

The road and the few isolated homes on it bordered Devils Canyon, which once was the hideout for a renegade mission Indian. "Pomponio's crime," Crowe would tell guests to his enclave, "was being too Indian for the whites. He was shot for stealing horses but the Indians didn't know what stealing was because they never owned anything to steal. Nobody owned the damn deer so why should the lazy ass priests own horses? They never fed them. The Indians cared for the horses, made the adobe bricks, cut the logs for the roof, worked the fields and grew the crops. And for what? The priests wouldn't let them even fuck. They put the girls in separate dormitories. It's amazing more Indians didn't have the balls that Pomponio did. Why didn't more do something against the system shoved down their throats? They'd been happily doing their own thing for hundreds of years."

Once he got going, Ophelia would have to start easing him down. "Dennis," she would tell him, "you can't win with politics."

"We're getting in such a goddamn hole that one day we're all going to get a knock on the door from some Beijing cocksucker saying how he now owns our land, and it's going to be just like what the Spanish sons-of-bitches did to the Indians."

But eventually Ophelia would always divert him off topic. She'd tell startled company that it was a good thing they lived where they did on the edge of the canyon, isolated from the Bay Area and the metropolitan millions close by. "Ask our neighbors who the real devil of Devils Canyon is and they'll tell you it's Dennis."

He didn't disagree. Last year, he had come close to losing it all. Gazing out over his deck, he was well aware how easily it could all slip away. He used to have a separate rant for bicyclists. That was until the deer came through his windshield last year. He was aware that without Ophelia, he might have lost his mind over it. Finding her was total circumstance. He had met her six years ago in Oakland at a café while listening to live jazz.

In the foreground seen from the balcony, she rose from the lounge and eased into in a narrow pool he had built eight years ago on the edge of the ravine. Nature began at the ravine, above which he had hacked back the coastal forest to carve out a lap pool where now Ophelia stood, stark-naked to the world, a fifty-two-year old black woman, as stout as a linebacker with long strands of black hair held by a scrunchie and draped to her lower back.

When he first met Ophelia, he had been stoned. Through his haze, he saw this gorgeous person in her mid-forties digging the music. An empty chair was all the invitation he needed. When they both stood after a break, she was all of five-eleven to his six-two. Since then, she would jokingly tell him and their friends that she'd been taken in by false advertising, seeing this mellow, graying white guy in an otherwise all black club. It wasn't an hour until he even spoke to her, but since then had never shut up. She loved him, loved where he brought her to stay.

Twenty-five years ago he had purchased a lot off Pomponio Ridge Road for peanuts and had slowly built his own carpentry shop and attached house while still working for wages as a carpenter in the Santa Clara Valley. His specialty eventually became high-priced doors, but also cabinets and railings as well as wood sculptures and carvings. He ran his shop off electricity generated on property, initially by wind-power but later by photovoltaic. Independent and a bachelor, he made time for work when he wanted and women when he needed. All he required was a stormy night, wind howling, trees dancing, a little homegrown and romance was easily kindled. Most women couldn't find their way back to his place if they wanted to and, if they could remember, the narrow one-lane road with slippery curves pasted on the canyon walls was pretty intimidating. He called his home the Crowe's Nest, naturally.

A painter, Ophelia also taught art at Skyline Community College. Dennis built her a studio behind his wood shop. She loved living on the ridge, so different from her Oakland neighborhood.

Before entering the water, she looked up and saw him watching her from the second-story deck attached to their house above his woodshop. He was smiling at her and she smiled back. They never wore swimsuits. Each was an artist of different disciplines; neither desired to live in an urban environment but they were happy to have one close by and able to afford their products.

She was pleased to have gotten in the swim before their guests arrived. Dennis had invited his favorite architect up to their place around noon and who had asked on behalf of her husband if he could bike to their place with his friends. A year ago Dennis would have had no use for bicyclists. That was before the deer crashed the windshield.

They also didn't talk about Katherine, the architect who sent plenty of work Dennis' way. Ophelia was sure that her husband had canoodled her back before Ophelia had met him. What she was not sure about was if he still was slicing off a piece every now and then. But she thought probably not, seeing how well they seemed to get along together on the phone. She'd only met Katherine in person a couple of times and had never met her husband, Boston, the road biker. Ophelia figured once she met Boston, she would know for sure if the woman was doing Dennis.

Chapter 2

Pomponio Ridge

Lupugeyun was a mission Indian who lived at Mission Dolores in San Francisco, where he was given the name Pomponio after a sixth century Italian bishop. Tired of the padres' continual punishments, he bolted, organized other bands of outlaw Indians into stealing horses and committing other crimes from San Rafael to Santa Cruz.

One of his hideouts was a cave in the upstream hills of what is now Pomponio Creek. Other caves were in Devils Canyon, located along the crest of the Santa Cruz Mountains. Homesites have been cleared on the long ridge served by Pomponio Ridge Road.

Having broken free of Spain in 1822, the new country Mexico's government was not pleased with the Spanish mission system and its treatment of native peoples. In 1824, Pomponio was captured in Marin County, taken as prisoner to the territorial government seat in Monterey and shot. In 1834, the government finally ordered the missions closed and the lands distributed.

October ride, part 2

Dennis Crowe heard the bicycles first, rolling through his finely graveled-topped driveway on the other side of the house, below the second floor deck where he was standing. There were four of them, whom he had never met including Boston Reed, husband of his favorite architect and former lover, Katherine Kirk.

"Welcome, welcome," he called down to the small group. They all looked about the same age, somewhere in their forties, all wearing helmets and dark sunglasses. "You guys are welcome to cool off in the pool. I'll be right down."

16

The riders rode across the lot toward the pool, shaded by an overhead trellis. They did not see Ophelia in the water, resting against the far side while they leaned their bikes up against the garage shed and kicked off their bike shoes. Starting to take off his jersey, one of the men approached the pool, suddenly halting at the sight of the naked woman, mostly underwater, watching them. "Oh, hi," he said nervously. "I'm Boston, Katherine's husband." Ophelia introduced herself in return.

From behind, Dennis came striding up to pool. "Honey, aren't you going to get up and greet these boys?" he offered with a smile, shaking hands with each of them.

"I think I'll just stay right here," Ophelia responded when the hand shaking was over. You boys can just jump on in." What she saw was four men, all somewhere in their forties, sweaty, watching her with various degrees of embarrassment.

"Guess I'll leave my bike shorts on," smiled Boston.

"Hell no," Dennis said, then added, "Well, actually it's up to my wife."

"Except we're not married," she corrected, then repeated Dennis' offer for them to take a dip. "Hell no. Don't worry about it," she laughed. "Nobody owns any swimsuits around here."

"Not too many people can bike up Pomponio Ridge Road," Dennis stated. "You guys make it without walking? I couldn't do it but you guys look like dedicated bikers. I'm just a dedicated wood-butcher. Go hop in the water. You've earned it."

Ophelia eyed the group, wondering who was going to get in the water with her? Boston hesitated for moment with his bike shorts. "We usually don't go swimming on our rides," he said, then quickly slipped naked into the pool. He's the leader, Ophelia figured, and he's not afraid, or maybe too dumb to be afraid. Twenty-five years ago, she laughed to herself, it might have been different. Two of the other men also stripped down and got in the water. That impressed Ophelia, but then she remembered that this group must have thought nothing of biking alongside highways so why should they be concerned about a middle-aged woman in a hot tub?

"Damn," said Ophelia looking the paler of the two. "You've to be the whitest white I've ever seen."

"You're even whiter than my Slavic ass," Dennis joined, sitting down in the chair.

"Erik's Icelandic," Boston said.

"We moved to America when I was two," Erik clarified, stepping down the short ladder into the pool.

"Erik the White," the tallest, oldest one said, moving through the four-foot deep water.

"You don't have that much of a tan yourself," Ophelia said.

"All those centuries of living in the Black Forest," the tall one replied.

"That's what I call Ophelia's privates," Dennis added.

"Watch it," Ophelia mock-frowned, bottom lip curling out in a slight smile.

Dennis grinned at her. "Sorry my fraulein," he offered, then turned to the tall man. "Are you a German?"

"I'm a Leunberger," he replied, "from Cedar Rapids, Iowa."

"At least the German's got a farmer's tan," said Dennis, commenting on the Iowan's brown arms and neck. "The Icelander is nothing but white." Then he turned to the fourth biker. "Aren't you getting in the pool?"

"It's ok," the fourth rider said.

"That's Carlos," said Boston. "He's old school Europe."

"Don't mind my old lady," said Dennis. "Nobody ever wears a swimsuit around here."

"You're wasting your breath ever trying to talk him into anything," Boston said. "Either he's going to do it or he's not."

"Well, if it's me he's worried about, hell, I'm ready to get out," Ophelia announced. Standing straight up, she rose out of the water and waded past the three men, pulling herself up by the short ladder. "You hop in there, Carlos. I'll go fix you men something to eat." With that, she picked a towel off the chair, gave herself a quick rub, wrapped the towel around her waist and then strode across the gravel driveway toward the house while everyone watched her in silence.

"How about that for a real woman?" Dennis said, as she entered the door to the stairway leading up to the residence above the shop. "We've been together five, six years here on the ridge."

"Carlos, you can get in here now that you've chased out the only woman," Boston announced.

"That's quite a canyon out there," Carlos said, ignoring him while facing the gorge beyond the forest. "Never knew it was here."

"Devils Canyon," Dennis told him. "Supposedly, Pomponio hid up here. He was an Indian outlaw and the canyon here was his hideout." Pulling a joint out of his shirt pocket, he lit it and took a big drag.

"Also Devils Slide?" Carlos asked.

"I think that was another devil," Dennis laughed, coughing out smoke. He offered the joint to the others but got no takers.

"No thanks," Boston told him, then turned to the Spaniard. "Carlos, are you getting in or not?"

"I'll wait." Carlos sat down in one of the extra chairs.

Dennis meanwhile sat back in his chair. "So, you're Spanish," he began, then turning to the others, "you're Icelandic, you're German. Boston, what the hell are you?"

"I'm pretty much English."

"So, German guy, what's your deal?"

"My name's Bert, I told you," Bert answered with an annoyance. "I'm from Cedar Rapids and I've never been to Germany."

"It'd be better visa versa, but I remember: Lupinberger."

"Leunberger, my friend."

"Ah, don't mind my short memory," Dennis answered, drawing on the joint. "What do you do for a living?"

"Psychoanalyst."

"Hello," Dennis replied, slumping down in his chair.

"When he's not robbing banks," Boston added.

"No shit?" Dennis asked.

"Wasn't me," Bert offered.

"So he says," Boston countered. "Then there's Erik."

"So, what do you do, pale face?" Dennis inquired.

"Gynecologist," Erik replied.

"Holy Christ," Dennis laughed, slapping his thigh.

"That's why he's so pale," Bert deadpanned. "Spends all his time inside." Dennis guffawed with a burst of smoke. Erik just shook his head, having heard Bert's joke several times before.

Boston meanwhile continued, "Carlos is an electrician."

Still chuckling, Dennis asked, "Spaniard, you got your own company?"

"Yes," Carlos answered, "but no employees, just me. I wire up home security systems."

"My home security has two barrels," said Dennis. "Like you, I work solo. What about you, Boston?"

"I'm partners in a civil engineering firm."

"Somebody else to watch the store while you're out biking. That's good. Katherine doesn't have time to bike, does she?"

"She used to," Boston stated.

"Until the ring," Bert added.

"Until me is more like it," Boston said. "She biked a lot with her second husband."

"He was an asshole," Dennis commented. Boston said nothing but stared at the grizzled, gray-haired host, reminded that Dennis had worked with Katherine for years before Boston had met her. "German, you married?" Dennis asked him.

"Bert's the name. From Cedar Rapids. Left Iowa when I was about ten. Not married anymore."

"Shacked up?"

"Here and there,"

"Spaniard, Carlos?"

"Just got divorced."

"Icelander, what about you?"

"Married," Erik answered.

"He married a Russian," Boston added. "She's should be arriving soon with Katherine."

"A Russian. You and I have to trade war stories," Dennis told Erik. "Ophelia can be a handful and a half, but what a woman. I met her in an Oakland jazz club. I was so stoned that I couldn't even talk to her for the first hour. What the hell did she see in my poor white ass? Thought I'd be a bachelor all my life."

"Must've been lonely up here," Bert said.

"Who says I was lonely? Actually, I'm still technically a bachelor. But don't tell my wife that."

Wearing a smock, Ophelia crossed the driveway with a bunch of towels in her hand. "If that's what you want to do, baby. Here's some towels, boys, when you're ready." She tossed the towels into an empty chair and left.

"Not me," said Dennis as she walked away, then added, "No, I never had it so good. Not that I wouldn't mind a stray every now and then. Who wouldn't?" The group was silent. "Don't mind me," he finally said. "I'm just a little ripped. You guys bike every weekend?"

"Pretty much," Boston answered. "This year we're training for the Death Ride."

"What's that?" Dennis asked.

Boston explained the ride to him that it was a hundred and thirty miles in the Sierra south of Tahoe, sixteen thousand feet vertical climb.

"How many days?"

"One."

"One?" Dennis exclaimed. "Where's this take place again?"

Bert spoke, "Markleeville."

"Hey," Dennis smiled. "I've hunted deer there." The moment he said it, he thought of the deer and the windshield of a couple years ago. There was a road biker involved then, too, and he was on the verge of telling them about it, but he didn't. "I balled a waitress in Markleeville. That was sweet. Took her out hunting the next day with me. She couldn't shoot for shit but she sure was hot in bed." He looked around the group. "Now, doesn't that sound a lot better than biking?"

The Spaniard looked over his head to the late afternoon sky. "Somedays anything sounds better than biking."

Boston nodded in agreement. Unknown to the others, he could have said the same thing about his work, or rather, his company. The civil engineering firm in which he owned with a partner was not doing well. Work had declined locally and they were in debt on several fronts, including the building they rented. His partner, older by fifteen years, was talking about putting their company up for sale if business did not pick up by the spring.

He had yet to mention any of this to the biking group. Road biking was his outlet away from business pressures. The other three in the group were all solo entrepreneurs, dependent also upon clients but without the overhead such as necessary to run his company. He preferred not to share his professional worries with them.

Discussing his company's decline with Katherine was even more daunting for him so he avoided the subject. Married for five years, they still kept separate finances. Their accounts were part of their pasts, as were their private lives. He knew that Katherine had been previously married twice, without children, and she knew he had a daughter from a former marriage to a woman now living in Stockton. Their courtship had been as swift as it had been hot. Neither had been effusive about their past histories to the other and neither had been curious. The attractions had been mutual and once they quickly discovered that their lives were compatible, they married.

As for being at Dennis Crowe's and meeting him for the first time, Boston merely understood that he was a woodworker whom she had been using for years. Neither had ever indicated if they had ever had a previous relationship with each other outside of work.

For a biking destination, his home was perfectly situated. The ride up to Skyline Ridge was taxing enough to take his mind off his engineering company as well as be more than enough challenge for himself and the other three riders.

On top of it all, Dennis seemed more than enough of a character to add zest to the day's visit, not to mention his extraordinary unmarried wife who had greeted them from the lap pool.

Chapter 3

Skyline Boulevard

Skyline Boulevard, also known as Highway 35, weaves north-south atop the Santa Cruz Mountain Range from Highway 92 in the north to Highway 17 in the south. The older east-west highways were built first, originally as stagecoach routes in the 1860s and 1870s, connecting the San Francisco Bay peninsula suburbs to the coast. Constructed for cars decades later in the 1920s, the ridge route linked the more traveled roads. It's a rural highway with only one small community at a midway junction of Highway 84, called Skylonda, which has the only gas station on the highway.

October ride, part 3

Katherine Kirk punched in the number code for the Portola Heights Road gate, happy to be finally turning off Skyline Boulevard and toward Pomponio Ridge Road. She never liked driving up to or along Skyline anymore—it just reminded her too much of her own past. Actually, she felt just as worried about bicyclists as a driver than when she biked, not wanting to either hit or to be hit. Her second husband, Mark Kirk, had seemed so cavalier about cars, whether on the narrow, hilly roads or winding two-lane highways like Skyline.

Picking up Irina Erikksson in Menlo Park, she drove up Highway 84 toward Skylonda. "Mark and I used to bike down this road," she told Irina, who expressed surprise that Katherine had been one of those taking the twisting curves on just a bicycle.

"Moscow is so flat," Irina commented. "Many trucks, buses, but no hills. I had a bike as a girl."

"When I left Mark, I was done with biking. Then, I met Boston, another road biker. Reluctantly, I got back into it. We did a century together shortly after we were married. Funny thing is, at that point, Mark was into golf. I was doing a century and Mark had quit biking. After I did it, I told Boston I was done."

"How did he take it?" Irina asked.

"Oh, he was okay with it. Truth is I don't think he enjoyed biking with me, not because he didn't like me but because I hated it so. He was always considerate, but it wasn't fun for either one of us. I told him we could only stay married if he didn't make me bike."

"Erik always wants me to bike with him," Irina told her. "We use to bike around town with the boys. Sometimes we'd bike to the farmer's market. Erik carried the food in a backpack. But it wasn't really biking for him."

Irina had enjoyed the view from Skylonda to Pomponio Ridge but Katherine did not, remembering those mornings and afternoons of biking on slim-shouldered highways with furious motorcycles, the too-close pick-up trucks, sightseeing motorists, and so forth, all the while having to struggle up long slopes.

When biking with her, Mark had always passed by Portola Heights Road, which was blocked by a private gate. Then she met the iconoclastic woodworker Dennis Crowe, who lived mysteriously up the mysterious road. Her architectural design business was just getting started and she came upon this tall, dark-haired, handsome hermit, who invited her to this edge of a wild ravine to visit his shop from where he built custom doors and cabinets. Sleeping with this crazy woodworker who lived deep in the forest was all part of the excitement of starting her own business. That their liaisons were hidden far from the main road, behind the closed gate, helped to ease what little guilt she might have felt cheating on a husband whom she was leaving soon anyway.

The gate opened automatically when she punched in the private number. Crowe's place was a few miles from the Skyline highway. The road dipped down before a very steep climb where it crested and intersected with Pomponio Ridge Road, which road hugged the mountainside next to a deep canyon, formed with high gray rock cliffs tipped back into the hillside. Turning into his driveway, Katherine parked her Ford Expedition near the familiar pool. There were four bikes against the garage but no bikers. "By those towels lying around, I'd say they're here and have already had a dip," she mentioned to Irina, Erik's wife.

"Looks that way," Irina agreed. "I wouldn't mind a dip myself. We should have brought swimsuits."

From the moment, the gathering was planned, Katherine had wondered how to handle the inevitable skinny-dipping probability. She had never entered Dennis' pool in anything but her own skin. "We won't need suits," she replied.

"First we have to take the food and drinks upstairs. I promised Ophelia she wouldn't have to do anything to feed my husband and his friends."

Katherine grabbed a basket of sandwiches and chips while Irina took up a shopping bag of plastic sports drinks. They entered the wood shop and ascended a heavy-timbered stairway to the second floor, which were the living quarters for Dennis and Ophelia. Upstairs, the four bikers were seated around a table already set with cheese, grapes and bread. Ophelia was swinging free underneath her smock as she cut up some bread. The two women had met a few times previously on jobsite. "Ophelia," began Katherine, "you weren't suppose to fix anything."

"Couldn't let these bikers starve," said Ophelia, smiling at her husband's architect. "This was just to hold them over."

"Hell," said Dennis, "these guys can go a hundred miles on a couple of cashews. I'm the one who's hungry."

Introductions were made and the sandwiches passed around. Irina had never met Carlos or Bert. Her husband Erik had only started riding with the group within the last year. She was Russian, still speaking with an enthusiastic accent although she had been in the country for twenty years. Five-foot-ten, she was slightly shorter than her husband, blonde, bosomy, forty years old which was four years younger than Erik. Their two boys were fifteen and thirteen.

Bert Luenberger's son was twenty-five and his daughter twenty-four. Both were out of college on their own. He'd been divorced for three years. He was exactly fifty years old, six-foot-two, short-gray hair that was rapidly receding, tanned face, rugged as if he were some sort of Marlboro man, minus the mustache, cowboy hat and cigarettes.

Six-foot-tall, forty-five years old, Carlos Cordova stood and sat stiffly with a fit physique. His three daughters were ages twenty-two, twenty and eighteen, all in college. He had been divorced less than a year and had just moved from his Los Altos home to an apartment in Cupertino.

"While you guys are eating," Katherine announced, "Irina and I are going to the pool." Those munching around the table nodded in response.

Boston still had his mouth full. "Want some company?" he asked.

"Up to you," Katherine stated.

"We already went in," Erik said, reaching for the grapes.

Boston looked to his wife, seeing that she was just as pleased to be able to have the pool to herself and Irina. The two women left the second story to go back down to the pool.

Stepping out of her sandals, Katherine quickly tossed off her linen top and skirt. Without any underwear, just like that she climbed into the pool. She was also tall, five-foot-nine, a Norwegian by two previous generations, with very fine, light brown hair, cut in a man's style, her body still thin at forty-six.

Irina followed her into the pool. She was taller than Katherine, heavier, her breasts larger though Katherine's were not small. Gliding through the water, she sailed to the other side. "This is wonderful," she told Katherine.

"I wish we owned one," said Katherine. "I'd be in it everyday. Actually, having a hot tub would be better. It'd feel so good after a day at the drafting table. Boston could do his weekend rides and then we could soak before dinner, after dinner, during dinner."

Paddling around, she stood against the side, staring out across the ravine. This was her favorite place on earth, she had years ago decided, back when Dennis had built the pool. Divorced from Mark, she had luxuriated in its warmth on several evenings. Had Dennis ever told Ophelia that they had been lovers, she wondered. Katherine certainly had never mentioned the pool's history to Boston. Had she not raved so much about Dennis Crowe's fantastic woodshop off Skyline, he never would have wanted to bike here with his buddies.

What did it matter? Katherine was back in the pool, a place she had not been for several years. She and Dennis were each getting more involved with their own spouses as the years progressed, though technically Dennis had never officially married Ophelia. Dennis wasn't the marrying kind, Katherine knew, but he was sure staying locked on this woman.

Was he now faithful to her? Katherine was sure of it, ever since the deer and the windshield. That was a watershed day all around as it ended their illicit relationship once and for all. Now, she was so pleased to be back in the pool, which Dennis had built solely for her prior to Ophelia, though undoubtedly he had used it for several of his concurrent Crowe's Nest conquests.

Upstairs still in table conversation, Dennis asked, "So how do you guys all know one another? Are they all head-shrink patients of yours, doc?"

Bert answered him. "I knew Boston from soccer and that he was also into road biking. His then fiancée Katherine designed a remodel for me many years ago, before my divorce. My ex got the house and I moved to Hawaii for a year. When I moved back, I called him up to see if he was still biking. He was and I needed something so I started riding with Boston and Carlos."

"Is Boston tough? He looks tough."

Boston was five-foot-ten, square shouldered, brown-haired and brown-eyed with a rugged build, obviously a jock in a previous life.

"He keeps up," Bert answered. "Boston's strong on the flats but I own the climbs."

"That true, Carlos?" Dennis asked.

"Sure, Bert's tough on the hills," Carlos replied, "on his good days."

"Every day's a good day," Bert responded. "But I have to admit that when we hit a headwind, we all duck behind Carlos. He's a one-man Spanish Armada. He can also downhill like a bob sled."

"What about you, Icelander? Are you as crazy as these guys?"

"He's getting there," Bert laughed. "Erik just joined us this spring. He may look kind of wimpy but he's coiled like spring. He's the second best climber, the second best downhiller and the second best sprinter."

Erik Erikksson was the same height as Boston but not as muscled, his skin coated a northern European white. He wore what he called a Nordic fu-Manchu, short of a wispy reddish goatee, no mustache with the hair on his head somewhat long and straight, a dark reddish. His countenance was bookish, inquisitive. "I've always biked alone," he said softly.

"This guy's a gynecologist," Dennis shouted out so his wife could hear.

"You're lunching with professional people, sweetheart," Ophelia called out. "Any lawyers in the bunch?"

"No, thank God," Dennis replied. He looked to Carlos, "This one does real work like me."

"Don't mind him," Ophelia said. "Does the g-y-n deliver babies? Not that I need to worry about it. My two daughters hopefully someday will pop out some grandkids."

"No babies anymore," said Erik. "I gave up my obstetrics business."

"Too many middle of night phone calls?" Ophelia asked.

"Too much insurance required," Erik answered.

Dennis interrupted. "I think it's about time to tell my deer story."

"Save it, honey," Ophelia said. "Everyone's in too good a mood."

Dennis got up from the table to help himself to a glass of wine. He stared out the window at the two women in the pool. "Anybody want to hear?" he asked the table.

"Ok, but I don't need to hear it again," Ophelia told him. Taking the bottle and three glass of wine, she left the room and headed down the stairs towards the pool.

At poolside, the two women were chatting. "Ah, perfect," Katherine said, seeing the wine in Ophelia's hand.

Ophelia replied, "I came down to drink with you ladies while Dennis told his deer story to your husband and friends."

"Deer story?" Irina asked.

"Dennis survived but a bicyclist was killed. It was in the papers a couple of years ago." She poured out three glasses and handed two to the women in the pool.

"I think Erik told me about it," Irina said vaguely, looking to Ophelia as she took a glass. "As I remember, a terrible accident happened on Skyline. Was your husband involved?"

"We're not married," Ophelia told her. "Yes, he was most definitely involved." She pulled the smock over her head, revealing that she had nothing on underneath. Setting it down, she got into the pool with Katherine now looking away, towards the trees, seemingly and surprisingly uninterested. That woman has a nice body, Ophelia noticed through the water, thinking, she's very comfortable in this pool and she has definitely slept with Dennis, maybe, probably even in our bed. Katherine was almost her height but thinner, an auburn brunette, at least on top, darker down below.

The Russian was also a big woman, almost the blonde version of Ophelia, except with large curls instead of Ophelia's draped rows. Ophelia doubted that Dennis had ever met her. While they chatted, the fact that Irina did most of the talking, asking how long she had lived here and so forth, further convinced Ophelia that Katherine by her silence was plenty familiar with the property and with Dennis.

Inside the house, Dennis sat down at the table with the other four. "All right," he began. "This is some bad business, if you want to hear."

"We're all ears," Bert replied.

Dennis proceeded to tell his story. He related that it was about dusk and he was driving on Skyline headed back to the Portola Heights Road turnoff. As he was rolling downhill through a series of dark, shaded turns a deer suddenly burst out of the roadside vegetation and leaped across the hood with a thud, slamming into the windshield with a huge bang, caving in the windshield and sending his truck careening across the road with the deer impaled.

Dennis was able to control the truck before it crashed into nearby trees. His seatbelt saved him as he was able to safely stop the truck. The deer meanwhile had flopped onto the highway, writhing in broken bone spasms. Having his rifle along, Dennis shot the animal and dragged it off the highway before any other cars came along. All of that took awhile. Then he examined the front of his car. The first motorist came up from the other direction and stopped, seeing the smashed front of Dennis' truck.

It wasn't until a motorist came from the other direction, which had been Dennis' direction of travel, that they discovered the bicyclist lying on the edge of the pavement with his bent bike tangled into the bushes.

The police report had said that apparently the deer had struck the biker at the same time Dennis' truck was passing by so that the deer and biker all hit the truck at the same time. He was exonerated from any blame for the biker's death, as he related to the four at the table, intently listening to this tale.

That was where Dennis left it with them. What he declined to say was that he never saw the bicyclist. Sure, it was dusk and that section of road was quite dark. He probably should have had his headlights on but he'd traveled the road so much that he knew every curve on it. Also, he knew that his thoughts were on the woman he had just made love with.

He had felt guilty from the start with Katherine, beginning back when she was married to her second husband Mark. He had plenty of single girl friends but none as vibrant as her. In honor of her finally divorcing, he had built her the pool on his property. But he was not about to marry and she met somebody else, this Boston who was sitting at his table. It was this husband whom she cheated on next, whom Dennis had never met until today, and whom they may have kept cheating on until the deer and the windshield.

Had he not been with Katherine that afternoon, he would have been home earlier, avoiding the dusk, the deer and the biker. He had not been unfaithful to Ophelia since then.

"We all knew about the accident," Boston said. "We even biked past the place a week or so later. I recognized your name in the paper. Katherine said she was going to get the details from you but she never did."

"The newspaper said it all anyway," Dennis told him, speaking just of the accident. The rest of it, he was not about to divulge. There was a small end of a joint in the ashtray. He was about to reach for it, but stopped. His next thought was to go down to the pool but then both Katherine and Ophelia would be there. His wine glass was empty and Ophelia had taken the bottle with her. He was stuck with these four. "So, you guys are doing all this biking just for the Markleeville ride?"

"No," Boston said. "We're doing the Markleeville ride because we do all this biking. Might as well count it toward something."

"Watch out for the damn deer," Dennis mentioned.

Chapter 4

Alpine Road

The former residence of Maximo Martinez was located at the current site of the Portola Valley Garage, address 4170 Alpine Road in Portola Valley. Slightly to the east, at 3915 Alpine Road is located a beer and burger place proclaimed by sign as "Alpine Inn Formerly Rossotti's." Built in the 1850s, the tavern was known for card games and grizzly bear-steer fights. Martinez carved out part of his Rancho del Corte Madera for his friend Felix Buelna, formerly the alcade, or mayor, of San Jose where Martinez served on the council. Buelna lost the tavern due to his gambling debts to American William Stanton in 1868, the same year that the Corte de Madera main road became part of the Menlo Park-Santa Cruz Turnpike. The road was extended alongside the creek, which retains the Corte Madera name, to the Skyline ridge and over to La Honda.

There were several owners and several names of the boisterous roadhouse until, following Prohibition, the saloon was operated by Enrico Rossotti and became a hangout for Stanford students, especially with liquor being outlawed in nearby Palo Alto. Though ownership changed from Rossotti in 1956, the name has hung on as "Zotts."

October ride, part 4

"So what about this bank robbery?" Dennis asked Bert.

"All a big mistake, many years ago," Bert replied.

Dennis turned to Boston, who just shrugged. "We don't know anything about it, really."

"It happened when I was in Hawaii," Bert began. "It was a bank I went to all the time and apparently they thought I sort of looked like the robber. I mean, he had a pulled down sailor's hat over most of his face and had a false beard. Give me a break."

"How much did you get again?" Boston asked.

"Wasn't me," Bert replied emphatically, ending the conversation.

Boston slid back his chair, which indicated it was time to go. The other three bikers got up, along with Dennis, who shook their hands and said goodbye from the living room, declining to go back downstairs. Instead, he went onto the balcony to watch the departure, staying a safe distance from the three naked women in the pool.

As the bicycles were parked against the garage wall close to the pool, the four bikers could not help but pass close by the three women. Katherine noticed that Carlos stayed focused on retrieving his bike whereas Bert nonchalantly freely viewed the mostly submerged female trio. Erik, the erstwhile gynecologist hardly gave them notice. Boston was last.

"No rush is there?" asked Katherine, seeing her husband slyly checking out the other women.

"No, but it's time to go," Boston replied.

"Why don't you join us instead? We can have a little party in here, right Irina?"

"Sure," Irina added. "I'm not shy."

"Me neither," Ophelia volunteered. "In fact, these boys have already seen my full monty."

"Is that so?" Katherine frowned. "You've been in already?"

Boston nodded, mounting his bike frame. "But remember, I asked you earlier if you wanted company."

"Well, now we do. Give yourselves a break. The Death Ride isn't until next July," she reminded him.

Again, he shook his head. "We have to go."

Katherine wanted him to stay. Built for her years earlier, she considered it a special place and wanted to share it with her current husband. But she knew she could not reveal the romance she had shared with Dennis, not after it had continued beyond her marriage to Boston.

She said her goodbye and reconciled to being in the water with Irina and Ophelia. She had no problem with Ophelia's presence, in fact, she liked her. After all, it was her, Katherine, who had cheated with her man whereas unsuspecting Ophelia was blameless.

The group put on their helmets, said thank you, goodbye and were gone. From the balcony, Dennis watched them depart while simply not being able to understand why they would leave three perfectly good naked women in a pool, with a bottle of wine no less, to go biking up steep roads as well as survive the infrequent but often speeding traffic. Even given the fact that two of the men were married, there were still two other women in the pool who were not their wives.

He was all for adventure but these were not his kind of outdoorsmen. Dennis was used to annual Wyoming elk hunts with whiskey and barmaids at night, as well as occasional Baja marlin fishtrips with tequila and flirtatious hookers. He watched the bikers leave his property the way a sentry might see a party of scouts disappear toward hills fraught with hostile Indians—admiring them, thinking them a little crazy and just as happy to not be part of the bunch.

On the other hand, how could he justify keeping to himself and staying out of the pool? He was in no hurry to go downstairs, where the woman he was living with was situated a few feet from a woman he had been screwing until a year ago, and both as stark naked as lighting. He was sort of secretly stuck.

With her back turned to him, Ophelia called out, "Honey, we need some more wine, don't we girls?" The two nodded. "Dennis?"

"Sure," Dennis answered, as he went back inside the second story.

"Will he be getting in the water?" Irina asked.

"I'd be surprised if he didn't," Ophelia answered. "Being the only male shouldn't bother Dennis any."

Katherine said nothing. Irina replied, "Good. I wouldn't mind seeing another man's cock." Then she covered her mouth. "Oops, sorry," she said, looking to Ophelia. "I didn't mean anything."

Ophelia just laughed. "Understood. I think you'll be impressed." She glanced at Katherine, who merely stared out into the forest.

Dennis soon arrived carrying a bottle of red wine with a fourth glass. After handing the bottle to Ophelia, he stripped and nervously climbed the short ladder into the water. Rather than acting politely surprised to see his long-time architect naked, he chose instead to mostly ignore her and stick to his wine. The only saving grace in the whole ordeal was the bosomy, blonde Russian, who seemed delighted to have a naked man join the group.

As Ophelia had predicted, Irina was impressed, which Katherine noticed as she settled into her refilled glass. She sipped her wine knowing that her former lover was just a few feet away, exposed in the pool where they had eagerly romanced each other several years ago.

—

Meanwhile, the four bikers back-tracked up Pomponio Ridge Road, which snaked alongside heavily treed Devils Canyon with its large massive cliffs of the canyon visible through the fir trees, such cliffs which they weren't able to notice on the descent.

The road was private, barely a single lane in spots. A Mercedes coming the opposite direction stopped and the driver, a male about their age, asked them what they were doing there. Boston mentioned that they were guests of Crowe's and the driver asked no more questions. The road intersected with Portola Heights Road as Boston led the riders up to the crest.

Though Katherine had wanted him to stay, Boston had felt awkward at poolside beyond the nudity involved. He had never seen his wife and Dennis together and thought, based on their long time acquaintance, that they should have been friendlier to each other upstairs than they let on. Instead, they hardly had any contact, as if toning it down on his account.

Once the group was through the private gate and biking on Skyline, he felt liberated from the whole experience, back on familiar territory doing his favorite activity. After a couple of miles headed north, the group took the right-hand turn on Page Mill Road down to the Palo Alto area. Riding the edge of the travel lane, they clung tight to the farthermost asphalt edge, tensing only when two motorcycles roared by with a screaming pitch well over the speed limit.

They stayed fairly knit together initially on Page Mill until the first drop, which fell away like a roller coaster. Bert began the descent first but was soon overtaken by Carlos, the fastest downhiller of the bunch. All three disappeared from Boston's view as he followed, ever more cautiously than the others.

As the group circled at the Arastradero Road T-intersection, Bert called out, "Got time for a beer at Zotts?" Everyone agreed, still circling like salmon gathering their strength for the next set of rapids.

"Outlined against a blue, gray October sky," Boston recited

"What's that supposed to mean?" Bert asked.

"The Four Horsemen," he answered. "Grantland Rice, you know, that photo of the Notre Dame backfield on horses."

"Who were they?" Erik asked.

"Football players and I forget their real names but Rice was referring to the four horsemen of the Apocalypse, who were War, Pestilence, Famine and Death. Book of Revelations."

"Consider me to be War. Last one buys!" Bert shouted and, running in his pedals, sped up Arastradero toward Rossotti's. Erik was right behind him with Boston and Carlos following. All four stayed together through the first few rises. Then as the road got steeper uphill, Bert and Erik pulled away. Boston and Carlos traded off cat-and-mouse positions until the turn into the Rossotti's parking lot and eased over the large speed bump.

By the time, they biked through the gate opening, they saw that Erik and Bert were already seated at a wood table, their bikes leaning against a fence. "Son of a bitch," said Bert to Erik. "I couldn't shake you today."

"But I couldn't quite pass you," Erik responded. "One of these days."

"How come you're not out of breath like me?" Bert asked. He turned to the other two approaching. "Who's buying?" he questioned in mock sympathy.

Carlos put his bike also along the fence and left to go get the pitcher of beer.

It was an Indian summer fall day and the outdoor table picnic area was still crowded, even for a late Saturday afternoon. Only a couple tables were empty, all others covered with pitchers, bottles, cups, hamburgers, French fries, and a lot of noise in the form of loud kidding and laughter from a mixture of Stanford students, alumni, Portola Valley residents, Woodside horse people, construction workers, motorcyclists, and two women in either late or mid-twenties, seated all the way across the picnic area, drinking beer also in their biking clothes with their road bikes close by. "Can't totally make them out," said Bert, "but they look hot. Maybe we could tell them we're the Four Horsemen of the Apocalypse. That ought to go over big. 'Hi, I'm War.'"

"So what am I then?" Erik turned to Boston.

"Famine," Boston replied. "You're the thinnest."

"Also there also can't be much to eat in Iceland," Bert added.

"Only if you like fish, then there's plenty," Erik told him and turned to Boston. "So, are you Pestilence or Death?"

"Pestilence, for sure," Bert interrupted. "He lays out these painful, torturous rides. That leaves Carlos as Death."

"Makes sense," Erik said. "Plus Death seems very Spanish. You know, the land of bull fights, civil war, Guernica, black dresses."

"Here comes Death now," Bert announced as Carlos arrived with the pitcher and four cups.

"What's that?" Carlos asked, setting down the pitcher and pouring the cups.

"The Four Horsemen of the Apocalypse," Bert stated. "War, Famine, Pestilence and Death. You get to be Death."

"I don't find that humorous," Carlos said seriously.

"No," Boston joined, "but that is how we arrived. War won the bike ride. Famine, Erik, was second. That usually follows War. Then comes Pestilence, disease, me. Death always finishes up."

"I'm not always last," Carlos argued.

"Can't we just be the Four Horsemen of the Apocalypse without the names?" Erik asked.

"Are you Catholic?" Bert asked.

"Lutheran. Was a Lutheran rather."

"I was Catholic," Carlos stated flatly. "If we're the Four Horsemen, why are we on bicycles?"

"What about the Four Bicyclists of the Apocalypse?" Erik asked Boston.

"I don't think bicyclists would have swept Army over the precipice," Boston answered. They all stared blankly at him. "That was how Grantland Rice described the game's outcome."

"Speaking of going over the precipice, I got my eye on that one," Bert said, changing the subject as he took up his cup, staring at the younger of the two women, pretty and blonde. "Twenty-five, tops."

"What makes you think she'd have the slightest interest in an old guy like you?" Carlos questioned him.

"They're bicyclists, too, aren't they?" Bert smiled. "Road biking has no age limits. What do you say, Carlos? There are two of them. Can't do it all by myself."

"I say you're so full of shit that you're eyes are brown. What do you say to that?" Carlos coldly asked him.

Bert did not answer as the two women rose and began to walk out with their bikes, taking a line far from their table. Finally, he spoke. "My eyes are hazel," he answered.

Watching the two women leave, Boston still thought back to the pool and Katherine's disappointment in his leaving. Typically, she would have insisted he stay at such a party, especially with the pool involved. But for now, he was one of the Four Horsemen, sitting in a beer garden under a blue, gray October sky.

"What's your objection to Death, again?" Bert asked Carlos, pouring him another beer. "Aren't we training for the Death Ride after all?"

"Doing the Death Ride and being Death are two different things," Carlos answered.

Let us hope, Boston thought to himself.

Chapter 5

Crystal Springs

Crystal Springs Reservoir lies in a long longitudinal valley, or cañada, south of San Francisco, west of the Bay. At one time, the cañada slowly drained the depression between parallel ranges, with the taller one being to the west. Near the junction where three creeks met was located the rustic Crystal Springs Hotel in 1851, catering to honeymooners, trout fishermen and deer hunters. San Mateo Creek came down from the western hills to meet San Andreas Creek from the north and Laguna Creek from the south. Nearby on San Andreas Creek was a camp on property owned by Leander Sawyer, serving refreshments and providing beds for hikers and horseback riders, and eventually for stagecoach passengers traveling past Crystal Springs and through the gap to Spanishtown on the coast, later named Half Moon Bay. The town of Crystal Springs first appeared on an 1856 map.

San Francisco's need for water grew while local springs within the City were overwhelmed by development. The cañada was purchased by the City for an ambitious water project, which ultimately brought Sierra water from Hetch Hetchy Valley in Yosemite. When the town of Crystal Springs began disappearing underwater in 1888, the road through Sawyer's property got moved uphill. The concrete dam, which was the world's biggest at the time at 149 feet tall, was finished in 1890. Sawyer's old road is now off-limit to vehicles and meets the current Skyline Boulevard at a junction with Crystal Springs Road just north of the dam.

Crystal Springs Reservoir, split by the Highway 92 leading to Half Moon Bay, divides two tectonic plates with the oceanic Pacific Plate traveling north and west, subducting the continental North American Plate to the east. North of the reservoir is Lake San Andreas, once a shallow sag pond on San Andreas

Creek, such feature being typical of earthquake faults, deepened by an earth dam constructed by the City of San Francisco in 1870. Years later in 1895 the contact zone between the two plates was discovered and mapped as the San Andreas Fault, named after the lake.

San Mateo Creek flows into the reservoir and spills out of the dam. During the Spanish period, it formed the northern boundary of the Rancho de las Pulgas, or Ranch of the Fleas, so named due to a deserted but infested Indian village discovered by Gaspar de Portola's expedition in 1769. Crystal Springs Road was built on the sidehill to connect to the top of the dam.

November ride, part 1

Entering November, the financial outlook at Boston Reed's civil engineering company had not improved. Boston's partner, Larry Dunne was almost sixty-two years old. He had started as a small surveying company almost fifteen years ago, then had asked Boston to join him ten years ago, back when all kinds of construction was booming. Larry had planned to retire at the end of this year by selling out to Boston.

But now they both needed an upsurge in business to make the company profitable. Boston had been working more than ever to keep the company afloat.

He depended upon the weekend biking excursions for a diversion. Rained out the previous weekend, he organized one last blowout foursome Skyline Boulevard ride before cutting back on distances due to winter. From Palo Alto, he planned that they would head inland north and drop into Pacifica, a beachside fog-wrapped suburb of San Francisco, then return along the coast to Tunitas Creek Road, where they would climb through the redwood forest back to Skyline Boulevard and down the other side.

Biking side by side with Carlos in little traffic, Boston took note of the ponderous clouds hanging on the Skyline ridge. "Feels like steelhead weather," he stated, "like a cool fall day in the Pacific Northwest threatening to rain, good for fishermen. That's what my father liked to do with his friends. You ever fish?"

"No," Carlos responded. "Not in Spain, not here either. My father gardened and took care of a little olive orchard we had in the country. If he was still alive, he'd think we're crazy."

"Fly fishing was my dad's form of exercise," said Boston. "Couldn't go every weekend but it was what men did in the generation before us, driving maybe hundreds of miles to their favorite streams. Also, deer hunting, duck hunting, that sort of stuff, with always a little bourbon involved."

"We used to watch the Vuelta de España when it came through Asturias. He couldn't see what the fuss was about or how professionals could live off just cycling. In Spain, I never biked. Not until I got here."

"My dad and his friends fished all over Northern California, Oregon, even Canada and Alaska. I got to go on a couple trips when I was older. Today feels like British Columbia. Thirty years ago, instead of biking, we'd be putting on waders and our raincoats, getting ready to hit the river."

Crossing San Francisquito Creek, they continued on Alameda de las Pulgas, translated as the Avenue of the Fleas. Ahead on the Alameda was a Starbucks coffee restaurant where Bert was waiting. It was 8:30 am and Erik was late, not unusual for him.

Erik was a gynecologist and his wife Irina a structural engineer. Boston met Erik through Katherine, who just this spring had contacted Irina about doing permit-required calculations. Now that he was no longer delivering babies, Erik kept a fairly regular schedule, except when it came to making the routine biking start time, which was no problem for the others. Boston was part owner in a civil engineering company that generally closed the office Saturdays through Sundays. As a self-employed home security-wiring electrician, Carlos could pick his weekends for work and, unless his general contractors were desperate, was almost always available. The psychoanalyst, Bert, didn't want to see his clients in the morning anyway.

"Saw 'Tombstone' last night," Bert said, sipping his coffee. "Another foursome like your Four Horsemen, only on foot, well at least at the OK corral. The three Earp brothers and Doc Holliday."

"So, who's who this time?" Boston asked.

"I concede Wyatt to you, only because you do all the planning. That leaves Virgil and Morgan Earp, plus Holliday."

"We had to read Virgil in school," Carlos said.

"Virgil Earp was sort of the strong, silent type. That about fits you," Bert said to Carlos "but I can't see myself as the third brother Morgan. What do you think?"

"I don't know."

"Have you seen the movie?"

"No."

"Ever hear of Wyatt Earp?"

"No."

"Sure you have," Boston reminded Carlos "We biked past his grave in Colma a couple years ago, sort of a pre-Death Ride, now that I think about it."

Bert grinned, "I think of myself as the spoiler, like the huckleberry that Doc claimed to be. But Wyatt was the man, a straight-shooter, just like Boston."

"I'd rather be John," Carlos said.

"John Holliday, the Doc?" Bert asked.

"No, the Apostle."

"How'd we move from gunfighters to apostles?" Bert asked.

"Why not? There were four of them. Mathew, Mark, Luke and John."

Bert paused. "Sounds pretty dull."

"How about Carlos as St. John the Apostle," Boston interjected. "That's more impressive. Like the Knights of St. John. Smacks of Crusades and all."

"What about going back to the fourth horseman called Death?" Bert countered. "We are training for the Death Ride after all."

Carlos said nothing and only glared. Bert asked him, "Why John?"

"The other three are just story tellers," Carlos answered, "whereas John bore witness to the life and light."

"Wish you could bear witness to Erik arriving on time," Bert stated.

"So, which of us would be Matthew, Mark and Luke?" Boston asked him.

"It doesn't matter," Bert said. "They all told the same story according to John here."

"Luke was a physician," Boston offered.

"Then that's me," Bert said.

"He was a doctor, not a shrink," Carlos told him with a slight sneer. "Erik's a real doctor."

"Jesus probably needed a psychoanalyst more than a gynecologist," Bert responded with an unflinching grin.

"Okay," Boston intervened. "Let's not lose it over the Four Apostles." The table quieted as Erik finally arrived, parking his bike outside and entering.

"You get to be Morgan Earp," Bert told him.

"Morgan who?" Erik asked.

"It's either that or you get Doc's Big-Nose Kate as your girlfriend," Boston told him, heading for the door without any further explanation.

"She sounds more like Bert's type," Erik called out as he trailed the group.

"Hey," Bert complained, kidding, "anybody ever seen me with a big-nosed woman?"

"We've never seen you with any women," Carlos followed, "only heard the stories you've told."

"Anybody ever hear me talk about a big-nosed woman?"

"What about that one in San Bruno?" Boston asked.

Bert thought about it for a moment. "Doesn't count. Her whole head was big," he finally answered. "So was her body. And her friend was even bigger. Carlos, she'd be the type to love you to death. Maybe I should look them up again." Carlos said nothing.

—

Irina arrived at Katherine's that Saturday morning to review a set of plans, drink coffee and, this morning, to a door design that Katherine wanted Dennis to build. They had never really discussed the visit to the Crowe's nest two weeks ago.

"What's you think of Dennis?" Katherine asked.

"He's good looking," Irina said, "in a cowboy kind of way. I can see why you like him."

"Who said I like him?"

"I don't mean anything by it," Irina apologized. "But you've been using him for years."

"All before I met Boston," Katherine reminded. She poured more coffee into their cups, even though they were still almost full. "You want the real story?"

"Of course," Irina replied, her voice hushed with anticipation.

She felt like she had to tell someone and Irina had become her closest confidant. In the kitchen, Katherine spelled out the situation, at least from her viewpoint, describing how she had met Dennis on a work recommendation. Unhappy with her second husband Mark, she pretty much jumped into Dennis' bed. Love did not have much to do with it, which was why she loved him, plus he built the pool for her.

But Dennis was too much of a pothead hermit for her and she didn't like living alone. Along came Boston, rugged, handsome, self-employed and she was attracted to him. But she never lost her baseline lust for Dennis, even after she married Boston.

"What are you saying?" Irina asked her.

"I kept sleeping with Dennis," Katherine confessed. "That is, up until that biker got killed in the deer accident."

"What did that have to do with anything?"

"We fucked that afternoon," Katherine said. "That made Dennis late. Hitting that biker took all the air out of our balloon. Of course, it didn't do the biker any good either." Then she added, "As far as I know, you're the only other person who knows about me and Dennis."

—

The self-proclaimed Four Horsemen approached the inevitable sprint beginning at the Edgewood Road intersection, alongside the stone towers of a grand estate. There was never any discussion that there would be a mini-race and never any official get ready-set-go. It had just become habit that the adrenaline would start to flow where the road first descended. Boston shot ahead, followed by Carlos and Bert. Expecting one or the other to slip by, he was surprised when Erik shot past.

Pushing as hard as he could, Boston caught and passed him as they neared the entrance to a rotund Grecian-style temple containing the rushing waters of Yosemite National Park, dammed at the Hetch Hetchy Valley reservoir. Once by the wrought iron gates, they both relaxed, breezing past.

Boston Reed had more athletic history than the others, playing team sports when younger, even rugby in his early twenties and then adult league soccer, all with a sense of team spirit but also with the individual joy of the burst, as occurs in the field sports, those precious few seconds of making a play. With memories of all that, he wasn't about to let these little make-believe finish line sprints occur without a challenge.

With Crystal Springs Reservoir now appearing on their left, the road leveled out and their pace eased as they neared the stoplight ahead. While waiting for the light to change, Bert asked, "What about the Cartwrights?" No one responded. "Another foursome. You know, Bonanza. I think Carlos could be Hoss."

"What's Bonanza? Who's Hoss?" Carlos asked.

"A western and he was the strong one,' Bert answered. "Boston is Ben, the father figure. I'm Adam, the tall dark, handsome one. Erik, sorry, you're Little Joe."

"I like being Wyatt Earp better," Boston stated.

Erik interrupted, "Maybe we could be the Three Musketeers . . ."

"There's four of us," Bert interjected, "just like the Cartwrights."

" . . . plus d'Artagnan," Erik continued. "Of course, I'm d'Artagnan."

"Why you?" Bert asked him. "That's a far cry from Little Joe."

"Two reasons," Erik stated as the light changed to green. He continued his reasoning on the other side of the highway. "First off, I was the last to join the group, as was d'Artagnan. But the second is that I'm the only one who can name the other three." Discussions ended as the group crossed over a highway merge lane, then descended to a stoplight where they turned north, avoiding the road's continuation across a narrow causeway between the two reservoirs.

"There was a Porthos," Bert replied as the four riders regrouped on the uphill.

"That would be you," Erik told him.

"Why's that?"

"He considered himself the ladies man."

"But how did the ladies consider him?" Boston asked. Bert did not reply. Boston continued, "So which one am I?"

"You would be Athos, the businessman," Erik smiled.

"I'm a civil engineer, not a businessman."

"Yes, but the other one, Aramis, was a priest."

"That's Carlos," said Bert. "Sorry, Carlos, but you'll have to hear my confessions.'"

"Could take awhile," Boston added, "including the bank robbery."

"My uncle is a priest," Carlos said, "and so is my brother-in-law."

"Ever think about joining?" Bert asked, a facetious gleam in his eye.

"Use to," Carlos stated. "Then I went to Madrid. No more priesthood for me."

"Maybe it's time to reconsider," Bert suggested, "if you insist on remaining celibate."

"I don't insist on anything," Carlos returned, staring at him, not friendly.

Coming from Spain, Carlos had played schoolyard soccer and had tried basketball on some very primitive courts. But his father never did any athletics and nothing drew Carlos to sports once out of school. After graduating from high school, he left home in the north for Madrid, where he did odd jobs and where he met and fell in love with a Germanic-descended red-head from the Bay Area, which is what brought him to California. Once his girlfriend became pregnant, Carlos quickly married and eventually got his own contractor's license as the babies kept coming, along with the fights with his wife, who possessed an explosive temperament that he had never noticed in Spain. Biking became his release from everything, but he had never fully explored the Peninsula until meeting Boston.

Conversation once again stopped as the road curved sharply down and across Crystal Springs Dam, holding back the headwaters of San Mateo Creek augmented by the captured and diverted Tuolumne River of Yosemite, fed by the unseen snowmelt of the Sierra to the distant east.

It was steelhead weather, Boston thought again, thinking once more of his father and his love of fishing, as he noticed the clouds hanging low across the reservoir while sea gulls rested flat on the still surface below where large trout lurked in the murky waters.

—

"Do you miss him?" Irina asked her, referring to Dennis.

It was a question Katherine had been asking herself for a year ever since the deer and the windshield accident. At first, when they quit, she had been glad to be relieved of the guilt in deceiving Boston. With her second husband Mark, she had been convinced that sleeping with Dennis on the sly was a result of a marriage gone sour. But in the case of her marriage to Boston, her continued love affair with Dennis was her weakness.

"I miss fucking in the afternoon," she answered, then immediately regretted the crassness of her own words.

"I miss fucking period," Irina said with a wan glance out the breakfast window. In hindsight, she was impressed that Katherine could have remained so stoic in Dennis' pool while her lover was a few feet away. She wished she had known the full story earlier so she could have observed Dennis more closely, not his body but his demeanor. His body, she had examined plenty, at least as much as she thought Ophelia might allow as harmless curiosity. However, Irina now considered him more than just a pot-smoking carpenter capable of blowing away an elk.

Chapter 6

Devils Slide

Devils Slide is the name of a short stretch of California State Highway 1 between Pacifica and Montara, two towns south of San Francisco, where the highway was built along a previous railroad grade across a steep, eroding slope that plunges to surf's edge far below. The slope was avoided by the Portola expedition of 1769, which crossed more inland, closer to where a tunnel is to be built, on their journey of discovery along the coast. Crossing over the slopes of Montara Mountain, Portola's group climbed the ridge above Pacifica where they spotted the huge inland bay to the east, of which the entrance had been missed by Spanish and English sailing vessels of previous centuries.

Subsequent coastal travelers also kept to the higher ridges in order to avoid the steep slope emptying at water's edge. One particular chute ended at a rocky promontory, still visible today, with a swoop shaped like a giant's slide, terminating into the ocean. Accordingly, it was called the Devils Slide. When the Ocean Shore Railway was built beginning in 1905 across the face of the mountain, the swoop was cut down for grade purposes. Due to the constant sluffage of the sandy slope, repairs and shutdowns were frequent. Devils Slide came to be the name of the deteriorating, steep slope, eventually helping to cause the railroad's demise due to all the problems of keeping it open but lending itself to the future roadway. The road's sharp curves, narrow shoulders and steep cliffs have caused many fatal automobile accidents over the years. For both safety sake and long-term maintenance costs, the State finally funded tunnel construction to bypass the treacherous section of Highway 1.

November ride, part 2

After crossing the Crystal Springs dam, the four rode past several parked cars before turning into the entrance to Sawyer Camp Trail. The gateway was crowded with joggers warming up, joggers cooling down, walkers, walkers with strollers—a whole cluster of people using the six-miles trail along the eastern banks of reservoir. Gazing at the body of water on their left, they saw the level was quite low due to the onset of winter and wanting to keep capacity for the storm season.

Around the first turn came two young women running in halter-tops and small shorts. After they passed, Bert questioned, "Why don't we take this route more often?"

"Because it was always so crowded," Boston answered.

"This kind of crowd I like," he replied. "Carlos, maybe we should go back and introduce ourselves to those two."

"You're older than they are combined," Carlos called out.

"Works for me, Bert answered, slowing down to let some parents and kids go past, then adding, "Carlos, you're a free man now. Don't age discriminate. You can never tell where you'll find true love."

"My oldest daughter's almost their age," Carlos replied.

"But that's only because you're an old man," Bert responded as he slowed down to get past some walkers in front of him. Returning to speed, they spotted ahead an attractive woman running, tall and athletic, in a white sports bra and dark gym shorts. Staring at the trail in front of her, she glanced over at Bert, who gave her a friendly smile. Sweating, she slightly smiled in return. Not much further along, Bert turned around to Carlos, "I think I just found true love."

"Why don't you turn around and go find out for sure?" Carlos told him.

"Find out if she has a friend, you mean," Bert answered as he continued straight.

Boston listened, unsure as usual as to how much of Bert's braggadocio was Bert and how much was his egging on of Carlos. Bert Luenberger had been a proficient adult league soccer player into his mid-forties until too much running and contact began to take its toll. Boston could remember playing against him years ago before Boston's marriage to Katherine. An aggressive player, Bert had his share of confrontations before learning to tone it down. When playing as a goalie, he was not one to wait but charged the shooter, often to a fault. Boston remembered once scored on him but Bert always denied it. When Bert got divorced, he had moved to Hawaii. Boston didn't accept at face value all of Bert's stories from there, just as he wasn't quite sure about the alleged bank robbery incident. However, once in California again, Bert met up with Boston and got hooked on biking. Bert had since claimed that it was either quitting soccer or getting divorced, but his back had felt so much better since doing both and that biking was the best therapy of all. It was his best way of dealing with the stress of psychoanalyzing others.

Crossing an earthen dam, the riders emerged from the cold shade to adjoin a brilliantly blue body of water named Lake San Andreas, an early source of San Francisco's drinking water, now filled with Sierra runoff pumped up from the two Crystal Springs reservoirs. Returning onto the two-lane highway, headed north, they continued beneath an undeveloped ridge to their left that had given the Portola band their first view of San Francisco Bay, now on their right.

After a few rolling hills, they turned into Skyline Community College, where Dennis' companion Ophelia taught her art class, and cut over to Sharp Park Drive, which led downhill to Pacifica. Often foggy in summer, today the sky was now totally blue, with a cool breeze blowing offshore. The descent to the coast began slowly but soon dropped rapidly. Always the fastest downhiller, Carlos shot out ahead, followed by Erik, then Bert with Boston behind, knowing he was being overly cautious. Death, Famine, War, Pestilence was their typical order going downhill.

After crossing the Highway 1 overpass, they turned off onto the Rockaway Beach area, where they parked bikes against the seawall, sitting against the sound of the ocean crashing nearby. Boston and Carlos had only been south of Highway 1 over Devils Slide a couple of times whereas Bert and Erik had never biked through here before. "The worst part," Boston told the group, "is not the Slide itself, because that's so intimidating that people get pretty cautious. The scary part is the climb before the Slide—there's no shoulder, it's uphill so you're going slow and, especially today, you're in and out of shade, not easy to be seen."

The other three listened to the danger explained. Eating one of his small russet potatoes, Erik changed the subject, "What about Mt. Rushmore for a foursome? Who's George Washington?"

"Got to be Boston," Bert spoke up. "Our fearless leader."

"Agreed. Thomas Jefferson?"

"A great thinker," Carlos stated. "The Declaration of Independence."

"Who also slept with his much younger slave for twenty years," Bert added.

"That had nothing to do with anything," Carlos proclaimed. "Plus his wife had died."

"Ok," Bert began. "Seeing how you've just declared your marital independence, you should be Jefferson." Carlos didn't answer.

"Who'll be Lincoln?" Erik asked.

"Remember I was the horseman named War and Lincoln was president during the Civil War," Bert stated. "He was also tall, like me."

"You're not that much taller than us," Carlos said. "And Lincoln wasn't a warrior, wasn't even a general."

"Right," Boston chimed in. "He was the architect of the peace. Erik should be Lincoln."

"Plus his beard is Icelandic," Erik added.

"You don't really consider your little scruff to be a beard, do you?" Bert asked him. Erik just rubbed his faint Fu Manchu, teasing with any response from Erik. "So, who's left?"

"Teddy Roosevelt," Boston answered. "Rough and Ready."

Bert laughed, "Well, that does sort of sound like me. Plus he did lead the charge up San Juan Hill, didn't he, like I lead the charge up our hills."

"I think the hill's been downgraded to San Juan Heights," Erik commented.

"Bully," Boston grinned.

Soon they were off again, following a light tailwind, biking past Rockaway Beach and into the heavy vegetated-lined climb on the narrow highway with plenty of cars. The four bikers were all aware that it just took one driver not paying attention and drifting over or misjudging an extra-wide-mirror to fatally knock one or all of themselves out. Cars continually passed to the other side within arm's length.

Each slow truck was typically followed by a half-dozen cars barely brushing past the bikers. Boston led the group to the crest ahead with a small shoulder, giving room and time to exhale while bunches of cars rolled by. After the last car in one such group, Boston and the riders started out on the now descending highway. Ahead the road surface was rough, having been patched over and over due to ground movement, until finally on top it became a twisty, bumpy stretch strung across a steep grayish landslide, bracketed by concrete railing on both sides, hundreds of feet above the ocean directly below on their right.

Cresting they careened downhill, slower than the cars stacking up behind the last rider but still ripping around the turns. Ahead was a comforting sight of straight highway, a striped bike lane, blue skies and, on their right, surfers bobbing between rows of white curls. Safety was now within sight.

As the road leveled, their anxiety passed as did the cars backed up behind them. Boston had been especially anxious about that stretch. Being the group's chief engineer, he planned the routes and studied the distances and grade percentages, blue-printing the designs mentally in time to inform the other three by Friday where and when to meet, envisioning the climbs and descents while hoping for the difficult stretches to be spaced by scenic distractions such as ocean and land provided them now.

It was a degree of professionally honed precision, which clashed with his wife's sense of spontaneity. "I work with plans and details all day," Katherine would often emphasize. "I don't need to do that in my play time."

"We both work on plans," Boston would tell her, "and because of that, it's natural for me to plan out other things as well."

"Not for me," she would counter. "I want to be able to take off when I want and detour to where I want. Actually, detour is the wrong word because that implies a route to begin with. I want to be able to head toward Texas but wind up in Utah if it feels right."

Boston felt that same way about road biking. Often, his groups took a variation on a planned route. Even if the plan took a deviation, he still enjoyed picking ride destinations and projecting a month's calendar well in advance. He wasn't a big vacationer to begin with and dreaded losing the bike training time, especially this year with their goal of the Death Ride set for the second week in July.

He knew Katherine saw it differently. A feverish worker, she would reach a work-stress critical mass and need to flee, not just mentally but geographically as well. Her Friday afternoon saturation points did not fit into his Saturday riding plan, perhaps made weeks before. Now with the Death Ride on the horizon for next summer, he needed even more biking time to train.

That she had no interest in Markleeville created a dissonance in their marriage, something that didn't present itself in their whirlwind romance, especially as she had biked with him the first year they married.

At least with Erik having joined the group, Boston figured that Katherine could connect with Irina during these Saturday mornings and be able to look ahead to her company in Markleeville next July.

In the meantime, road bikers follow roads and the one ahead led toward Half Moon Bay.

Chapter 7

Tunitas Creek

Tunitas Creek Road leads from the creek's mouth at the ocean to the skyline ridge, several miles uphill to the east. Beginning as an extended logging road out of Woodside, Kings Mountain Road crested and leveled out at a logging camp called Grabtown, located on a steep ridge between the Tunitas and Purissima Creek drainages. By 1875, the downhill Tunitas Creek Turnpike Road had reached the coast. The timber company owner built a chute for his logs to reach awaiting ships but the operation was difficult and the eventually abandoned chute was finally destroyed by storm in 1885.

By 1908, the Ocean Shore Railway terminated at Tunitas Creek, from where passengers continuing south from the Tunitas Glen station to Santa Cruz had to travel by Stanley Steamer automobile-bus. From their home at the lonely terminal, the Easterday family served passengers. Marrying at age 39 in 1915, family's exotic poet daughter Sybil operated a saloon at their home with her husband for only a year before he committed suicide. Within a few years, the Ocean Shore Railway closed, victim to high operating costs but also increased automobile use, which include a touring car that had been making a Tunitas Creek Road run since 1913.

November ride, part 3

Being off-season November, highway traffic was relatively light with few cars parked on the shoulders opposite the beaches, popular in summer. With a tail wind, there wasn't much need to change leads. Carlos overtook Bert and the trailing riders were content to let him slice the air in front. Devils Slide was behind them and all they had to do now was make it up Tunitas Creek Road, miles ahead, and the hard part would be over.

Past the Half Moon Bay airport on their right was the little hillock, which served as the spectator lookout for Mavericks, the hole in the ocean a half-mile off shore where some of the biggest swells in the world broke, triggering an annual worldwide surfing contest.

Approaching the boat harbor meant Half Moon Bay was nearby. After refilling water bottles, they rejoined Highway 1, forming a draft line headed south, soon passing a golf course along the highway. "Speaking of foursomes," Bert said to Boston, biking alongside, "golf's my father's game now. Same bunch of cronies in Arizona every Saturday around dawn."

"Maybe that's next for us," Boston replied, not seriously.

"You think?" Bert asked, speeding up to overtake Carlos, who had been going as fast as ever. Without much change in road grade ahead, it was a good stretch on which to make time. After about a mile, Erik took a turn in the front, then Boston before Carlos stormed back in front, pushing harder than ever until reaching the turnoff, which quickly forked right across Schoolhouse Creek.

Soon all four were huffing and puffing up the steep pitch, then descended into the Tunitas Creek drainage. Like all roads returning from the coast to the Skyline ridge, the first part was relatively gentle, traveling the flood plain. Then there was a little rise that was an ominous foreshadowing of what was coming. They were still biking hard and fast as the road disappeared past the last homesteads and into the redwood tree shaded forest.

Boston hung with the other three as the first really steep grade began but then started seeing a gap that he wasn't able to keep closed. Soon he noticed that Carlos had also lost contact with the other two. As the first steep, sharp right-hand uphill turns came in sight, Boston was well back of Bert and Eric, who were side by side. He saw Carlos glancing over his shoulder at him, which he only did when tiring.

Gaining on Carlos with every pedal, Boston caught up before the next hairpin as the other two were barely in sight ahead. Knowing that Tunitas was not forgiving of exhausted riders, he began to inexorably pull away from the Spaniard.

Alone, he was too far behind the other two to be a pursuer and had gained too much on Carlos to be the pursued. Instead, he was in this middle layer, alone and working hard to keep his momentum. These long climbs had their own agony-in-place, slowly, slowly gaining asphalt to the next bend, always wanting to stop for a rest but never grabbing the moment to do so. Starting to waver, he thought of the Death Ride waiting some eight months away and that each incline earned and locked away was going to pay off when the time came. The uphill strain was not fun, not even enjoyable, but necessary now that they had locked onto next July's ride.

More right-hand turns came until finally the road dipped slightly, crossing the upper drainage with a gentler grade. Not wanting to be caught from behind, he pushed his legs harder, shifting upward only a couple of gears. Ahead, the road's grade eased. Keeping a steady pace around the curves, he finally rounded the last earthen bank on his right to see the Skyline Boulevard intersection open up dead ahead.

Erik and Bert were sitting down on the side of the big turnaround, shaded by the nearby pines. Boston biked over to them, then got off, set his bike on the ground and plopped down beside them. "Where's Carlos?" Bert asked.

"Coming," Boston said, pleased to have finished in third. The thought then crossed his mind that maybe Carlos had a flat, or worse, some kind of medical problem. But, looking back at the near bend, he saw the Spaniard slowly arriving.

Bert scoffed. "Erik killed me. Famine took out War today."

"D'Artagnan," Erik corrected. "Today I earned my Musketeer's uniform. Finally was able to edge Bert on a climb."

"Carlos," Bert started, changing the subject, "what happened to you?"

"I don't know," Carlos shrugged.

"Too much Highway 1 headwind for even the Spanish Armada," Boston interjected. "You led most of the way."

"Tunitas was my Trafalgar."

"We all get to be sunk now and then," Bert said, rising up from his seat in the dirt, brushing off the bottom of his shorts. "You the man, d'Artagnan."

The four put on windbreakers for the descent, crossed Skyline Boulevard and headed down Kings Mountain Road, stopping at the historic Woodside Store on the corner of Tripp Road. "To Rossotti's?" Bert asked. Erik declined, saying that he was overdue at home as it was.

The other three continued on Woodside Road westward toward Menlo Park, turning onto Tripp Road, leaving the 1850s store where Yankee lumbermen used to gather, and headed south toward Alpine Road and the 1850s roadhouse, where Mexican herdsmen met during the same period, both ethnic groups carousing separately.

Continuing on Portola Road, they biked over an arm of the lake which drowned the little lumber town of Searsville, then past the corner of Old La Honda Road which was once dirt wagon tracks to Dennis Martin's mill, and around the loop to Alpine Road, which was once Maximo Martinez's trail from the coast leading to Rossotti's, the former grizzly bear arena of a hundred and fifty years ago.

"I never use to give my wife a time frame," Carlos remarked, referring to Eric's departure.

"I tell Katherine when to expect me, but I allow myself a couple hours past when I think I'll be home for sure," Boston said.

"When my marriage was going sour, I always tried to make it home for breakfast," Bert snickered. "Eric probably doesn't even notice other women."

He's also the only one who's never been divorced," Boston noted.

"Bite me," Bert shouted, standing in his pedals as he turned left, racing toward Rossotti's.

Boston chased after him.

—

Erik Erikksson biked through Menlo Park, hurrying to make it home on time. He promised Irina that he would accompany her shopping for a new Persian carpet. He had been reluctant to leave the other three though he had never been comfortable with a group mentality, large or small, and had never played any team sport. Even in Iceland, he had eschewed shotgun hunting parties to stalk game on his own. Competition had never been his thing, preferring instead the quiet and solo concentration required for use of bow and arrow.

For his own sons when they were younger, Erik encouraged them to participate in the same sports as other boys their age, glad that he had talked Irina out of naming their youngest son Ivan, being able to foresee the teasing nickname "Ivan the Terrible." Eventually, the two boys no more liked team sports than he had, preferring instead to go on family hiking and backpacking expeditions. As teenagers, they were less inclined to go on family day trips, giving Erik time to bike. Until meeting up with Boston, he had never considered biking with a set group.

Previously, he had thought of himself as the methodical archer, patiently waiting for his prey, which never showed, or else painstakingly, slowly releasing the arrow at targets. But today he admitted to himself that he had enjoyed besting Bert to the top of Tunitas Creek Road, realizing that maybe his veins contained the slash and burn Viking blood that had landed on Iceland's shores on his father's side, refined by his American mother, detoured by a romantic summer in Reykjavik.

When he arrived home, Irina was very eager to leave, not even allowing him to shower. When he asked what the rush was, she told him that they had an appointment. "Don't you realize it's hard to get a good deal when you give them the upper hand?" he asked her but other than that remark, he went along with her program, rapidly changing his clothes, realizing that she had waited patiently all day while he did his activity.

Instead of going to the carpet store however, she drove them to a massage and private hot tub room establishment. "My treat," she simply said when he question why they were there. As beat as he was, he figured a massage might feel pretty good but instead she had rented one of the private rooms.

Though the hot tub would feel welcome also, he could sense that she was feeling fairly amorous. That was confirmed when she nuzzled up to him in the shower. Revived by the hot water, he headed toward the hot tub but she went to the table bed where a clean sheet was stretched. "In the mood? I am," she announced.

"We don't know who else has been here?" he told her.

"Don't be so clinical," she replied. "You never want to do it at home because of the boys."

"As your gynecologist . . ." he began.

"You're not my doctor," she told him, "and don't use that as an excuse. You're either too tired from biking or too exhausted from work."

"What about getting in the hot tub first?" he tried.

"No, then you'll be a limp dishrag. I want to make love in the afternoon and I want to now." Hopping up on the table, she leaned back on her arms, opening up her legs. "Why don't you give me your own private pelvic?"

"Let's just get in the tub," he answered, shaking his head.

Frowning, she dropped her hand down. "I'm going to make love to somebody, even if it's to myself."

Erik walked over to her, standing between her legs as she squeezed her knees against his thighs. He resigned himself, asking, "Do we still have to shop for carpets afterwards?"

"The only carpet you have to deal with is mine," she responded, leaning back as he climbed onto the narrow table.

Chapter 8

Arastradero Road

Arastradero Road was formerly a logging haul road from the redwood-treed slopes above Portola Valley to the county roadway later designated in Palo Alto as El Camino Real. The timber was dragged southwards to build the Mission in Santa Clara as well as to construct houses in the Spanish colonial settlement of San Jose. The arastradero, from arastar meaning "to drag," was a shortcut from Rancho del Corte Madera beginning at Buelna's Casa de Tableta, or Card Table House, then a gambling/gathering locale, now a beer and burger roadhouse known as Rossotti's. Immediately crossing upper Los Trancos Creek, the haul road continued over low lying hills, traveling through the headlands above Deer Creek then followed Dry Creek, later named Barron Creek, until it veered southeast, dipping through the Adobe Creek bed near the current La Mesa Cemetery. To avoid paying a new bridge tax to the Mexican government but still accommodate oxen-pulled wagons, the arastradero was rerouted from the southeasterly veer directly to El Camino Real, which itself crossed Adobe Creek further downstream. The former alignment is now an easement for the piping of Hetch Hetchy water to Crystal Springs Reservoir.

The road's most famous resident was Juana Briones de Miranda, a daughter of a soldier Marcos Briones stationed at the Presidio by San Francisco Bay. At age eighteen, she married a Presidio soldier Apolinario Miranda. Allowed by the church to separate from her abusive husband, Señora Briones owned the first private house beyond the military grounds. Her residence was located on the sandy hillside above Yerba Buena Cove, where she cultivated the area around the future Washington Square to grow fruit trees, vegetables and corral her cattle. She sold produce and milk to whaling vessels and also administered to sick sailors. Two years before California was seized by the Americans, at age forty, she used her profits to purchase a 4400-acre rancho farther down the peninsula and had a rammed earth adobe house built on a small hilltop just south of the dusty arastradero road on what is now 4155 Old Adobe Road in southwestern Palo Alto. Her residence was famous for its hospitality with the local Mexicans. She continued to practice medicine and was rumored to have befriended Joaquin Murieta, a Mexican bandit in gold rush times. She sold part of her rancho herself with the rest eventually sold off by her descendents after her death in Mayfield at age 85. Juana Briones was the first person buried at Holy Cross Cemetery in Menlo Park.

November ride, part 4

Boston entered the outdoor table yard at Zotts, followed by Carlos with Bert trailing last. "No fair," Bert protested, putting his bike also against the fence next to the others. "You guys drafted me most of Alpine." He glanced over at Boston. "How do you always come up with that power at the end?"

"A lot of wind sprints," Boston replied. "Football, rugby, soccer."

"Guess having been a stationary soccer goalie didn't help me," Bert responded, leaving for the bar. "Get us some women while I'm inside, will you?"

While he was gone, the two women road bikers whom they saw in October arrived in the picnic area. They parked their bikes at a close-by table. Taking off their helmets and gloves, both headed toward the building's back door. "Will you watch our bikes?" the younger, blonde woman said to Carlos and Boston.

"For a price," Boston told her. "You have to later sit at our table."

She smiled her approval. The two continued through the back door of the bar while shortly after, Bert returned, carrying a large pitcher and three glasses. "Those two babes from a few weeks ago are here again," he announced as he put down everything down.

"They're going to sit with us," Carlos informed him.

"Carlos, you dog, I didn't think you had it in you."

"Boston asked them."

"Boston," guffawed Bert, "the married guy?"

"Thought I'd help out you poor miserable bachelors."

"Anytime, buddy, appreciate it." Bert poured all three glasses and they moved to the bench on the other side of the table, giving room for both women to sit across from them when they returned.

The two soon were back with a small pitcher and two glasses. "Offer still good?" asked the younger woman. She had very blonde hair, thick and straight, cut short stopping above her neck, piercing blue eyes on high cheekbones. Her face was clear, clean and beautiful, while her body was small, square-shouldered and muscular. In short, she was built like a jockey and looked like a model. Mid-twenties, Bert's previous estimate, seemed about right to Boston, who motioned for them to sit.

Drawing a deep breath, Bert said, "Glad you could join us. These are my friends Wyatt Earp and St. John the Apostle," nodding to the two of them. "D'Artagnan also rode with us but he had to go on home."

"What about your name?" the young girl asked, pouring her own beer.

"Teddy Roosevelt," Bert replied.

"Swell," she said, taking a sip. "I'm Calamity Jane and this is the Queen of Sheba," gesturing to her friend who appeared maybe a few years older, also attractive but shy, bigger than her younger friend, taller with the curved shoulders of a swimmer.

"Jane, Sheba," Bert replied, lifting his paper cup, "Cheers." They all tapped paper cups. "So, is this a regular stop after your ride?"

"Sometimes," said the young blonde said. "We saw you guys here before, right?" Then she turned to Carlos, "I've never met a saint before."

"He also an apostle," Bert added. "But we've never met a queen either." Turning to the dark-haired woman, he asked, "How are things in Sheba?"

"Got me," she smiled. "I live in Palo Alto actually, sorry."

"So do I," said Boston, "on Charleston near El Camino. My name's Boston." She appeared doubtful. "No, really. It's Boston."

"Bethy," she replied, "and I live off Arastradero, just the other side of El Camino."

"Hi, I'm Caitlin," the blonde woman beamed. "And I live on Arastradero, also close to El Camino so we're all pretty much neighbors. What about you guys? Teddy?"

"East Palo Alto. Real name is Bert but also known as Rough and Ready."

"Rough?"

"Think of me as always Ready," Bert countered.

"Is that so? And St. John?" Bethy, the dark-haired woman, asked.

"Carlos," answered the Spaniard.

"From Cupertino," Bert added.

"You still have a ways to go," Bethy told Carlos.

"That's what we keep telling him," Bert insisted.

"Are you the group wise-ass?" Caitlin asked.

"It's a dirty job but somebody's got to do it."

"A dirty guy for a dirty job, eh?"

"Eh? What's that, Canadian? You or your husband?"

"My boyfriend," she told him. Bert responded with a mock frown.

"Ex-boyfriend," Bethy corrected. "I'm the one with the husband."

"Soon to be ex-husband," Caitlin added. Bethy shook her head no. "We'll see," Caitlin hemmed. "So where'd you boys go biking today?"

Boston explained their route. The two had no idea where Pacifica was, much less Tunitas Creek, other than obviously on the coast. Bethy had been to Half Moon Bay but not Caitlin. They had never biked to Skyline but stayed mostly on the Loop and around Los Altos Hills.

"She kills me," Bethy told them.

"Does the name Calamity Jane really suit her?" Bert asked.

"More than you know."

"No, that was just off-the-cuff," Caitlin interrupted. She asked about their distance today, which Boston told her was about seventy miles. Impressed, she questioned if they were in training. Bert and Boston both answered back and forth by describing the Death Ride's 130 miles of distance and 16,000 feet of climbing, all in one day.

Appropriately impressed, Caitlin then asked if she and Bethy could join them. "Are you crazy?" Bethy told her. "How are we going to be able to do that ride?"

"We have until July to train," Caitlin responded. "Maybe these guys will let us train with them."

"Maybe we could use another pitcher?" Bert replied.

Carlos stood up. 'My turn to buy," he said and left the table, taking the empty pitcher with him.

"What a beautiful accent—where's he from?" she asked.

"Spain," Bert replied, then turned to Caitlin. "Really want to do the Death Ride with us?"

"I do," she answered. "I use to bike in college. A lot."

"Done with college?" Bert stopped her. "I figured you for a freshman, tops."

"I'm twenty-five, buster."

"Just as Bert guessed," Boston joined in. "Last time we saw you here."

"I'd be a little old for a freshman, huh, Bert?" she responded, raising an eyebrow in Bert's direction.

"Be a little old for Bert," Boston laughed.

"Don't mind him," Bert told her. "There's lots of time to get ready if you really want to do it."

"Now, that I've started again, I'd love to go for it." She paused, seeing how Bert and Boston would react and if they would object. "Bethy, too," she added, nodding toward her friend.

"Not me," said Bethy. "How am I going to do that and why do they call it the Death Ride? Henry's worried enough when I go out with Caitlin."

"It's just a catchy name," Boston answered.

Bert added. "It's a better title than The Will-Make-You-Feel-Like-Crap Ride."

"Ok, Mr. Wise-ass, what do you do for a living?"

"I'm a psychoanalyst."

"So am I," Bethy replied. "What's your doctoring name?"

"Bert Leunberger. What's yours?"

"Elizabeth Kono. Bethy for short."

They both stared at each. Then, on cue, both said, "Never heard of you," and laughed, along with the rest of the table.

"Seriously," said Caitlin, smiling. "I want to do this ride. But we'll need you guys to kick our butts."

Boston did not give her a strong reply, which Bert noticed, knowing that including the two women would alter Boston's carefully conceived training schedule, not to mention bringing single women into a male group that was half married.

Carlos meanwhile returned with a pitcher, which he distributed to all four, excluding himself. As he poured, Caitlin reached into her tiny fanny pack and pulled out a business card. It read: "Caitlin Carter, Associate Professor of Art, San Jose State" and had a cell phone number listed. "You have to promise to call me in February," she told Boston. Bert made sure he got a card also.

"Even if I can get in shape to do it, which I can't," Bethy started, "I don't know if my husband Henry will let me do it."

"What do you mean?" Caitlin told her. "He's gone on a lot of weekends and he's always gone in July. This will be perfect. We need a goal." She lifted her glass. "Here's to the Death Ride."

"Here's to new blood," Bert replied, clicking his plastic cup against hers, then added, "if it works out."

"So," Caitlin began, "why all the names from the past, Wyatt?"

"We were playing around comparing famous foursomes. Like the Earps of Tombstone," Boston answered.

"Like the movie?"

"Right," Boston smiled. "Also Bonanza, Mount Rushmore, the four Apostles."

"You guys are missing the greatest foursome of all," Bethy added. Bert and Boston wondered to each other. "A famous band," she told them.

"CSNY?" Boston asked but she looked blank. "Crosby, Stills, Nash and Young?"

"Sounds like a law firm," she told him.

"Ever hear of Neil Young?" Bert questioned her.

"Sure. Ever hear of the Beatles?"

"How could we forget the Beatles?" Bert turned to Boston. "So who gets to be Ringo?" Bert said, following his beer with a little drumroll on the table. Boston only shook his head.

With the sky darkening due to shorter daylight, they soon got ready to leave together. Bert decided to also take Arastradero to stay with the group.

Winding up a short climb, all five of them stayed together up toward the crest. Feeling like he owned the upcoming downhill, Boston stood in his pedals, pumping as hard as he could before dropping into a tight tuck. Bent over the bars, he felt at first like he had broken away, but once at the bottom and up a small rise, he sensed being trailed. Still, he thought he had enough energy to keep being slipstreamed. With Page Mill Road far in the distance, he was passed on the left as, unexpectedly, a tight female bottom in black-spandex swung in front. Drafting for a few moments, he then overtook Caitlin a hundred yards from the intersection ahead.

When the group reassembled and caught their breaths, Boston turned to Caitlin. "You're fast."

"It was the beer," she grinned. "Beer sometimes makes me feel feisty."

"Where did you say you biked before?" Boston asked.

"In college," she replied. "UCLA."

"Bike to class?" Bert asked.

"Yeah, to class," she admitted. "And on the team. You know, against other colleges."

"A ringer," said Bert.

"A ringer is right," said Bethy, biking with Carlos up to them. "You ought to see her trophies."

"I hope to," Bert smiled, with a wink.

"Wise-ass," Caitlin grinned.

There was no more racing as they continued to the Foothill Boulevard stoplight, where Carlos said good-bye and turned south.

Continuing on Arastradero, Bethy turned left at Donald Drive, waving good-bye as she rode off. A few blocks ahead on the left was Caitlin's apartment house. Stopping, she reminded the two, "So, you'll call me in February."

Boston nodded. "Yes, I'll call."

"I'll be ready in February, don't worry. Thanks for the ride," she told them, waiting for a break in traffic, "and the beer."

"February," called Bert as she left. The two men continued on Arastradero. "Good," Bert said. "It's about time we had some women join us. And a good rider to boot."

"Your dad ever golf with women in his foursome?" Boston asked him.

"No, but that's different. You can't add someone to a golf foursome."

"That's beside the point," Boston responded. "No women ever went on my dad's fishing trips. How am I going to tell Katherine that two women in their twenties have joined the group?"

"Bethy might be thirty," Bert raised a grin. Boston gave him the unappreciated sarcasm look. Maybe that'll make Katherine want to start riding again," Bert tried.

"You know, I don't think she ever enjoyed it, not with her second husband and not with me either. She certainly never had the exhilaration Caitlin showed when she passed me."

Bert pondered for a while, then added, "My dad use to play mixed doubles in tennis."

"So how'd that turn out?" Boston asked.

"Come to think of it, that was how he met his second wife," Bert responded. "Maybe that's why he had to switch to golf. You'll think of something to tell Katherine before February."

"Sure," muttered Boston, wondering to himself how Katherine would respond once he figured out how to tell her. For the past five years of their marriage, she had conceded him the Saturday morning bike rides with whatever male acquaintances who were along. That was granted, he felt, because she had begged off after they had ridden together during a year's dating and marriage. Though she had never ruled out his riding with other females, it had never come up before in the four years since she had quit biking herself.

Recently, she had not been pleased with the extra hours he was spending at work. He had yet to introduce to her the possibility that his civil engineering company might be sold and that he would be then seeking employment elsewhere, especially in a down market. Remarried so suddenly at middle age, he was not confident in their relationship to share downbeat personal concerns.

They knew about each other's previous marriages but did not interact with the former spouses, except for various situations involving Boston's daughter, now in college. Katherine had always been congenial with his ex-wife Shannon, remarried and living in Stockton. No other women from Boston's past had ever reappeared in his life and so the opportunities for Katherine to exhibit jealousy had been limited.

Having the two young women along would definitely add some interest to the training rides, Boston contemplated, as well as provide still another diversion to the same old financial bind at his company. Still, he was not prepared to announce the addition to his wife, waiting in their house a few blocks away as he and Bert approached the El Camino Real stoplight, a bright red in the evening gloom.

Chapter 9

Old La Honda Road

The road to La Honda originally followed the wagon tracks to Dennis Martin's sawmill, built in the ravine in which the creek has been named in his memory. Born in Ireland, Martin arrived in California in 1844 along with his father and brother-in-law as part of the first wagon party that crossed the Sierra Nevada. The expedition ran into snow by Donner Lake, not as much as the Donner Party did two years later, but enough to leave a leg sore, seventeen-year-old Moses Schallenberger behind along with their wagon goods as the rest of the party traversed the mountains. Three months later, the twenty-three-year old Martin had a heroic crossing on self-made snowshoes to successfully retrieve him.

With money made from the gold rush and as working as a lumberman, Martin began to purchase property in the redwood area of Portola Valley. Besides starting his lumber business, he built a church on his property on San Francisquito Creek near the base of Jasper Ridge. Services at his small St. Denis Church were performed by the Jesuits of Mission Santa Clara beginning in 1856. He also built a cemetery on the hill, first burying his 86-year-old father and later the local pioneer Maximo Martinez, former owner of the surrounding Rancho Corte de Madera.

Other Martin holdings however fell victim to an adverse Spanish land grant court ruling and then, now widowed, he was forced to sell his two sawmills in the ravine. In 1882, broke, he moved to San Francisco where he died, penniless, eight years later at age 69 and was buried in his own cemetery. In 1953, any graves that could be identified were moved to Holy Cross Cemetery in Menlo Park.

A narrow, twisty toll road, called the Redwood City and Pescadero Road, was built close-by in 1874 to La Honda en route to Pescadero, using Martin's sawmill approach for its initial leg. When a new road was built in 1914-15, the original road became the Old Road, intersecting the new route, now Highway 84, on the west side of Skyline a few miles north of La Honda.

About a mile from Skyline, Old La Honda Road passes by Upenuf Road, so named because stage coach passengers, having walked "up enough" through the steepest sections of roadway, finally had reached a break in grade where they could get a breather as well as a drink at a saloon conveniently awaiting.

December ride

Bert Leunberger arrived at Boston Reed's in the front yard on Charleston Road about 9 am as scheduled. Boston's wife Katherine Kirk invited him inside as her husband finished getting dressed for the ride. He accepted a cup of coffee. She asked him about his son and daughter. Since the divorce, he had not much contact, Bert admitted, due to their both living out of state. His daughter Jaqueline was working in New York and his son Michael in Seattle. Katherine asked if he was planning to visit them and he replied he hoped to next year but the divorce had not gone well and contact was still a little uncomfortable, even three years later.

The sky was gray and heavy. Maybe it would rain although it was not predicted. Carlos and Erik weren't riding today due to other things. With just Bert along, Boston opted to take Arastradero Road to eventually Old La Honda Road.

Out the door and on the bikes, Boston asked, "Do you miss the contact with your kids?"

"I miss a lot of things," Bert said abruptly and was silent for a couple minutes. Then he added, "I miss the family times I guess, but that was years ago. Jackie and Mike are grown, adults. There's a lot of anger around still. With me, too," he added. "But what I really miss is this lady friend I had in Tacoma. When I'd visit Mike, I use to knock a homa in Tacoma."

"That's real cute. You and Mike also double date?"

Bert ignored the sarcasm. "She married some smuck."

"So, why didn't she marry you?" Boston continued. "You're smucky enough."

"Not quite," Bert replied. "Anyway, I got other lady friends here and there. Although lately, buddy, the herd is thinning out."

Coming up on Arastradero, they crossed the road and continued toward the foothills, slowly. "How's married life?" Bert asked. "You were a single guy. Do you miss the action?"

"I get plenty of action," Boston replied. "All at home."

"Not sex," Bert responded. "I mean the action of meeting somebody new, getting turned on, making your move. That kind of action."

"I forget, Bert, are you fifty or fifteen?"

"Fifteen, definitely. Why else would I be doing the Death Ride?"

A woman's voice from behind them called out, "Did somebody say Death Ride?" As they partially turned, Caitlin rode forward alongside. "I thought I recognized you two, even if you were going so slowly."

"Good morning, we were just warming up," Bert said.

"Just gabbing away like old hens, I noticed. Where're you headed?"

"Old La Honda," Boston answered. "What about you?"

"I was just going out for a spin. Old La Honda sounds good. Bethy and I started up it once but we didn't know how far it went, so we turned around after a mile or so. It looked pretty hard. Mind if I tag along?"

"Not at all."

"Where's your friend?" Bert asked.

"She and Henry are doing something so it's just me today. Where's your Spanish pal?"

"He thinks it's going to rain so he's working today."

"And what if it does rain?"

"We get wet," Bert said.

"Oh yes, Mr. Wise-ass still at it."

"You remembered."

"Couldn't forget you."

A car passed them on Arastradero Road, lightly honking the horn, convincing them to bike single file. There was one big hill where all three went into low gear, then down toward Rossotti's.

This section of roadway Bert considered his specialty. Passing Boston, he sped up but not in full racing mode, just enough the test the other two. At the crest, Caitlin passed him and led all the way to Alpine Road, biking hard to stop sign. "Hey," she said as the other two pulled in behind her, "no challenge?"

"Got to let you win something," Bert grinned.

"You guys are all heart, I can tell."

Crossing, they continued around the loop to the Old La Honda Road entrance on the left.

Allowing a couple cars to pass by, Bert turned and then biked to a halt near an old stone bridge adjacent to Dennis Martin Creek. Stuffing her jacket into her jersey back pocket, Caitlin asked, "So what's Old La Honda. Sounds like a ghost town."

"La Honda's the town," Boston told her. "It's the road that's old. Highway 84 is the 'New' La Honda Road?"

"How old is 'New' La Honda Road?"

"About a hundred years old," Boston answered.

"Wow," she said. "Then this 'Old' road must be really old."

"Yeah," said Boston, "kind of like Bert."

"Hey!" Bert objected. "Just try to keep up with this old man." He took off, pedaling hard, with the road dark with a heavy tree canopy and thick clouds above. Caitlin quickly followed with Boston trailing.

As a rugby player, Boston was solid and fast, but his physique and weight worked against him going uphill. Bert was taller, slimmer, with his longer legs and arms working with more leverage. Caitlin hardly weighed anything, efficient and muscular. Boston quickly lost sight of her and Bert.

When he reached the top, they were off to one side, standing over their bikes.

"How do you like the road?" Boston finally had enough breath to ask Caitlin.

"It's a good hill. I like it."

"A good hill?" Bert gasped. "She dogged me the whole way and then passed me."

"He passed me back. I blew it," she said. "Misjudged the end."

"You about killed me. What do you weigh, about a hundred pounds?"

"A hundred and five. But I'm trying to diet."

"You're kidding?" Boston exclaimed.

"Yes, I am," she smiled at him. "Ok, where to now? I'm getting cold."

"Wait a minute," Boston said, still huffing. "Put your coat back on. We'll be going downhill."

She glanced around, seeing the highway rise in both directions. He pointed across Skyline to where the west side of Old La Honda dove into a hole between trees. With jackets on, all three crossed the highway and started down the backside in the darkness of the canopy. Finally, they broke out from the forest as Boston came to a stop at a left turn bend. The view ahead was distancing staggered valleys, now turning green with seasonal rains. Bert and Caitlin stopped along with him. "When it's clear," said Boston, "you can see the ocean from here."

"It's beautiful," Caitlin said.

"That reminds me," Bert interjected. "I have to take a piss." He set down his bike and walked over to the shoulder, which had small dirt level area lined with thick brush. Only a few feet away, he turned his back to the other two and reached down his shorts.

"Right here?" exclaimed Caitlin.

"Nobody's coming," Bert replied, daylighting and letting the stream go.

"Bert doesn't believe in going behind trees," Boston told her.

"There's too much poison oak," Bert said. "Snakes, ticks."

"What about me?" she said. "I have to pee, too."

Finished, he pulled up the front of his shorts. "Can't be modest and be in the group."

"Are you daring me?" she asked, setting her bike on the ground next to his, then again, "Are you?" Striding over to the shoulder, avoiding the puddle he had just made, she stood, gazing at the two of them before turning her back. "Little trickier for a girl," she said, then lowered her shorts to her ankles and squatted down with her leggings still over her knees, stopping at mid-thigh. Nothing happened at first and then she gushed out.

For a moment there was silence. Finally, Bert joked to Boston, "Ever read about the Johnstown Flood? Maybe somebody should warn La Honda."

"Shut up, Wise-ass," she answered, still going. Then, finished, she stepped forward, pulled her shorts back up and turned around. "Much better. I've had to go since the bottom of the climb."

"So, what's the tattoo?" Boston asked.

"What tattoo?" Bert asked.

"You weren't supposed to be watching," she scolded.

"Only for a second," Boston stated sheepishly.

"Com'on, what tattoo?" Bert repeated.

Turning around again, she pulled down her shorts, exposing both buttocks. "Can you tell?"

"I better get closer," Bert told her, putting his face right next to her bottom, seeing a blue feature off to the right. "It looks like a cub or something."

"It's a Bruin. You know, UCLA," she answered, allowing him to keep looking. "All the bike team girls got one."

"Bear-ass," Boston deadpanned.

"You got it," she grinned, pulling her shorts back up. "Go Bruins."

"Boston, did you get a good enough look?" Bert asked. "Oh that's right, you're married."

"I think he got a good look anyway," Caitlin said, picking up her bike.

"Only at the tattoo," Boston responded, starting out once again. The three of them sped downhill to Highway 84. From there, turning right, they rode single file the few miles back uphill toward Skylonda, going fast but not racing, all three sharing leads.

They paused at the Skyline stop sign. "Ever been down 84?" Boston asked Caitlin.

"Not even by car."

"The only rule is don't try to keep up with Bert."

"Why's that?"

Bert answered, yelling as he took off, "Because he's so damn fast!" She pursued with Boston behind. Highway 84 started out gently but then quickly cut and twisted into sharp turns with long straight-aways in-between. Boston lost sight of Bert and Caitlin after the first few turns. As always, he just let the faster riders go, staying always cautious, especially with the road a little damp. He knew of others who had crashed on the descent, winding up with broken arms, collarbones, concussions. The real danger, however, was losing it into the oncoming lane.

Only a couple of times had he ever missed a turn to jump the centerline and never on this road. Most downhill riders on 84 were able to stay ahead of trailing cars. Boston preferred to ride more cautiously, slowing over to let cars pass, thereby negating the additional danger of being run over in case of a fall.

Arriving at the bottom without incident, he found Bert and Caitlin waiting just past the stop sign below. "She shadowed me the whole way down," Bert told him.

"I love following somebody who really knows how to downhill. I learn a lot that way," she said.

"Did you ever brake?" Bert asked her.

"Not as much as you, I'm sure. Remember, I'm only a hundred and five pounds."

"And dieting," he reminded her.

"Wise-ass."

Boston directed the route back to Palo Alto to the Stanford golf course junction where Bert usually continued straight home. With Caitlin along, Bert chose stay with them, veering to the right toward Arastradero Road. After a half-mile, they started to feel raindrops. "Thought you said it wasn't going to rain this morning," Bert told Boston.

"We'll be home before it hits," he replied.

"You'll be home, not me."

"If you take off now, you might make it."

Bert sighed, "Can I trust you two kids?"

"Don't worry, big guy," Caitlin told him, "we won't party without you."

Bert smiled. "Ok," he told her. "Good ride. I'm glad we linked up."

"Me, too," she said. "Thanks for showing me Old La Honda."

"Thanks for showing me the tattoo!" he hollered as he took the next left on Page Mill Road toward the bay.

Boston and Caitlin continued on Foothill Expressway to a left on Arastradero, now headed toward her apartment house. "When can we ride again?" she asked him as they casually followed the bike lane.

"February for sure."

"Not before?"

"Holidays, weather. The rest of this month isn't usually very good for riding. Neither is January."

"Well, keep me in mind," she told him, "just in case." With a smile, she checked traffic and then crossed the street to her building. Boston gave a little wave and continued toward home as the rain began to sprinkle, lightly dousing himself and Bert riding to his apartment, on the other side of town.

—

Alone in his apartment, fresh from the shower with glass of wine in hand, Bert contemplated calling his son Michael in Seattle, seeing how Boston had asked him about his kids earlier in the ride. Bert mused that his "homa in Tacoma" was a good line even if it was a one-night stand in a Holiday Inn with a woman of whose name he had absolutely no memory. That she had gotten married was true also, if she kept to her engagement of a few months away, as she had confided that evening. Out drinking in a motel bar did not show much fidelity to the upcoming ceremony, nor did sharing a room for the night with Bert Leunberger.

She was cute with long black hair, thin, mid-thirties and somewhat glassy-eyed after the two drinks Bert bought her. He did "knock it homa" then, and with someone ten years younger, but that was that. Trying to meet women through singles web sites or personal ads had only cost him a lot of time and money with rare result over the few years he had been divorced. For the last year, he had pretty much given up on strangers, preferring to circulate only amongst a group of several long time acquaintances who still were not opposed to taking him in, at least for a night or weekend.

He would have loved for Michael to call him to invite him up to Seattle for Christmas. His daughter Jackie already had plans to go to the Caribbean, but Michael, as far as Bert knew was free, except for the fact that he would probably spend Christmas with his mother, Bert's ex-wife.

If by chance, he did make it to Seattle to visit his son over the holidays, he knew he would somehow have to check out that Holiday Inn to see if his anonymous one-night lover was still there at the bar. If so, that wouldn't say much for either one of them but it had been a grand night back then. Thanks to a little coke, from her purse, they were still screwing when the sun rose.

His remaining holiday possibility was to hook up over Christmas with an old friend's ex-wife now living in Los Banos. Beyond that, the prospects were grim. Looking at his phone table, he noticed the business card of the blonde biker from UCLA, Caitlin Carter. Shutting his eyes, he pictured her pants down tattooed ass for a moment as he sipped his wine. Then there was that inelegant moment when she followed his rule and squatted unladylike with her pants around her ankles.

For a moment, Bert thought about dialing her but decided against it. Los Banos would be quite chilly later on in December and it was a long drive, but he would be welcome between the sheets there, at least for a night or two. Meanwhile, he got up and searched for his one and only x-rated DVD.

Chapter 10

Joaquin Road

Joaquin Murieta was shot by a band of California Rangers led Captain Harry Love on July 25, 1853 in the Arroyo Cantua near the town of Three Rocks on the western edge of the San Joaquin Valley, so Spanish-named in 1805 for the Virgin Mary's father, Joachim in English.

The short, steep road called Joaquin in San Mateo County connects the upper stretch of Alpine Road with the ridge of the Los Trancos Woods tract, where the top road was to be called Murieta but was changed to Old Spanish Trail to honor its previous use. The ridge was once a well-traveled Indian trading path that Antonio Buelna later used to drive cattle between his two ranchos, granted to him in 1839 by Governor Alvarado. Born in Monterey in 1790, Buelna's western rancho was on the coast at San Gregorio and the other bordered the Arroyo de San Francisquito, or San Francisquito Creek, on property later acquired by Leland Stanford for his university in honor of his son's name.

The ridge trail was more easily traveled than the current Alpine Road alongside Corte Madera Creek, which slopes are subject to slides and deadfall trees. The ridge, dividing the drainage between Corte Madera and Los Trancos creeks, was later named Coal Mine Ridge and was mined from 1855 to the early 1860s. Though the paved road stops at residences on Vista Verde, the open ridge continues uphill to Page Mill Road. In 1823, Spanish soldiers reportedly followed the ridge trail in pursuit of the Indian outlaw Pomponio before abandoning their chase at Devils Canyon.

The trail and later Buelna's cattle path passed through the wooded surrounds called Corte Madera, meaning Place of Cutting Wood, which was a rancho granted to Maximo Martinez. Born at the San Francisco Presidio, also in 1790, Martinez had been a soldier there from 1819-23 and later was a regidor, or councilman, for the City of San Jose from 1833-34 before receiving the rancho grant in 1834. Wanting to oust American interlopers logging the valuable redwoods, the Mexican government granted huge tracts of land to its leading citizens, especially those who had served its military.

Also running through the former Martinez' property is a creek, which was then called Arroyo de Maximo in the 1850s. In 1852, Martinez transferred some of his property on the bank of the small stream to Felix Buelna, Antonio's nephew, who built the Casa de Tableta at that location, also the junction of Arastradero Road and the main road, later named Alpine Road. After several owners and name changes, the roadhouse was eventually called Alpine Inn.

William Stanton acquired the establishment in 1868 from Buelna as compensation for gambling debts. The Arroyo de Maximo was designated as Stancos Creek on an 1876 map, possibly referring to the new owner. (A Stancos River exists in Romania but there is no Spanish name origination). In 1933, the United States Board on Geographic Names rejected Stancos Creek, allowing instead the name Los Trancos, which means "a bar," such as might be placed behind a door to prohibit entry, which in a way refers to the original rancho grant that was intended to bar the Yankee woodcutters from further intrusion into the redwoods.

January ride

Bert Leunberger and Boston Reed rode westward on Charleston toward the hills on a morning that seemed sure to rain. Instead of chancing bad weather, Carlos Cordova decided to work while Erik Erikksson had gone skiing with his sons and Irina. Boston figured that Bert and himself had but a short time before it downpours to do a quick hill, like Joaquin at the end of Alpine Road.

Stopping at the El Camino Real stoplight, Bert mentioned to Boston, "Can we make a little detour?"

Boston eyed him. "What kind of detour?"

"Go by Bethy's house to see if she and Caitlin want to join us. I told Caitlin there would just be the two of us today."

"I thought we were going to wait until February to ride with them."

"We can but, what, it's only a couple weeks away. I called her last night to see how their training was going. Anyway, February was to start the group rides. This is just you and me."

Just you and me, thought Boston, and two other girls. He felt he could always explain to Katherine the past La Honda ride with Caitlin because they had met by chance. Finally, he rationalized that they both were Bert's guests and he, Boston, was not sleeping with either one so there was nothing to feel bad about.

Donald Drive was only a couple blocks ahead. They turned and went to the given house number. Boston waited at curbside while Bert parked his bike and rang the doorbell. After the door swung open, Bert motioned for Boston to follow him as he went inside. Grudgingly, Boston parked his bike next to Bert's and went through the door left open. With the living room empty, he continued into the kitchen and saw Bethy and Caitlin standing outside under a large overhang as Bert was taking the front wheel off a bike. Bethy's bike had a flat tire and Bert was fixing it.

Boston looked around. Bethy's house was two-story, more modern than his own single story Eichler. "She has a hot tub," Caitlin told him. "I love it." Boston saw the tub in a corner of the yard, large, covered, shielded by lattice and thick vines from the view of other houses.

Soon Bert was done with the repair. He put the wheel back on and pumped it up while Bethy finished getting ready. Boston announced they were riding to Joaquin, at the end of Alpine Road.

"It's steep," Boston warned the two girls. Today will be short so we can beat the rain later this morning."

"Can't we bike in the rain?" Caitlin asked.

"We'd get soaked, but it's also harder to brake, which makes it tricky doing hills."

"No rain," Bert said. "Don't worry. Tell them about Joaquin."

Boston related the story of Joaquin Murieta, a Mexican bandit around the time of the gold rush who used to visit Juana Briones on her rancho off Arastradero.

"Makes it interesting," Bethy commented. "I never heard of Joaquin the bandit."

"Just wait until you see Joaquin the road," Bert told her.

Boston directed them over the usual route to Rossotti's, then up Alpine where the road wound around several curves until it turned left at Corte Madera Creek, continuing as a single lane alongside the deeply cut stream. "It's beautiful back in here," Caitlin said. "I never knew about this road."

"Look at those logs in the creek," Bethy stated. To their right were many landslides with several trees over a hundred feet long crashed over the creek. Meanwhile, on their side of the drainage, the upslopes had been regraded and supported by retaining walls.

"This Indians and Mexicans used the ridge to avoid slides and fallen trees. This road was made for stagecoaches," Boston informed them.

As the road steepened slightly, Bethy began to fall behind. Boston stayed with her while the other two ambled ahead. "Thanks," she told him as she struggled alongside. "I'm not anywhere near in shape as you guys." He found a sweet sadness about her and he appreciated that she was trying hard.

"Caitlin's a natural," she continued. "Making a good comeback, don't you think?"

"Comeback?"

"She only gave birth two years ago."

"Birth? She's never talked about her child?"

"Oops," said Bethy. "Forget I said that."

"How can I do that?"

"Look," said Bethy, "don't tell her I told you. She has a two-year-old daughter."

"Where's the daughter now?"

"Oh God, it's a long story," said Bethy. "I'll tell you but don't ask me anymore. Her daughter lives with her dad, the daughter's dad. He was Caitlin's biking coach. They were never married. I'm sure she'll spill the beans to you and Bert someday. Or not. I don't know." Then she changed the subject. "This road's doesn't look as steep as it feels."

"It only gets harder," he told her, biking in the shade of redwoods and firs, thinking of his own daughter when she was two, now twenty and not much younger than Caitlin. Caitlin's sweet demeanor had not revealed any inner turmoil.

Standing on a couple short pitches, they reached a wide spot at the base of Joaquin Road, where Bert and Caitlin were circling, regaining energy. Off to the side, Joaquin looked an immediately formidable fifteen-to-twenty-percent grade.

"I don't even know if I can walk that," Bethy stated, "much less bike it."

"Looks worse than it is," Bert told her. "Once you get going, it's not so bad."

"Com'on, slow poke," Caitlin called to him, quickly turning up the hill while getting a jump on Bert who had just circled past the bottom. Instantly, he took up the chase.

Meanwhile, Boston made enough traverses to keep Bethy in sight but still, even while going slow, was much faster than she was going. Bert and Caitlin disappeared around an uphill turn. When Boston got to the same turn, he lost sight of Bethy below. One last climb and he reached the other two. Bert was looping back and forth while Caitlin was straddling her bike, leaning on her handlebars.

"I didn't know if I was going to make it," she stated.

"You started off so damn fast," Bert told her.

"I ran out of breath midway. That sucked. Good," she said, gasping, "I love it."

Boston paused where he could keep an eye out for Bethy. Finally, she reached him. "I made it," she exhaled, stopping. "I never quit."

"Good girl," said Caitlin, admiring her. "Bethy's tough. She just looks like a sweet softie."

"That hill's insane," Bethy sputtered. "Caitlin, what have you gotten me into?"

"Two words," Bert responded instead. "Death Ride."

"Death Ride," Bethy repeated. "Well, that should've been a red flag."

"We better go," Boston announced, one palm up. "I'm starting to feel raindrops."

"Let's go back Arastradero before we get soaked," Boston announced. Taking the lead, he took the group down the steep and narrow residential streets of hilly Los Trancos. With moisture on the road, all four checked their speed through the tight turns until reaching the bottom and then Bert and Boston took off rapidly with Caitlin chasing from behind. Boston hung right behind Bert, then outsprinted him to the Alpine Road stop sign. Caitlin was right behind them both. All three were panting, catching their breaths while waiting for Bethy.

"You guys are just what my girl Caitlin needed," said her dark-haired friend, arriving shortly. "I could never race her."

With more rain falling, all four took it easy, turning at Arastradero, staying close together as the rain got heavier, staying in a silent, soaked draft line all the way to the Foothill Boulevard stoplight, where they waited.

"I'm drowning," Caitlin shouted to the others. "Let's all go to Bethy's and get some hot chocolate. Is that ok?" she called to Bethy, who said it was fine with her.

"Sounds good to me," Bert said. "I'm soaked to the skin and I'm freezing." Just as wet and cold, Boston did not commit however.

"Remember the hot tub," Caitlin added.

"Tally ho!" Bert shouted as the light changed, taking off before Boston could say anything. He trailed the group as the three turned onto Donald Drive and then into Bethy's driveway. Opening the side gate, she led them to the backyard where they all parked their bikes. With it pouring, Boston was not inclined to rush home. Besides, it was so early yet that Katherine would not be expecting him until a couple hours later.

"Everybody has to take off their wet shoes before you go inside," Bethy told them, flipping off her shoes and yanking off the wet socks underneath.

"If we're getting in the hot tub," Caitlin said, "we might as well take off everything." She began unzipping her wet windbreaker.

"Somebody has to help me with the hot chocolate," Bethy announced.

"I will," said Boston, removing his footwear.

Windbreaker off, Caitlin began tugging her jersey over her head. "Bethy, help," she cried. Bethy took hold of the sleeves and pulled the jersey off. Caitlin then flipped off her jogging bra. "I know I'm built like a boy," she said, bare-chested, staring at Bert.

"I wasn't looking," he responded, turning away.

"Yes, you were," she contradicted, slapping his arm. Then she turned to Bethy, who was shaking her head. "You know, these guys made me pee in the middle of road last time we rode together."

"Not true," Bert protested. "Not exactly. It was on the shoulder."

"Ok, right." Caitlin pulled down her bike shorts and kicked them off, standing there now just in her leggings up to mid-thigh.

"I confess to looking now," Bert admitted, stepping back so he could eye the young girl.

"So I'm shaved, big deal," she replied, only partially covering herself with both hands.

"No, I mean the leggings. Very sexy."

"You see a naked girl and you think her leggings are sexy?" Caitlin stated, hands away and starting to pull one down.

"So I'm a stockings kind of guy," he shrugged.

"Wise-ass," she responded as she took the other one off, standing now totally naked. "Com'on, slow poke," she hollered, running down the path in the rain to the hot tub corner. Bert began quickly undressing as, now barefoot, Boston followed Bethy inside to the kitchen.

"I think she likes your friend," Bethy told him, searching for the chocolate.

"Kind of obvious, I guess, but it's looking mutual."

"You're married, right?"

"Yep," Boston said, "and my wife Katherine's a big fan of hot tubs."

"Why don't you invite her over?" she replied, pouring dry chocolate into four large coffee cups.

Doubting that such invitation would be good idea, Boston struggled. "I wish I'd known about it in advance."

"Spontaneity not your thing? Not her thing?"

"She doesn't even know I'm biking with you two. Bert sprung that on me at the last moment."

"Oops. How long have you two been married?"

"Five years." As he answered, he thought of their first months together long ago. Both he and Katherine had been divorced for a couple of years with hers being her second. From the moment they began dating, they were mutually exclusive and soon living together within weeks. Boston's daughter had since graduated from high school onto college, but he and his wife had merely moved from just turning forty to mid-forties with little attitude change toward one another. Having come across one another by chance, both had recognized that they were two independent persons who had joined each other.

"Five years is one year longer than my marriage."

"Where's your husband? Is he coming home soon? What will he think?"

"He's away," she told him, then changed the subject. "You think everybody wants whipped cream?"

"I guess so, although it's going to be a little tricky drinking it in the rain."

"We'll use little saucers. On top instead of on bottom." She filled up the cups with an instant-hot faucet. "You take two and I'll take two," she told him, then led him to the patio door. Outside, she quickly disrobed and walked through the drops to the hot tub, where the other two were almost hidden by the tub's steam. Holding two cups and saucers, he watched her from behind, shapely hips shifting back and forth and the rain strung her black hair down her bare back, a sight he somewhat ashamedly had all to himself.

Part of the lure of biking is unexpected adventure, Boston told himself. And didn't Katherine just hop into the pool at Dennis Crowe's? I'm not sleeping with these girls, so what's the deal? Finally, he put down the cups and proceeded to undress, soon walking absurdly naked in the chilly rain while carrying in each hand a cup of hot chocolate with the saucer on top.

The three others were waiting as, handing over two cups, he climbed into the tub. The water was very hot with cold drops splattering the surface. Boston quickly submerged to his shoulders to join the others.

"Here's to Joaquin," said Bert, taking off the saucer and holding out his cup in the rain. "The road and the outlaw."

"And to the Death Ride," added Caitlin, arm up and tapping her cup to his.

"Oh God, don't remind me," Bethy muttered, rising up to tap her cup, her dark hair wetly draped onto her shoulders, breasts bobbing at the water's surface.

Chapter 11

Sierra Road

Sierra is the Spanish word for "mountains." Sierra Road is located above Milpitas, which is an Indian derivative for little cornfields, with a rancho of the same name granted in 1835 followed by the town founded in the 1850s. Local maps identified the sierra as an eastern landmark. Sierra Road begins on the lower flatlands and continues eventually to Calaveras Road, which also rises from the urban flatland before snaking into the eastern hills.

February rides, part 1

Katherine Kirk arrived at Irina Erikksson's house Friday with a set of plans for Irina to provide structural design and calculations. Irina's house also being her office, the two sat down for coffee in the breakfast nook. Katherine resumed a conversation she had started by phone once she had learned from Boston about the female additions to the biking group. "So, Erik has never told you about those women they're biking with."

"He says he wasn't there at Rossotti's when they met."

"I thought he went on the big Half Moon Bay ride that day."

"He did but says he turned off before they went to Rossotti's. So, who are they?"

"Boston says they're pretty good riders and that they want to do the Death Ride, also."

"So, why do they have to join our guys?"

"I don't know," said Katherine, sipping her coffee. "You know they have to be good looking for our guys to agree."

"Erik hasn't met them."

"I meant for Boston and Bert to agree. Well, for Bert I doubt they would necessarily have to be good looking."

"And what about Carlos?"

"Carlos was also at Zotts that day. But he would no more extend an invitation to a woman than he'd fly to the moon. I think he's scared of women."

"Doesn't he have a bunch of daughters?"

"Three of them. But his wife was very temperamental." Katherine gave Irina a look. "So, it's all Boston and Bert and I suspect more Bert than Boston."

"I think so, too," agreed Irina. "Are you going to stop it?"

"At least Boston had the balls to tell me. I give him credit for that so I doubt he's sleeping with either one." Irina raised an eyebrow. "Please," objected Katherine. "I'd know."

"No new jewelry?"

"No, damn it," Katherine smiled, then seriously went on. "In the first place, he wouldn't do that to me. In the second place, if he did, he'd have to know I'd figure it out. I told him that I wanted to meet both of them Saturday morning before they take off. So everyone is coming by our house."

"Wish I could be there, too."

"I'll tell you all about it. I imagine they're cute as hell. One was on the UCLA biking team. The other is married but no kids."

"And if they're both beautiful?"

"If they're both beautiful, probably not a problem," Katherine laughed. "If just one is cute as hell, that might be a concern. The other one would just be a cover. Anyway, I'll know tomorrow."

"These guys were just supposed to bike, not meet girls."

"They're men," said Katherine. "Moth to a flame."

Irina poured more coffee into their cups. "Erik hasn't been circling my flame recently, or else maybe my flame has gone out." She went onto to explain that there had been no more trips to the for-rent hot tubs and, in fact, Erik had been more or less turned off by the whole experience. He never really even liked motel rooms because others shared them.

Katherine listened, measuring what Irina was saying against her own feelings about Boston. Actually, he had been very passionate at times lately but his life still revolved around his biking, which now seemed to be expanding with the addition of these two women, whoever they were. Katherine had tried to get him excited about a trip to Europe in the fall. She wanted to see what was new with the architecture of Europe, not having been there since she was in college.

Recently she had met Dennis for lunch and had discussed with him how unsuccessful she had been in getting Boston excited about a vacation trip after his July Death Ride. Though he sympathized with her, talking to Dennis about traveling abroad was fairly pointless. He was ensconced in his Crowe's

Nest, except for when he went hunting in Wyoming once a year. Thinking of Dennis' pool, she mentioned to Irina that she wished she and Boston had their own hot tub.

"Erik says they're too expensive."

"If he feels that way then reserving a room for an hour is cheap," Katherine commented.

"I agree but he's uncomfortable with other people having just used the room."

"I don't worry about that," Katherine told her. "I'd love to go."

"You and me?"

"Why not?"

"Yes," Irina smiled happily. "Why the hell not?"

—

Saturday morning, Carlos arrived first at Katherine's and Boston's, waiting politely outside until Boston noticed him and waved him in. Bert was next, also entering the house, just a few minutes before Caitlin and Bethy arrived, parking their bikes. Boston introduced them to Katherine. Bert held his breath while Carlos watched from across the room.

It only took an instant for Katherine to size up both girls and figure out why they had been asked along on the Saturday rides. "So, these old dogs talked you into riding with them, huh?" she thinly smiled, shaking their hands.

"We want to do the Death Ride," Caitlin explained. "But we need help training."

"You know these guys are masochists? They might discourage you."

"Better to find out now," Bert jumped in. "Why waste time training with somebody who'll quit later?"

Gazing at the two women, Katherine replied, "They don't look like quitters."

"No, "Caitlin replied. "We're looking forward to it."

"Hmm," mulled Katherine, then turned to the dark-haired woman. "You, too?"

"We'll see," Bethy shrugged.

"I used to bike with the big dogs myself, well, never any Death Ride though I did a few centuries. It's hard work, more power to you." Katherine turned to Boston, "Well, you better get going." That was her way of saying she wasn't going to veto the plan.

"We have to wait for Erik," Boston said. A minute later, the Icelander arrived, apologizing once more for being late. He was introduced to the two women, politely meeting them for a moment before the group left.

Off on residential streets, Erik continued chatting with the two women, one curious question leading to another. Ahead, Boston commented to Bert, "No fireworks."

"Yeah," Bert answered. "Katherine was very nice but she knows."

"Knows what?"

"That these two are a turn-on. It's not just biking."

"For you that is," Boston replied. "For me, it's only a bigger training group."

—

Meanwhile at the house, Katherine answered Irina's phone call. "Ok," said Irina, "what are they like?"

"They're both so young," said Katherine. "One looks about fifteen, totally flat as a board as I can tell."

"Cute?"

"Absolutely darling, damn it."

"What about the other one?"

"A little older, maybe a little pudgy. Hard to say because the blonde one is so slight. The older one's a little morose but nice enough features. Boston said she's a psychoanalyst, like Bert."

"Bert needs analyzing more than anybody," Irina commented.

"She actually looked a little depressed," Katherine continued.

"Probably thinking about the hard rides ahead. Anything about these two for us to worry about?"

"The blonde is a dead ringer for you, maybe at age twelve. She's too young. The brunette is not for Erik. So, you're in the clear."

"And you?"

"They're pretty enough for Boston, but not old enough, ultimately that is. I never really got to figure out Boston's type. Who knows if I even am? So, when are we going to rent a private room? What about today?"

"Sure," Irina said. "But when will they be back?"

"Who cares?" Katherine said. "I'm sick of work and just want to soak."

"Alone?"

"No, no," Katherine replied. "With you. But we can't discuss anything having to do with our projects." Irina agreed and said she would call for something available in the afternoon.

Katherine hung up pleased. Though she had considered Irina more of a business associate than a friend, the Russian woman had become her confidant, mostly by default, and she was eager to spend some private and personal time at least with somebody. Boston was busier than ever at work and, of course, would never miss a Saturday biking opportunity, especially now with the Death Ride targeted and the two young women aboard.

She felt that Dennis might have understood her best of all, both her career and her bad-girl side. But they had not had intimate contact in over a year since the deer-biker road accident. She didn't mind no longer feeling the guilt of an affair but did miss the intimate contact with Dennis. With Ophelia still at his side, Dennis hardly seemed in need of either her companionship, in bed or otherwise.

Hot tubbing alone would not do it for her. She wanted somebody else there and Irina had plenty of vitality. Katherine looked forward to it.

—

It was all surface streets, some quiet and some busy, as the six rode through Mountain View, Alviso and into Milpitas. Still in the urbanized area, they turned onto Sierra Road, totally flat, lined with apartments, nothing special about it. As they neared the cross street of Piedmont, ahead was a hillside that seemed to have a gray ramp shooting up it. Drawing closer, they saw that ramp was the straight, vertical continuation of Sierra. "We're supposed to do that?" Bethy asked, astonished.

"This is only the start," said Boston. "It'll get worse before it gets better."

When the light changed at Piedmont, the group started up. Soon, all six were standing in their pedals. The hill was so long that they all were up and down on their seats until reaching the brief level area on top. Bert had led the way, followed by Caitlin and Erik. Carlos and Boston kept a little further behind with Bethy struggling. After a moment's respite, they turned to face another steep climb.

That was how it went for several miles as they had biked past all the houses into open country between cattle grazing hills, quite green from the winter's rains. Both Boston and Carlos stopped several times waiting for Bethy, encouraging her to continue up the especially tough road. Boston noticed that Carlos seemed especially solicitous of the thirty-year-old woman.

It's probably the first time in a long while, thought Boston, that he's been in a social situation with a new woman. After all, she's biking, something that Carlos has complete knowledge of, plus she needs some help and, on top of all that, she's married and not a threat. Carlos demonstrated a patience that Boston had never observed before, not even with Carlos' own daughters.

Finally, they reached the true top where the other three were sitting by the road.

"So what'd you think?" Boston asked.

"Good hill," Bert said. "I can see why they put it on the California Tour."

"A bitch," Caitlin said. "How're you doing, Bethy?"

Bethy's cheeks were bright red as she was taking a big drink from her water bottle. "I hope that's the last of that for today," she finally said. "I have to pee. Where's the ladies room?" The hilltop was treeless and the road lined with barbed-wire fences on both sides.

"You don't know the rule," Caitlin told her. "You just step off the road, drop your pants and go." Bethy looked at her waiting for the joke. "No kidding," Caitlin continued. "I already went." Bethy still looked very unsure, eyeing Caitlin as well as the barbed wire lining the road. We all went," Caitlin affirmed. Bert and Erik nodded their heads in agreement. Bethy still stood frozen, squirming next to her bike.

"Nothing to it," Boston finally said. Leaning his bike against the fence, he pissed against one of the posts.

"Well, seeing how they're no trees on top of this god-forsaken hill, might as well," Bethy stated. Leaning her bike against the fence as the others had done, she stepped off to the side, dropped her drawers and squatted down.

As Bethy finished her business, Bert turned to Carlos, who just shook his head that he wasn't about to join this scene. "Well, if we're all done with the pissin' party, let's hit it," Bert yelled, getting on his bike.

Boston remembered a very steep drop ahead with a quick uphill transition that was screened by canopy. The others in front of him were caught off guard at the bottom when the climb suddenly appeared. Boston sailed up it, passing even Bert at the front.

In the lead now, he wondered if he could hold them off all the way into Milpitas, which would be a rare coup for him to keep ahead of the fast downhillers. The part that they were on now still had unmarked sharp turns.

Suddenly, Caitlin shot by him. Boston instantly sped up, gaining on her as she whipped through a left hand turn. He was still closing on her as she slowed for the next right hand turn. Approaching with a lot of speed, he saw the second half of the turn getting sharper. Braking too little too late, he began drifting toward the centerline. No cars were coming so he chose to sweep wide into the oncoming lane rather than skid. But he kept drifting, now to the outer edge of the asphalt where the hillside fell away. Knowing his line was no good and still too fast, he braked too much too late. His bike waffled back and forth and then he went down hard, sliding on his hip like a baseball player for a few thumps and then stopped.

Bert was immediately off his bike and right with him. "Jesus, are you ok?"

Boston got up on his own, looking first at his injured right hip, which felt sore, the shorts scraped with a few holes in the fabric. Next he examined his right forearm. Through a big tear in the windbreaker, he could see blood but it wasn't dripping, just a huge oozing road rash. Picking up his bike, he saw that it looked a little scraped but had been mostly protected by his hip slide.

By now Erik and Carlos had arrived. Seeing blood on the asphalt, they asked what had happened. "I blew the turn," Boston told them. "But I'm ok. I can still ride." Sensing that nothing was broken, he got on his bike and started pedaling. His right forearm and hip ached somewhat but, other than that, he was riding all right, soon meeting Caitlin, returning from the other direction to see where everyone had gone.

Not stopping to explain to her, he felt stupid to have missed the curve. At almost two hundred pounds, he had so much more momentum than Caitlin in front at half his weight. Going the same speed, he never had a chance.

The cool February air rushing by as he pedaled was somewhat comforting. When he finally reached the busy streets of Milpitas, Carlos was right behind him with the rest of the group closely strung together. Stopping at a Starbucks, once inside the restroom, he removed his windbreaker and saw that his forearm was fairly shredded. Running water and soap over it was awkward with the small faucet and stiff paper towels. When he lowered his shorts, he found a bloody mess on his hip, which seemed impossible to attempt to clean at the sink.

Torn windbreaker back on, he returned to his group, waiting outside. Carlos handed him a coffee. Asked how he was feeling, he responded remarkably good considering the speed at which he fell. Raising his forearm, he gave them a look at his road rash through the tear in the sleeve.

"I never saw anybody fall as hard as that." Bert told him.

"All I did was lay it down, just a little slide."

"Thank God no car was coming," Erik said. Boston nodded, thinking that was one of the benefits of biking lightly traveled back roads for those having crossed the centerline.

Caitlin and Bethy stood to the side, having seen his forearm. "Are you going to be ok?" Bethy asked him, grimacing. "Should we get you a ride home? Call your wife?"

"I can bike the rest of the way fine. The road rash will heal," Boston replied.

"That was a nasty turn," Caitlin added. "I was going way too fast but was able to brake just enough. Then I heard or felt something behind me and should have stopped then."

"He's an old rugger," Bert grinned. "You've seen the bumper sticker: Rugby players have leather balls?"

Finishing the last of his coffee, Boston thought back twenty-years ago to the fallout of distant rugby games: sore shoulders, sprained ankles, black eyes, jammed wrists, a broken foot—hard-fought Saturdays and long Sundays recovering. "Give blood, play rugby," he finally said, tossing his empty cup into the trash.

—

Irina was able to rent a private room from 1 to 2 pm. Picking up Katherine at the Charleston house, she drove to the massage and hot tub establishment across town. Irina put the rental on her credit card. "Next time it's on me," Katherine said.

"It's my pleasure," Irina told her as they walked down the hall. "This feels very naughty. It's wonderful."

Katherine agreed. "It's like motel sex, which I haven't had for a long time." She could remember the last time, which was with Dennis the day of his accident. She thought of their typical scenario, which was waiting in the car while he paid for some cheap room far away from Palo Alto, always wondering if they would be spotted.

Inside the private room, they began to undress. "It feels like a slumber party, but without the pajamas," Katherine stated.

"Are we going to shower together or separately?" Irina asked, already down to her underwear.

"Together," Katherine smiled. "Much more fun." Off came her clothes, leaving her naked as she watched Irina fully undress. "You have a wonderful figure," she told her.

"So do you," Irina replied. "Don't women always say that when what we really want to do is try to find the flaws in each other's bodies. Stay there so I can really study you."

Katherine stood still, letting Irina examine her. Then she demanded equal time to study the Russian woman's body. Finally, they were ready for the shower. "Can we soap each other?" Irina asked.

"Of course," Katherine told her, turning on the water.

"Wonderful," Irina said. "Erik hates washing each other."

That was the worst part of motel sex, thought Katherine. The showers were too small and the water pressure too weak. After making love with Dennis, she could never quite rinse off the tainted residue of lust. At least at home they had a large shower where she and Boston had their best frolics together. Soaping Irina's back, she thought of her husband's back. Then Irina turned around to have her front lathered.

Chapter 12

Charleston Road

A Scotsman, George Charleston, arrived in northern Santa Clara County in 1852, purchasing 160 acres of marshland around Adobe Creek for his farm, which did poorly and was abandoned. In the 1860s, Arastradero Road was detoured to meet with Charleston Road on the other side of El Camino Real, then known as Old County Road.

February rides, part 2

The return route from Calaveras Road in Milpitas was fairly direct, skirting bike trails and paths in Alviso along Highway 237, taking urban streets back toward Palo Alto. As they neared Charleston Road, Bert pulled alongside Boston. "You know," he began, softly so no one else could hear, "a hot tub might feel pretty good."

"Ice will feel better, at least for today," Boston replied. For a while neither spoke, the Boston added, "You go ahead."

"Without you?" Bert asked.

"Take Carlos with you."

"The shy Spaniard? Think he could handle it?"

"He seems to like Bethy. Encourage him. You're the psychoanalyst. Consider it a professional challenge."

The group turned onto Charleston, soon reaching Boston's house. Katherine came out with Erik's wife Irina beside her. "How'd it go?" she asked.

"Ok," said Boston, "except I crashed a little." He held up his slit windbreaker, showing his wife the bloody, oozing forearm underneath.

"Good lord," she sputtered. "What did you do to yourself?"

"Like I said, I crashed a little."

Erik looked to his wife. "Hi, honey, what're you doing here?"

"I always meet Katherine on Saturdays," Irina answered, with her interest in meeting the two young women replaced by the shock of seeing Boston banged up. As Katherine continued wincing over Boston's wound, she took Erik aside. "Aren't you going to introduce me, Erik?" Irina smiled, gazing at the women.

"This is my wife, Irina," said Erik to the two, standing at curbside with their bikes, and then to his wife, "This is Caitlin and Beth."

"Bethy," the dark-haired woman corrected.

"Nice to meet you," Irina nodded, studying the two women. "I hope these rough guys aren't too tough on you girls."

There was a little silence. "They've been very patient. I'm much slower than everybody," Bethy responded.

Meanwhile Katherine was all over Boston. "Well, I guess this is the end of your Death Ride."

"No way," he gently disagreed. "This'll heal up in a couple weeks. Nothing's broken."

"Half your skin is gone," she responded.

"Time for us to go," Bert stated. Irina told Erik that he should put his bike in the car and ride home with her. Soon everyone had said goodbye and were gone.

Once inside the house, Boston took off his sliced windbreaker and jersey, fully revealing his arm wound. He then lowered the ride side of his shorts, exposing a dripping red hip, every bit as raw as his forearm, causing Katherine to exclaim, "You definitely skinned the hell out of yourself. I can't believe you want to keep riding."

"It was my fault," he said. "I just took a curve too fast."

"How come nobody else crashed?"

"I was going too fast because I was following Caitlin around some tight turns," he answered, knowing the moment he said it that he shouldn't have. Why was he following Caitlin and where was everybody else? That wasn't his point and he didn't want to get in a fight over it. Instead he mentioned how he had played rugby games with worse injuries than this, which wasn't true but he was making a case.

"Have you ever thought that maybe you're pushing this biking a little too much?" she asked him. "If it's not crashing chasing some young girl then it could be getting hit by a truck like Dennis did to that biker."

"That was a freak occurrence."

"Nobody plans to get killed biking," she exclaimed. "Of course, unless they enter something called the Death Ride." With that, she stormed out of the room and into their bedroom. He followed. With her back to him, he gently held her shoulders. Softly, she told him, "I know you love riding. Though I've never loved it, our first year riding together was, well, it had its moments. But now I've quit. If you quit too, we could do a lot more things together. We could travel more."

"I'll be more careful in the future. But I want to do the Death Ride," he told her. "That's all I want to do."

"You say that now, but you'll keep riding."

Kissing the back of her head, her hair was still somewhat wet with a heavy smell of chlorine. "Have you been swimming?" he asked her.

Of all the times she had dodged being caught with Dennis, now she debated whether or not she should lie about soaking in the private room with Irina. "Just got out of the tub," she replied, not telling him exactly where was the tub. "You better wash yourself clean. I'll go hunt down some disinfectant."

"I'm going to need a lot," he told her, taking off his bike shorts as she left the room.

—

Meanwhile, the other four bikers continued on Charleston toward the El Camino Real intersection where Bert suggested that they all take a hot tub together, looking to Carlos to see if he would go along. Before Carlos could respond, Bethy spoke, "Henry's home tonight. I'll have to start fixing dinner soon."

"No time for a little tub beforehand?"

She laughed, "He doesn't mind it when it's just Caitlin and me, but you two might be a little much."

"He gets in with you and Caitlin?"

"No," she smiled. "He's too much of a gentleman."

"Not like you, Bert," Caitlin told him.

A block ahead they stopped at Caitlin's apartment house. "Do you want to come up for a beer or some wine?" she asked the group.

"Thanks, sweetie," Bethy replied, "but I really do have to be going."

"No, thanks," said Carlos.

"Com'on," Bert told him, "have a beer."

"Please, Carlos," said Caitlin, "it'll give me a chance to know you better. Plus you'll save me from this masher."

To Bert's surprise, Carlos agreed to one beer. With her house just a short distance away, Bethy said goodbye to ride home alone. The three took their bikes into the building and up the elevator to Caitlin's apartment.

"Here it is," she told them, waving to her small living room. "Just put your bikes against the wall." She put hers there then walked around the corner. "Should I put on a robe or just get naked?"

"No need to overdress," Bert grinned. "Where's the beer? I'll get it."

"In the fridge. Help yourself," she called out. Going to the refrigerator, Bert put his helmet on the counter and took out three bottles from a single six-pack, bringing them over to the nearby coffee table. When Caitlin returned, wearing a green terrycloth robe, the two men were sitting in chairs with all three bottles opened on the coffee table. Sitting alone on the couch, she lifted up one of the beers. "Here's to the ride today."

"To Sierra," Bert said as all three tapped bottles together.

"So, Carlos, Mr. Spaniard," Caitlin began, beer in hand, "tell me about yourself."

"Not much to tell," Carlos replied.

"Are you married? Divorced? Kids? How'd you get to the United States?"

"Wow," said Carlos, "that's a lot."

"No, it's not," Bert said. "He's divorced with three daughters and I don't know how they let him in the country."

"I came here about twenty years ago," Carlos began. "I met my wife in Madrid. She was going to an American university and I was bartending when we started hanging out. She invited me to visit her in California. We got married and started having babies."

"And what do you do?"

"Home-security wiring," he told her.

"Let me speed this up," Bert began. "He owns his own company. Last April, he finally divorced Gertrude. So he's footloose and fancy free."

"How's that been going?"

"It's been hard on my daughters," he replied. "They're teenagers. It was nobody's fault. I don't want them to take sides. Hopefully, it'll be better for my family."

"Definitely," Bert told him. "He needs to be introduced to some women."

"I was hoping you'd set me up with one of yours," Carlos said, sipping from his beer. "You can't possibly take care of them all."

Caitlin titled her bottle toward Bert. "So, what about all these women you have?"

"None at the moment," Bert replied, scowling at Carlos, who looked like he didn't quite believe him. Then he turned to Caitlin. "Where's your boyfriend?"

"What boyfriend, eh? The last one is long gone," she said. "Good riddance." She sipped from her beer. "I guess we're just three loners."

"I thought you were going to say 'losers'."

"Maybe that too."

"No, com'on," Carlos said. "I think we're all where we want to be."

Bert gazed around the room. "Works for me."

"Wise-ass," Caitlin smiled.

Soon Bert finished his beer first, asking her if he should get out a second round. "No," she told him, "I'm throwing you out. It'll soon be way too dark for you to ride."

"You could give us a lift," Bert suggested.

"Not a chauffer," she said, "plus I haven't eaten so one beer already has me buzzed."

"Dinner?"

"No, get out," she smiled. Bert nodded. Taking a last swig, Carlos thanked her. Both men said goodbye and left with their bikes, taking the elevator down.

In the lobby, Carlos strapped on his helmet. "Where's yours?" he asked Bert.

"Damn," said Bert, turning around and pushing the elevator button. "Catch you later."

"See you," Carlos replied, walking out of the building, sure that Bert had forgot his helmet on purpose.

Bert felt nervous riding the elevator back up to Caitlin's floor. Usually, he had choreographed his game plan but now he was not even sure of his objective. The girl was so young but he still retained a vision of the bear tattoo next to the crack of her ass.

As he returned to her apartment, he saw that the door was slightly ajar. Pushing it open, he saw her standing there, holding his helmet in her hand. Her terrycloth robe was slightly open, revealing a narrow glimpse of skin and a trace of panty. "Forget something?"

He cuddled up to her in the doorway, ignoring the helmet in her hand. "What would you do, if I loosened your belt?"

"I don't know," she said softly.

Leaning the bike against the wall, he tugged gently on the robe belt, causing both ends to drop, widening the gap. "What would you do if I kissed you?"

"I don't know."

Wrapping his arms around her small waist, being much taller, he bent down and kissed her. She put one arm on his shoulder, the other continuing to hold his helmet. Still kissing, he lightly rubbed one hand under her robe across her bottom. Reaching back, she pulled his hand back outside the terrycloth. Then she gently broke loose the kiss and stepped back from his embrace, her robe still hanging open. "What will the neighbors think?"

Bert stepped back, looked up and down the empty hallway. "Should I come in?"

"No," she laughed, extending forward the helmet. "Here, Wise-ass."

He put it on. "Forgetful, huh?"

"Flattering," she smiled, then flashed open her robe, revealing her small breasts. "The hot tub would have been fun. Good night." The door closed.

Outside, the streetlights were on already as it was quickly darkening. Bert biked carefully back to his apartment in East Palo Alto, sorting his thoughts: of course this girl was too young for him. After all, she was at least ten years younger than the woman he left his wife for, whose age even then had astonished his friends, not to mention upset his kids. When that relationship ended, he met a wide age-range of women in his few years on his own but none were bicyclists, at least not real road bikers, until this one and of course she was ridiculously young for him.

He negotiated through the shadows and dark corners to the bike bridge overcrossing to the east side of the freeway, then biked along the pavement edge, trying to hold a narrow straight line while avoiding the glare of oncoming headlights. Cars approaching from behind meanwhile lit up the street ahead as if each were a colossal truck imminently ready to run him over.

Finally, he reached his apartment. Seeing no message blinking from his answering machine, he put a frozen dinner in the microwave. Debating if he should call up Caitlin, he phoned his daughter instead, reaching her in New York just before she was going out.

Chapter 13

Kings Mountain Road

Frank King bought the Mountain Brow House, located at the current Kings Mountain Road-Tunitas Creek Road intersection with Skyline Boulevard. As the establishment evolved into a popular resort, the road became known as Kings Mountain Brow House Road, later shortened to its current name. There's no mountain nearby named Kings.

The Redwood City and San Gregorio Turnpike was built in 1868 up Kings Mountain Road and down Tunitas Creek Road as far Star Ranch Road where it turned to the coast. Currently, Star Ranch Road is gated off at private property a few miles below the Tunitas Road connection.

Summit Springs Hotel was located on Kings Mountain Road on the eastern side near the top. At the bottom of the hill was a hubbub of three little communities: Woodside which surrounded Robert Tripp's store, now a historical building restored to its 1850s condition; West Union, which was located northerly along West Union Creek, now the back entrance to Huddart Park; and fronting on Kings Mountain, Greersburg, so named for Irish sea captain John Greer, who married Maria Louisa Soto Copinger, a recently widowed landowner. She had inherited from her late husband whatever was left of Rancho Cañada de Raimundo that had not sold. John Copinger had been granted the rancho located in the Cañada de Raimundo, which was the same cañada traveled by Portola and named for its Indian resident.

Copinger had built a primitive adobe on the Kings Mountain Road property a year after marrying Maria, the twenty-two-old daughter of a Mexican landowner. Two years after Copinger died, Greer sailed up San Francisquito Creek, stopping on the banks of Soto land, in future north Palo Alto, where Maria, now both Soto's daughter and Copinger's widow, sold vegetables from *a small wharf. Renting a small plot from the widow, Greer married her a year later and decided to move to Copinger's vacant adobe, near Kings Mountain Road. As it was primitive to begin with and hardly lived in, Greer traded 1200 acres of the widow's land near Sand Hill Road to Dennis Martin for ten dollars worth of hardware in order to fix up the decrepit adobe into a honeymoon cabin. Those 1200 acres later fell victim to a title dispute based on which Spanish land grant was deemed valid.*

The widow's daughter, Manuella Copinger, who was three at the time of her mother's remarriage, at age twenty married Antonio Miramontes, a grandson of Maximo Martinez. Demanding part of her late father's estate, Greer granted to her a lot in Greersburg, identified now as 3333 Woodside Road, known then as the Miramontes Mansion. Manuella, Miramontes, Raimundo and Greer are all now streets in the Woodside area.

February rides, part 3

Boston's injury caused him to cancel the group ride for the week after the spill. His road rash took a week to heal, running its course from bloody gauze on Sunday to dry bandages by Friday. Fortunately, he spent all his weekdays in the office that next two weeks. Work remained slow, made even more so at this time of year. Boston sought new clients while his partner, Larry, began a search for possible buyers of their small firm.

For one weekend the riders all were on their own and the following weekend, still in February with the weather remaining cold, Boston scheduled a return to Old La Honda Road, choosing the same road climb as he had done with Bert and Caitlin in December.

Racing out the door, just minutes late, he thought he might see Caitlin and Bethy already on the road during his short ride up Arastradero to Foothill. Instead, nobody else was biking as he arrived at the Foothill intersection a few minutes late, finding only Carlos there. Then the time dragged with no sign of the two women. Minutes later, Boston and Carlos headed back down Arastradero to Donald Drive, where they found Bethy's house dark and quiet. Next, deciding to check Caitlin's apartment, Boston rang the buzzer, Caitlin said she'd be right down and emerged with her bike five minutes later. Apologizing, she told them that Bethy was not riding today.

Biking the few miles to the Sharon Heights, they found the two guys inside Starbucks, where it was warm, drinking coffee. Caitlin apologized to them her being late, to which Bert remarked it was the first time Erik ever had to wait for anyone.

Skyline Boulevard was freezing cold and the five didn't wait long to push onto Skylonda and descend 84 back to Woodside. Caitlin kept up the whole way. Taking the Loop and bypassing Rossotti's, they split with Erik, who headed back to Menlo Park. Later, Carlos turned onto Foothill Boulevard while Boston and Bert stayed with Caitlin to her apartment house—Boston because he lived a few blocks away across El Camino and Bert on account of, obviously, Caitlin.

"Asking us up today?" Bert asked when they arrived.

"Not today, I have some classwork to get done. Some other time, sweetie," she smiled as she gave him a little peck on the cheek then waved goodbye to Boston and crossed the street to her place.

"What was that all about?" Boston asked, seeing her go inside the building.

"Just being friendly, I guess," Bert answered, also gazing in her direction. "Don't look at me that way."

"That was pretty friendly, all right," Boston agreed. "You know, she's about twenty-four years younger than you."

"Twenty-five," Bert replied, "if you're keeping score, which I guess you are. Biking age, though, we're the same."

"Meaning?"

"Meaning don't worry about it," Bert told him. Boston did not say anymore, staying alongside Bert the rest of the way to his house where he said goodbye. He was not surprised, given Bert's wide-range propensity for dating and that he usually kept company with her on their steeper climbs.

—

The following week, Boston decided he would stop at Caitlin's on his way. Leaving a little early for once to play it safe, he biked to her apartment house. Buzzed inside, he rolled his bike to the elevator and up to Caitlin's floor.

With her having left the door partly open for him, Boston peered in and called out a hello. She appeared from the hallway holding two water bottles and wearing a small tank top with bikini panty bottom. "Running a little behind," she said calmly, passing him on her way to the sink. "Come on in, close the door."

"Anything I can do to help?"

"Well, you could pump my tires as I get changed. The pump's right next to the bike." Caitlin stuck the full plastic bottles in her two cages, then disappeared down the hallway. He had the tires filled before she returned to the living room, now fully dressed in her bike clothes. Checking his watch, they were about fifteen minutes late. Together on the elevator, he asked her, "Think Bethy's riding for sure?" he asked her.

"Yes," she said, "but I have something to tell you. Bethy and her husband have separated. He moved out last weekend."

"Wow," he said, "sorry to hear that."

"He's an asshole," she said. "He's an old guy," she started, then looked to Boston, "older, I mean, even older than you guys."

"Thanks."

"You know what I mean. Not that there's anything wrong with their age difference but he's all caught up with his work and travels all the time. I don't know why he even married her. It was like he wanted a housekeeper, not a wife. It was his second marriage. What a jerk," she fumed.

"Think she'll even want to ride?"

"Sure, she needs to."

"Is she getting divorced?"

"She should," Caitlin said. "But Henry's too busy to even discuss it with her. He just got pissed and left. Best thing to have happened to her. Don't say anything to her though."

So, mused Boston, I now know that Caitlin's a mother of a two-year-old and Bethy's separated, which I learned from both of them but am not supposed to let each other know that I know. All I'm trying to do, he thought to himself, is get these two women trained for Markleeville.

When they arrived at Bethy's house, she came out the door already wearing her helmet and dark sunglasses. Saying hi, she quickly got on the bike. She might be getting divorced, he told himself, but this one knows how to be on time.

Boston was glad to see that Carlos was still waiting. They rode Foothill to Sand Hill, same as the previous week. At Starbucks, they only found Bert waiting there. Before they could dismount, however, Erik arrived, his tardiness now equal to the Caitlin's. Bert finished his coffee and they took off.

Crossing over I-280, Boston led the group, turning at Whiskey Hill Road to the town of Woodside, then west at the Pioneer Saloon road crest toward the westward hills and Kings Mountain Road.

Passing the historic Woodside Store, the girls paused to see a building restored right out of the 1850's as the other riders began to press uphill. Turning to Caitlin, Boston advised, "Better get going if you want to stay with the big dogs."

"You're all big dogs," she replied, but sped up to catch Erik, trailing Bert in front. As with the steep ride up Sierra, Boston hung back with Carlos and Bethy. Having been told about the separation, Boston could see that she was somewhat distracted, understandably, her face sad even with eyes hidden behind dark sunglasses.

After awhile, the pace was too slow for him. He pulled ahead of Carlos and Bethy, but made no effort to chase after the three in front. They were all waiting at Skyline as he arrived. Bert was fairly beaming. "Caitlin kicked Erik's butt," he announced to Boston.

"Practically a tie," she corrected. "Couldn't catch Bert, though."

"Dream on," Bert said.

"She'll get you soon," Eric grinned. "Don't worry."

"Nah," he said. "Never happen on a climb."

After a giving Bethy a chance to get her wind back once she arrived with Carlos, they turned north. After a series of rolling contours, a constant downhill began and Boston and Bert suddenly bolted at the same time with Boston making the quickest jump. He could feel Bert right behind as they hit the initial curves together. Once out of the woods, the road straightened, pitching downward, exposed to a stiff crosswind. Beautiful views on both side of him—ocean on the left, bay on the right—but Boston was pedaling too hard to look. His head pointed forward with shoulders tight and legs pumping, trying to compress a lifetime of athletic fitness into acceleration. Focusing only on the asphalt ahead, he wondered how much he could push himself for how long.

Ahead was a little hill, which led to a series of sharp turns where Boston felt he might be able to better hold off anyone trying to pass him. On the open ridge, he was buffeted by the strong offshore wind. Slowing just slightly, he was startled by Erik shooting by on his left. Rocking in the wild breeze, Boston stood on the pedals to catch him.

Beginning to close the gap, his bike rattled when a car whooshed by from behind, blocking the side wind for instant, sucking him and then Erik to their left. But it was gone so quickly that they both instantly regained control. Straining, Boston was able to catch Erik's draft and conserve some energy with a little forested hillock approaching. When Erik slowed slightly at the hill's base, Boston stood and outran him once again into the lead but then Erik overtook him on a short section between alternating headwind and tailwind curves. Boston tried to recatch a draft but Eric was too fast, eventually making the last headwind turn in front toward the Highway 92 intersection ahead, serving as the finish line of the unofficial contest.

It was pure, unadulterated competition. Clinging to Erik's back wheel with a straight section ahead, Boston slingshotted Erik perfectly, moving out a bike length before both had to begin slowing for the rapidly approaching stop sign, where both finally halted, exhausted.

Within a minute, Bert was also there, huffing and puffing. "Somebody's been eating their Wheaties," he exclaimed. "You guys were really going for it."

Arriving next, Caitlin exclaimed. "The wind shifted me over six inches!"

"No ballast," Bert commented, patting his gut. They waited a few minutes for Bethy and Carlos to arrive.

"That was insane!" Bethy enthused. "Caitlin, didn't it feel like you'd be whisked off your bike?" The two girls went on about it and the group stayed chatting excitedly at the stop sign with the wind rushing from ocean to bay over the low point of the ridge.

Boston meanwhile kept an eye on the steady stream of traffic on the highway ahead returning from Half Moon Bay toward the direction the riders would be headed. He told everyone about the narrow shoulders ahead but that they should be able to slip into the line of traffic. Carlos volunteered to stay behind Bethy so she wouldn't feel pressured by any trailing vehicles.

After their descent, they regrouped at Cañada Road before beginning the eight-mile return to Woodside. The cross breeze that they had on the ridge began converting to a tailwind as they started south. As the group began to string out, once again Carlos hung back with Bethy.

Following Bert, Boston was then surprised to find Carlos on his back wheel. The Spaniard had been shepherding Bethy pretty much during their entire rides. Being freshest of all, Carlos soon rode into the lead. "The Spanish Armada is back!" Bert called out as Carlos passed him. "What happened to your pupil?"

"She said I've been too easy on you guys!" Carlos shouted as he started picking up the pace.

"You guys are all animals!" Caitlin told them.

"It's these married guys who have all this bottled up aggression," Bert replied.

"You're the worst one," Caitlin cried out. "They're just faster than you on the flats!"

"We'll see," said Bert, winking at her as he overtook Carlos.

"You're as much of an animal as we are," Boston told Caitlin, pulling alongside her.

"I only draft," she said. "Following you guys is like being behind semi's."

Passing underneath Interstate 280, Carlos overtook Bert going up a small rise. Then the real sprint began downhill toward Woodside. Bert slipstreamed a tiring Carlos only to have Boston whip past with nothing but a short knoll left before Woodside Road. Suddenly, Erik shot by without leaving a chance to overtake him before they both had to slam on brakes at the stop sign.

"Ok," said Boston, pulling alongside him, "you got me that time."

"I know I cheated," said Erik, a little ashamed. "I drafted you the whole time."

"That's ok. I thought I could just out-last you."

"I learned that lesson from you up on the ridge."

"Ever consider playing rugby?"

"I'm Icelandic, not crazy."

The other three arrived right behind them, having given up the chase. Bethy soon showed and the group turned west to a speedy descent toward Alameda de las Pulgas. Erik eventually turned off in West Menlo Park while the others continued south to Arastradero Road, halting at the stoplight.

"Hot tub?" Bert asked.

"Mr. One-track Mind," Caitlin joked, then looked to her friend.

"Sure," Bethy said, cheeks red. "Why not?"

"Carlos? Boston?" Bert asked.

"I don't know," Carlos answered. "Where is it?"

"My house. You're more than welcome," she told him but he only shrugged. "Even if you just stay for a little while."

Without making a commitment, Carlos kept with the group making the left-hand turn onto Arastradero and then again onto Donald Drive. While everyone got off their bikes at Bethy's house, Boston stayed on his.

"Coming?" Bert asked him.

"You guys go ahead," Boston told him.

"No hot tub?"

"Not today," Boston replied, surprised and pleased to see Carlos apparently accepting the invitation. That was his sole consolation as he watched the four walk their bikes behind the side garage gate.

Returning to Arastradero, waiting alone at El Camino for the light to change, he regretted leaving the group and the post-ride comradery, hot tub or not.

Katherine was working on a set of her drawings as he entered the house after putting his bike away in the garage. Coming out of her office, she asked him how the ride went and if he would like a sandwich as she was going to make herself one as well. She asked if his fall of two weeks ago bothered him.

Boston responded that his injury was all healed. Sitting in chair in order to take off his shoes, he then told her about how he was not sure if he could keep beating Erik in a long sprint if Erik didn't want to be beaten.

"How important is that?" she asked.

For a moment he thought about the four riders now lounging in hot tub, about which he still had not told her. "It's not that important," he told her. "I don't need to win. But I do need to be in the hunt."

"Were you?" she asked.

"All the way," he answered, "at least up to the very end."

"I guess that means you're still set on going to Markleeville," she said, working on their sandwiches.

"I felt good," was all he replied, still dwelling on the post-ride party he was missing.

Chapter 14

Donald Drive

Donald Drive, located off Arastradero Road in southwest Palo Alto, was built as part of the subdivision in 1956, named after the son of one of the principals of Moerdyke, Hardy and Anderson, who developed the tract.

The subdivision was part of the early 1950s state wide building boom. Arastradero Road borders part of Barron Park, a long time unincorporated area of Palo Alto named for Edward Barron, an Irishman who arrived in San Francisco in 1851, first making his fortune with cattle and later with Comstock Lode silver mining before settling in Palo Alto, where he purchased Mayfield Farm, a large estate south of the former town of Mayfield, once centered around El Camino Real and California Avenue, formerly Main Street and Lincoln Avenue.

February rides, part 4

"How'd we lose Boston?" Bert asked, wheeling his bike around the back of Bethy's house on Donald Drive.

"He's married," Bethy told him.

"Didn't stop him before."

"What do you mean 'before'?" asked Carlos.

"The once before when you weren't there," Bert replied. "When you were worried about the rain that didn't happen. Actually, what's more amazing, you joining us or Boston not coming along?"

"Maybe you don't know either of us very well," Carlos told him.

"Guess not," Bert shrugged, unzipping his windbreaker.

"Mr. Eager-beaver, why don't you wait to undress until we help Bethy?" Caitlin told him.

"With what?" he asked, taking off his windbreaker.

"Snacks, something to drink, you know, whatever?"

"You two get the hot tub ready," Bethy said. "Carlos can help me." She motioned for Caitlin to go ahead with Bert. They began taking off shoes and socks while Carlos followed Bethy into the kitchen. Going to the refrigerator, she gathered some cheese and took out a six-pack of beer. Then she told Carlos to at least take a couple beers out to the tub.

Carlos did as asked, finding that the Bert and Caitlin were already in the tub, visibly naked in the clear water. Embarrassed he averted his eyes as he handed off the beer bottles.

"Could you turn on the jets?" she asked.

"Why don't we leave them off?" Bert grinned.

"You just want a peep show," Caitlin smiled, crossing her legs.

"What's wrong with that?" he grinned, arms resting on the high sides of the tub.

Leaving the two to themselves, Carlos turned on the jets and went back to the house, not really sure why he stayed but it certainly wasn't to scope out any young woman almost his daughters' age. Also, he wasn't interested in seeing Bert flirt with someone half his age, especially without any clothes. As a divorced father of three girls, he knew he wasn't quite ready for hot tubbing with these women and Bert. Instead, he went inside to say goodbye to Bethy.

She was sitting at the nook, sipping a beer, waiting for his return, looking a little forlorn. Seeing that she expecting him, he sat across from her. During their private time together on the ride, she had told him about the separation. Now she began explaining that Henry Kono had been married once before, to someone who worked at the same company he did. She had met Henry and his former wife during a single counseling session, which didn't go well. It ended so abruptly that she didn't consider them to be clients. A year later, Henry, then in divorce proceedings, called her up. His pitch to her was that he wanted to date somebody totally outside of the computer industry in which he was employed.

That sort of seemed like a good match at the time, Bethy told Carlos, but in essence it shut her out of his work. It is not that they drifted apart; it was more like he set sail, using their house for a homeport. She kept to her career and entertained him when he was around, which was less and less. The only fun in her life had been biking with Caitlin, whom she met when taking an adult art class taught by the young woman. For herself, Bethy was glad to be part of a group as long as she didn't aggravate everyone by being so slow.

Carlos told her not to worry about that. As for her personal life, he had little to offer. Having lived with women his whole life, he still felt as if he had very little understanding of them. Not getting much feedback, Bethy asked him about his background.

"There's not much tell," he said, sipping on his beer.

"Remember I'm a therapist," she told him. "All I know is you're from Spain and you're divorced with three daughters. What are their names?"

He responded that his daughters were Marlene, Marga and Maria, with the first two named by his German wife Gertrude. He finally got to choose his third daughter's name, which was in honor of his grandmother. Maria liked it but Gertrude did not. The girls were seventeen, nineteen and twenty-one, which Bethy commented was a lot in a few years.

Carlos admitted as much, having been married at twenty-three. "I met Gertrude when she was going to school in Madrid, then followed her to California. Marlene was born a year later."

"Is that why you got married?"

He didn't answer, didn't look at her. Instead, he was back in Madrid, just in his twenties, scared to death of Spanish women, or rather, his feelings for the women of Madrid, who reminded him of his dark-haired sisters, one older and one younger. He had little money, very little courage and pounding hormones, which he had been taught were indecent. It was only later in life that he learned most men feel the same urges, at least most young men. But by then, he had married Gertrude, a free-spirited redheaded German, nothing like his sisters, which was unfortunate in the long run.

"How did the divorce proceedings go?"

"We've settled everything. I have one year left of child support. But you know, she still calls me up to complain. I tell her, 'You win. We're divorced.' But she still has to yell about the most idiotic things."

She sighed. "Living with Henry has made me a basket case. If my clients only knew how screwed up my personal life was, they'd never come see me." She paused. "Why am I training for this bike ride? Want some more beer?" She reached for the remaining two bottles of the six-pack.

"Sure," he replied, answering one question and ignoring the other as he finished his first beer.

Suddenly the door opened. Dripping wet, stark naked, Caitlin took two steps into the room, holding two empty bottles. "Any more?" she asked. As the young girl faced Bethy, Carlos eyed her, surprised that she was completely shaven.

"Sure, honey," Bethy replied, laughing, exchanging the two in her hands for the wet blonde woman's two empties.

"Aren't you two coming out?" Caitlin asked of Bethy as she took the beers, then suddenly her full front turned to Carlos. He quickly looked away.

"Later," Bethy shrugged. "We're discussing divorces."

"No fair conversing privately, Carlos. You have to join us," Caitlin murmured she departed from the room.

Carlos did not reply but Bethy chuckled a little. "For somebody who raised three daughters, you seem pretty self-conscious."

"They never ran around like that," Carlos responded, allowing himself a little smile.

—

Farther down the street on Charleston Road, Katherine had brought Boston a sandwich while she sat with her own. "It's not often we have a Saturday lunch together," she told him. Sitting, still wearing his bike shirt and shorts, he had plopped down in an easy chair. "You're usually not done this early. No Rossotti's?"

"It was really windy on top. Everyone's at Bethy's. Kind of a post-ride wind down."

"Why aren't you there?" she asked, biting into her sandwich.

He gazed over at her. "She has a hot tub."

"And?"

"I came home instead."

"Hmm, I sense some regret here." Going into the kitchen again, she returned with a half-poured bottle of red wine and a couple glasses. "So, you came home," she began. "That's commendable, I guess, unless you're some kind of martyr to marriage. Is that how you feel?"

"Not really," he told her, taking a filled glass from her.

"They must be pretty hard up to ask you old guys to bathe with them."

"Hot tubbing, not bathing. Anyway, it was Bert's idea."

"How'd he know she had a hot tub?" she asked. Drawing a deep breath, Boston went through the whole explanation of the spontaneity of the rainy day when they biked Joaquin Road. "Meeting them was spontaneous," Katherine voiced, "but getting into the hot tub with those two was deliberate. And isn't the older one married?"

"Separated."

"Swell," Katherine said but stopped there. During her second marriage, she would have gone through the roof. But now, she was surprised at her own calmness. Having recently visited the private hot tubs twice with Irina within the last few weeks, she felt as if an edge had been taken off. The idea of sitting underneath noisy foam with Boston's biking guys didn't exactly appeal to her at the moment. Imagining what the two young women looked like naked however did perk up her interest.

Irina was to blame, Katherine thought. Her touch was just right for her. She asked Boston, "Now, tell me the truth. Have you ever made out with those girls?"

"Com'on, what do you think?"

"What if you weren't married? Would you want to fuck either of them, both of them?" He raised his eyebrows, staring at her. "That question's unfair, I know," she said. "One last question. Do you want to fuck?" She watched his face. "Right now?"

"That's two questions."

"Don't push your luck."

"Can I finish my wine first?" he asked, tilting his head at her.

"Why don't you—," she began but he sprang from his chair before she could finish and took her by the hand, pulling her up from her seat and kissing her. Wine glasses set down, he led her to the bedroom, picked her up and tossed her on the bed. She just lay there as he undid her shorts and pulled them down. Usually they just made love underneath the covers, now he just stared at her. He's checking me out, she realized. We're going to have afternoon sex. Like we used to. Finally.

Off came his bike shorts as he joined her.

—

Returning to Bethy's hot tub, Caitlin re-entered with water holding two beers while Bert sat above on the edge, dangling his legs. "Mr. Immodest," she told him, handing him a bottle.

"Me? Who went bare ass to get the beer? Did you spook the hell out of Carlos?" he asked.

"He looked awfully shocked," she replied.

"I bet," he said, softly adding, "You looked pretty sexy walking across that lawn."

"You look pretty sexy yourself," she murmured, still holding his beer above the foam, gazing at his mid-section. "It's been a long time for me," she murmured, seeing him totally exposed to her, sitting on the tub's edge. "Too long." Taking a long drink from the bottle, she put it down alongside him and floated in between his legs, reaching out and gently taking him into her hand.

He expected some hesitation but there was none. Her fingers squeezed around him and she took him into her mouth. He leaned back, allowing her whatever she wanted while he kept watch on the kitchen back door, which stayed closed. It didn't exactly feel right but it did feel good. He thought he was probably too nervous to finish but he wasn't.

When she was done, she rested her cheek on this thigh, slowly opened her eyes and gave him the beer bottle before gliding back to her side of the hot tub.

"Hey," he said, softly, "can I have another?"

"Another?"

He lifted up the bottle. "Wise-ass," she told him. Taking a swig from her half drunk beer, she passed it to him. Without hesitating, he drank from it, eyeing her. Seeing how that was over, now what?

"What's keeping those other two?" she asked.

"Good thing, they stayed inside," Bert stated softly, sipping on his new bottle. Caitlin gave him a sly look. "Anyhow, Carlos is probably spilling his life story. His wife was a real terror. Too bad Bethy's married. She has a much more suited temperament for him."

"Does my temperament suit you?"

Bert stared at the naked young woman, blonde hair pasted alongside her head as he wondered, do you really care? With their age differences, he had a difficult time reading her. "Definitely," he answered.

As Bert was finishing off his beer, Bethy appeared with a couple of towels. "Don't feel like you have to come out," she told them. "Carlos is leaving however. I guess we wore each other out talking about our divorces, although mine is still in the works. You two want anything?"

"We're full," Bert grinned. Caitlin stared toward the back fence, betraying nothing.

Bethy dropped off the towels and went back to the house as Carlos left. Bert also came to the back door soon after, dressed and left on his bike. Seeing Caitlin still in the tub, Bethy joined her for a beer and a discussion of both men.

Chapter 15

Bohlman Road

Bohlman Road is located in Saratoga, a Santa Clara County village incorporated in 1856. In 1848, William Campbell built a sawmill about two-and-half miles upstream in the canyon, which was then known as Campbell's Gap. The mill was leased by Irishman Martin McCarty, who put a toll gate in town on his road to the mill, causing the settlement below to be known as Toll Gate, then later McCartysville, a rough frontier town with seven saloons on its main street then named as Lumber Street.

Springs below the mill were found to have the same chemical content as Congress Springs, one of almost a hundred springs around Saratoga Springs, New York. The tollgate was not popular, nor was McCarty who owned it. In 1865, the townspeople changed the name to Saratoga, in honor of the springs' similarity to the one in New York.

Frank Bohlman was born in New Almaden in 1854 to a German father, who came to California with the 1849 gold rush, and an English mother. Following his father's vocation, he was a teamster and did all the teaming for the Quicksilver Mining Company of New Almaden, owning 130 horses at one point. He also controlled the stage line and freight deliveries to New Almaden, which route had ten saloons in eight miles.

March ride

Boston Reed liked to think Caitlin Carter was getting better about being on time for the rides but this Saturday she was still in her underwear as usual, running around her apartment gathering her gear while he pumped up her tires once more. At least Bethy was ready, as always, when they stopped by her house. Both Bert and Erik, surprisingly on time, this time at Foothill Expressway, from where they turned south to pick up Carlos in Cupertino on their way to Saratoga and one of the hardest roads Boston knew.

Over the previous weeks, they had ridden Old La Honda Road so Bethy could experience it, and once again up Kings Mountain Road. Boston felt they were all ready for Bohlman Road, a ridiculously steep climb that he and Carlos had done only once before.

Carlos was waiting in front of his Cupertino apartment house on Homestead Road. The two women were eager to see what the inside of his place looked like, but he declined. "Next time?" Bethy asked.

"It's nothing special," Carlos downplayed.

"Nothing about Carlos is special," Bert added, "which is what makes him special."

After a couple turns upon reaching Saratoga, they were at the start of Bohlman, pausing opposite Madronia Cemetery. The climb began steadily that they stayed together, talking, excited. Then the first curve came and the road suddenly steepened. Bert, Erik and Caitlin began pulling ahead, slowly increasing the gap. Standing often, the other three slogged on up. One steep section led to another. It was as difficult as Boston had remembered.

Bert asked him, "How in the hell did you ever find this son-of-a-bitch?"

"I love it," Caitlin smiled, sweating. "How're you doing, Bethy?"

"All right," she responded with a deep gasp. "I'm making it at least. Not setting any records, except for slow maybe."

"No," Carlos disagreed, "you're doing far better than even last week."

"Not really. This is much harder."

"It gets even worse up ahead," Boston announced. "Remember to take On Orbit to the left. Get your money's worth."

"Com'on, slow poke," Caitlin said to Bert as she began pedaling hard while he and Erik followed.

The two groups of three soon spread out. Advancing slowly but still ahead of Carlos and Bethy, Boston reached the intersection of On Orbit first, circling and recouping strength while he waited for the other two. This was by far their hardest ride. He liked to think he was improving but he felt as if he just barely was able to keep pedaling up the raw steepness. The climb was punishing and he felt punished. The last two Saturday rides had been relatively short, due mostly to the seasonal morning chill. That was one reason whereas the other reason was that Bethy had difficulty keeping up.

When he broached the subject of possibly cutting Bethy from the team, so to speak, he met resistance from both Carlos, who consistently stayed behind with her, and also from Bert, who was fearful of Caitlin quitting the group for her friend's sake. Also siding with keeping Bethy in the group was Erik, who was doing plenty of training during the week and who stated that they, meaning Boston, should demonstrate a little more resiliency. Perhaps they were right, Boston considered. He accepted it, even if it meant slower and shorter rides.

Carlos and Bethy soon arrived at the junction. After a couple minutes, they and Boston took off, immediately standing for the steep beginning of On Orbit. The grade eased as they passed a few houses perched on the outer slope edge, situated with panoramic views of the Santa Clara Valley. Then the road curved around the hillside to an uphill-snaking twenty-plus-per-cent grade.

Boston immediately stood and slalomed as did Carlos alongside him, both taking full advantage of the road's width, keeping an eye out for any cars approaching from above. For a couple pedal strokes he was not sure if he had enough power left to stay upright. Carlos barely kept the same pace. Farther down the hill, Bethy tried to maintain progress.

Finally, Boston spotted Bert, Caitlin and Erik resting just beyond the crest. He and Carlos continued together all the way to the three on top, then stopped, fairly collapsing over their handlebars. After a minute, Carlos headed downhill back to find Bethy.

After awhile, Caitlin was thinking about going herself but then Bethy appeared, walking her bike alongside Carlos walking his. Nearing the group, she told them in a quivering voice, "Sorry, guys. I just couldn't make it."

Caitlin put down her bike and gingerly trotted downhill in her cleated shoes. Giving Bethy a big hug, she told her, "That's ok, honey. This road kicked all our butts." Then she reached for her friend's bike, "Here, let me take that."

"No way," Bethy answered, still shaky behind her sunglasses. "At least let me finish walking it up this damn hill." Caitlin stayed alongside her until Bethy reached everybody. At that point, they all dropped their bikes for a snack break. Bert began to urinate on the bushes by the road. "Somebody pee for me," Bethy said as she sat on the curb. "I'm too tired."

Soon refreshed and back on their bikes, the group rode up to the ridge before reaching a gate at the dirt access road. The sign stated that the road was a public trail closed only to motor vehicles. Knowing about this dirt stretch but never having taken it, Boston led the group around the gate. They proceeded along a fairly smooth surface until coming upon a series of small gully washes. Everyone made it except for Carlos, who caught his tire in a rut and went over, landing hard but without much speed. Bethy dropped her bike and went to him. "Are you all right? You're bleeding."

He looked at his forearm, trickling blood. "Just a little. How stupid of me."

Arriving alongside and getting off his bike, Boston looked down at the fallen Spaniard and then at the dirt road ahead. "This is a bad stretch. I didn't know."

"Are we training for the Death Ride or the Marines?" Bert asked.

Meanwhile, Bethy kept fussing over Carlos, who had two long blood trails on his forearm. "It's stopped," he told her. "It's not dripping."

"Yes, it is," she said, studying his forearm. "It's not gushing, but it's bleeding."

Reaching in her back pocket, Caitlin pulled out an unused headscarf. "Here use this." Worried about bloodstains, Carlos didn't want it. "I never wear it. Use it." Reluctantly, Carlos wrapped his arm.

"What're we doing here?" Bethy asked, still fraught as she watched Carlos. "This isn't even a road."

"Oh, it's a road for Boston," Bert answered. "We haven't really had a ride unless we go off pavement somewhere."

Back on their bikes, they soon crossed through another gate to paved Montevina Road, on which they made a long and windy descent to eventually Lexington Reservoir, the main body of which they reached by an overpass, with the northbound lanes on-ramp to Highway 17 pointed northward to Los Gatos.

Boston explained their two choices of either taking the turn off the highway and down the face of the dam to another dirt road leading into town or else legally staying on the highway for about a half-mile, tight to the shoulder as was allowed on freeways without readily accessible paved alternatives. "Carlos, you might have gotten hurt for nothing," Bert said. "Boston's finally figured out how to have us all killed."

"If you don't like the off-road, the freeway's much quicker," Boston stated. "For most of the way we have a few feet of shoulder. One stretch gets tight to the guard rail so you can only grit your teeth and hang on."

Bert was all for it as was Caitlin. Having fallen in dirt once already, Carlos was ok with taking the highway. Everyone turned to Bethy, who looked a little pale and very glum. Caitlin said that if Bethy wanted to take the safer, off-road route, she would go along. It surprised Boston when Bethy chose the highway, opting to follow the group's choice.

Starting out together, Boston was in the lead, beginning with lots of room due to a merge lane between the shoulder and the nearest travel lane but that soon faded out. Gathering speed, he traveled the narrowing shoulder only a few feet wide as the roadway began curving downward. Suddenly a large trailer swooshed by him, close enough for the airwave to rattle him. He watched the trailer's right side pass close to the guardrail exactly where they would have been had they gotten their first. But there was nothing else to do at this point but finish the next couple hundred of feet blind to anything coming from behind.

Hardly pedaling, he was still speeding as he hugged the guardrail while streaming ever so slightly into the travel lane as little as possible, knees shaking whether from fear or adrenaline or the fast curve itself, not expecting but dreading an impact from the rear. But nothing happened as the end of the guardrail approached and then he was past it, back onto the resumed shoulder now looking wider than ever.

Elated, he followed the shoulder around the off-ramp, stopping finally on top where it met the cross street. Erik, Caitlin and Bert arrived right behind him. "Oh my God, I've never been so scared in all my life!" exclaimed Caitlin.

"Boston," Bert shouted. "You madman!"

Erik merely said, "Wild," waited and then repeated, "Wild."

Calming down, they turned to look back down the on-ramp. Two cars exited but there was no sign of Bethy or Carlos. Caitlin started to turn her bike around. "Wait," Boston said. "Give them a minute." Fretting, Caitlin stayed.

Then Bethy came into view, slowly, followed closely by Carlos. As she rode up to them, they saw she was sobbing. She stopped, tears flowing from behind her sunglasses. Carlos plopped his bike into the ice plant and walked up to her. "Just a little scared," he told the others.

As she stood with the bike between her legs, Caitlin took her in his arms and gave her a big hug. "It's ok, you made it. It's ok," he repeated.

Resting her head, bike helmet and all, on his shoulder, she finally sobbed, "I know."

"That was scary," Caitlin told her.

"I swear that trailer only missed me by an inch," Bert proclaimed.

"Thank God he passed us before the guardrail," Boston added. "Next time we'll take the dirt road instead for sure. You ok, Bethy?"

She lifted her head from Carlos' shoulder. "I'm sorry for being such a baby," she said. "I'd never done anything like that."

"You don't have to apologize," Bert told her. "That was pretty crazy. And I'm not blaming you, Boston. Wait, yes I am even though we all agreed to it."

Bethy coughed. "Thanks for staying with me, Carlos," she told him, releasing the hug finally. "I began slowing down at the worst, scariest spot but you yelled at me to keep going. That helped. Without you, I'd be a nothing more than a grease spot in the road." She wiped her cheeks and nodded her head that she was all right. "One thing I'll say is that the freeway made me forget all about Bohlman."

Carlos let her go and picked up his bike. "I don't think we should ever do that again. Boston, we count on you. This isn't supposed to be terrifying," he stated, then turned to Caitlin. "Your scarf came untied off my arm and blew away."

"Big dogs playing in the street. Don't worry about it," Caitlin commented, then turned to Boston. "Luckily, we all made it."

Boston was silent but Bert countered, "We stayed alive in order to make the Death Ride. Isn't that ironic? I say we go to Bethy's hot tub and celebrate surviving that death trap."

"Hot tub?" Erik asked.

"It's a long story," Boston said, too tired from the freeway tension to tell him any more about experiences at Bethy's. Aware that only Erik had refrained from criticizing the choice of taking Highway 17, Boston appreciated him for it, realizing that the Icelander was the only male rider in the group, besides himself, without a female interest along.

—

They arrived at Donald Drive still early in the afternoon. Boston told the group that he was continuing to his house to see if Katherine wanted to join them. Erik decided to stay with Boston while other four went off to Bethy's. As they biked, Boston told Erik that he had informed Katherine about being at the hot tub and she was, amazingly enough, ok with it. Actually, she very well today may want to go with them.

In fact, she did, stating that she had been drawing all morning and was ready to be surrounded by naked men, leaving out mention of the two young women. Then Boston noticed that she had her bike all ready, tires pumped with helmet and gloves nearby.

Erik was less sure about going along until Katherine told him that she had spoken with Irina about his hot tub possibility, and who said it was fine, as long as Katherine went as well.

"Doesn't she trust me?" Erik asked.

"Yes, but not those girls," Katherine replied.

Erik agreed to go along and, with Katherine along, they biked back to Donald Drive and Bethy's, where they found the other four already in the bubbling waters of the hot tub. "Welcome, Katherine," Bethy called out, bouncing up in the waist high water, wet breasts jiggling. "Boston, there's beer inside the fridge," she said, pointing toward the kitchen.

"Hello," Katherine replied. As they parked the bikes, she imitated Bethy's bosoms with her hands and whispered to Boston, "You know, I'm not twenty anymore."

"I'm not either."

"Yeah, but there aren't any twenty-year-old guys here either."

"Hush," he said, removing his jersey. "Anyway, she's thirty and your body has hers beat. Let's just strip and get in the damn water."

"Yes, sir," she replied, undressing while her husband went inside the kitchen.

Glancing up, Erik saw her totally naked before turning away. "If I see any more, I'll have to charge you a doctor's examination," he uttered, smiling at his socked feet.

Boston emerged from the kitchen with three beer bottles, handing them out to Katherine and to Erik before leading his wife to the hot tub. The other four were seated up to their necks in the foaming water. Entering first, Boston quickly sat.

Katherine was next, stepping shakily over the edge. "Hello, ladies, good to see you again. God, it's tough to enter this lady-like. Hello Bert, Carlos."

"Welcome," said Bethy as Katherine seated herself next to Boston. "Glad you could make it."

"I even biked over," Katherine responded, "just to keep in the spirit of things, to be on the team so to speak. Of course, I biked a lot, back in a different hot tub era."

"You used to hot tub after biking?" Boston asked surprised.

"With Mark and many more people than this in a tub, too, I might add." What she didn't expand upon was that she was married to her first husband at the time when she met Mark, the hot young college professor known for biking around campus.

Meanwhile, Erik was still at the kitchen door, drinking his beer in the shade of the overhang, having proceeded no further than taking off his shoes. Seeing him there, Boston called out, "Aren't you getting in?"

"No," he shouted, "not without Irina. I'm going to finish my beer and go."

"Noble," Katherine told him, looking at Boston, then back to Erik, adding in a loud voice, "She said it was ok."

"Get in here, Icelander," Boston responded. Then he turned to Katherine, "Did she really say it was ok?"

"Yes," Katherine answered softly. "As long as he was blindfolded."

Bert shouted to Erik, "This is a team event. Get undressed and get over here."

"It's not like you can see anything," Caitlin offered. "The bubbles hide everything." Just then the jets stopped and the foam quickly subsided, leaving the group exposed under the calming water. "Whoops," giggled Caitlin. The group all looked around each other. She got out of the tub to reset the air jets timer.

As she climbed back in, Bert raised his bottle, announcing, "Here's to doing Highway 17. Thank you, Boston, for scaring the shit out of us." Hearing about the freeway venture for the first time, Katherine glared at her husband while the rest of the group clicked their bottles.

"Boston didn't make anybody ride it," Bethy defended him. "Seeing how I'm alive to tell about it, and I'm no longer crying. I'm glad I biked it."

"You're all crazy, you know," Katherine declared, sipping from her bottle. I don't even like to drive 17."

Boston stood, raising his arm "Here's to something much safer: The Death Ride!" The group in the water stood cheering, breasts bouncing, and tapped bottles together once more, Katherine included, not missing an opportunity to out-chest the two other women. Boston called out again, "Erik, come sit with us for a beer at least?"

Eric announced, "I've had one beer to be polite and I've kept my clothes on. Now I'm leaving." Putting his bottle down and his shoes back on, he started to leave.

"Were the Vikings afraid of their wives back home as they raided and pillaged Europe?" Bert asked.

"Viking woman we can handle. She's Russian. See you all later," Erik replied, getting on his bike.

Meanwhile, Katherine glanced across at the Spaniard. "Carlos Cordova, I can't believe you are in a hot tub with naked women."

"Well, why not?" he asked shyly.

"You don't even like to look women in the eyes. How can you stand it when their tits are exposed?"

"Sometimes it's easier to look at their tits," he smiled.

"What about in my case?" she asked, rising slightly up out of the water.

"Especially," he smiled, red-faced as he slunk down until his head disappeared into the foaming bubbles,

"You have a beautiful figure," Bethy interrupted. "You're so tall and slim. I'm short and pudgy."

"At least you have curves and boobs. I sure as hell don't," Caitlin said. She stood up, letting the water trail off her small bosom as she rose out of the water.

"You ladies aren't shy, I give you that," Katherine said.

"You're not shy either," Boston reminded her.

Never have been, Katherine thought. Being in the group reminded her of a time long ago, well before she married Mark, meaning also before Dennis built her the lap pool. She had been younger than even these two women when enjoying herself at several young adult backyard parties long ago. Now, over twenty years later, she was amazed at how comfortable she felt in this group. There hadn't been anyone in their forties joining them back then. She realized that she could care less about being in the water with Bert and Carlos, or even Boston. It was the two young women who were making it fun for her.

"You should bike with us," Bethy told her. "You can't be any slower than I am."

"Yes, I can be," Katherine replied. "There was a time when I could keep up but I lost all urges to do so. Can you two really ride with these animals or do they drag you along just for the hot tub afterwards?"

"Just for the hot tub," Bert interjected, earning a splash from Caitlin. "Hey," he laughed, wiping his face. "Just for that, you have to get us another six pack."

"No problem," the young blonde woman said, bounding up the steps and out of the hot tub toward the kitchen.

"She shaves," Katherine said with Caitlin gone. "Oh Bert, how will you be able to stand it?"

"Iron will, Katherine. Iron will."

"We'll see," she quietly replied, tipping the beer up to her mouth. Irina would definitely enjoy this, Katherine told herself. As much as she likes being in the private room with just me, she would really love it here. Besides, these two girls are no threat to steal our husbands away.

Caitlin soon returned, clutching another six pack above her taut, smooth midriff. Of course, Katherine pondered, if that blonde keeps flashing herself around, it could be a whole other story. Studying her for a moment, Katherine observed to herself, "That girl has had a baby." But without any mention of that, she simply asked, "How often does everyone get together like this?"

"Today is a special celebration," Boston answered.

"Yeah," Bert began, "we survived Boston."

"Don't pick on him," Caitlin retorted. "He got us here all in one piece." She tipped her bottle in Boston's direction, then added with a giggle, "Carlos only lost a little blood plus my blood-soaked scarf."

Nobody better lose anything else, Katherine mused with a sip of beer.

Chapter 16

Mt. Hamilton

On August 26, 1861, while accompanying two surveyors hiking in the east San Jose hills, the Reverend Laurentine Hamilton rushed to the top of the highest peak, waving his hat and calling down to the others. The two surveyors so named the mountain after him.

Actually, the mountain had already been named as the highest peak in the Sierra de Santa Isabel on local maps. An 1895 Geological Survey discovered a peak a couple miles to the southeast that was fourteen feet taller than the 4,209-foot tall Mt. Hamilton, and gave the name of Mt. Isabel to that peak.

The Reverend Hamilton died in the pulpit, giving his Easter sermon in 1864. The mountain named in his honor was chosen as the site of the Lick Observatory, for which a twenty-mile road was built in 1876 at a relatively easy gradient of seven-per-cent so that materials and equipment could be hauled by horse and wagon to the top.

On October 1 of that year, the observatory's benefactor and namesake, James Lick, died in San Francisco. His body is buried under the main telescope building, the white dome of which is visible from throughout the Bay Area.

No easy gradient was required for the construction of the steeper eastern descent, which drops only a few miles before the road crosses Isabel Creek.

April ride, part 1

Boston Reed had the group all sign up for an organized hundred-mile ride up and over Mt. Hamilton to the east of San Jose through the hills to Livermore and back to the Bay Area. Since doing Bohlman Road the previous month, the group had continued to bike the hills on the west side of the Bay and never more than fifty to sixty miles per ride. Their rides since then had been repeats of the same Old La Honda and Kings Mountain climbs. Ready for a bigger challenge, Boston chose the century ride, which required them driving across the south end of the bay to the start in Milpitas.

To make sure they would be on time, Boston picked up Erik in Menlo Park, Bert picked up the two girls and Carlos drove alone from Cupertino. Driving in his Honda Odyssey, Boston asked Erik, "Do you ever miss just our original foursome? The Four Horsemen?"

"I like it better this way," Erik replied.

"Bethy does slow us down. However, she does have that hot tub," Boston stated, although she had not offered it since the Bohlman ride of weeks ago. Usually at the end of each Saturday ride, the riders split off for home at various points, although Bert always made a point of biking to Caitlin's apartment, where she left him and Boston on the sidewalk.

"Irina's been doing a little hot tubbing herself," Erik announced. "She's been going to that spa place downtown on Saturdays when we've been riding. They called one morning when I was late and she'd already drive off to meet Katherine. The receptionist asked if Irina was coming in at noon as usual. That's awfully early for a hot tub, isn't it?" He paused. "I haven't asked her about it. She always tells me about new things she's discovered."

"After she meets for coffee with Katherine to discuss projects, then she probably relaxes with a hot tub. Sounds good to me," Boston responded, then glanced over at Erik, still consternated. "You upset?"

"Strangely, I'm not," Erik answered. "I'm really not into hot tubs. It's just that she's kept it all to herself. Would Katherine do that?"

Boston thought about it. Married to Katherine for five years, he felt as if he still had little clue as to her inner self. "If she didn't think I needed to know about it, sure she'd keep it to herself."

"Irina knows I'm just not a hot tub guy."

The group was to meet in Milpitas at the local Starbucks, where they had stopped after Boston's Sierra Road crash. Carlos arrived in a new car, his first major purchase since the divorce. Once Boston saw it was a Nissan Armada, he gave the Spaniard a thumbs up. The subtle humor was also duly noted by Bert once he parked his Silverado alongside and got out with the two women.

Heading south on Piedmont Road, the group soon passed the Sierra intersection, all turning to gaze up the initial steep section, then continued to begin the twenty-mile ascent up Mt. Hamilton Road toward the four-thousand-foot summit. The highest peak surrounding the Bay Area, it was clearly seen from either the valley floor or western ridge, an isolated massive meeting of heaven and earth, which was a constant visual target for bay area bikers.

The morning was cool although the day was predicted to be hot. Bert and Caitlin began pulling away as they usually did. Unsure about the difficult of the climb, Erik hung with Boston while Carlos stayed back with Bethy, as he had been doing for weeks. Boston had no idea if those two were striking up a relationship. Bethy's dark, apple-shaped face typically revealed little, except for the strain of grinding her way up.

Eventually, the three pairs each came to a series of long switchbacks at the base of the final climb, leading to a junction at the top with small buildings. To the right was the main observatory where the top of the mountain was an unaesthetic, empty parking lot overlooking the entire Bay Area to the west. Around the corner of the heralded observatory, a crowd of bikers busily filled water bottles from the spigot of large yellow containers, while getting fruit and bread from large trays, walking, sitting, sprawling—basically regrouping for the remaining seventy-five miles. Bert and Caitlin were sitting on brick steps, eating food they selected from the tables when Boston and Erik arrived.

"So who won?" Boston asked, setting aside his bike.

"We didn't race up," Bert told him. "Saving energy."

"Don't believe him," Caitlin said. "He took out after these four guys who roared passed us."

"Had to hold up our group's honor," Bert replied, biting into a cantaloupe slice. "We were almost at the top anyway. Plus they weren't really going all that fast."

"What about you?" Boston asked Caitlin.

"I tried. My bike let me down," she added with a smile.

Carlos and Bethy soon arrived, setting down their bikes, getting some food and joining the other four. Boston pointed out that the backside descent was supposed to be really steep until it reached the creek bed below after a few treacherous miles. When it came time to go, he started early with Carlos and Bethy, all slow downhillers. Riding along the Mt. Hamilton ridge, they came upon the expansive view to the east, seeing a desolate landscape of distant rolling hills, just before the roadway began to dive toward a dry valley below.

Boston took off first. The first hairpins were sharp and they had not gathered much speed yet, slowly and easily making the tight turns. But soon the downhill straightaways got steeper with the unmarked corners much sharper. Coming through a banked turn, Boston was suddenly passed by whom he guessed would have been either Bert or Erik but it was another male, wearing a red windbreaker, leaning hard into the next turn to the right, which they both leaned through, leading to a sharp left turn ahead.

Braking in preparation for the upcoming turn, Boston heard a woman's voice, "On your left." He moved over to his right as the woman, also in red, whipped by him and into the turn where her bike quivered before going off the asphalt onto a sandy shoulder. Quickly slowing, she almost got it back onto the roadway but her tire bounced off the lip and she toppled over hard onto her hip.

Able to halt his bike just past her fall, Boston hurried over to her with Carlos and Bethy stopping right behind him. She was sitting, weeping slightly. Kneeling alongside her, he asked if she was ok. Dizzy but otherwise fine, she seemed more concerned about her bike lying at her side than herself. Checking it out, Carlos said it wasn't damaged. The sand had cushioned her fall and protected the bike.

Bert, Caitlin and Erik arrived, asking what had happened and if she was hurt. "I'm causing quite a scene," the woman spoke, somewhat woozy but laughing a little, tears still on her cheeks.

Bert spoke, seeing no obvious injury, "What'd Boston do, run you off the road?"

"No, it was my own dumb fault. I was trying to keep up with my husband and I screwed up. He's probably halfway to Livermore by now."

"He's probably coming back uphill for you," Caitlin said. "We can go tell him what happened." Boston told the two to look for a red jersey like hers.

She appreciated that and started to get up, but only sat back down. "His name is Raymond. Raymond Delzio," she called out to Caitlin and Bert as they left. "Thank you all so much for stopping. I'm Lina Delzio." Taking off her helmet and sunglasses, she was Hispanic with black, shoulder-length hair.

Boston introduced himself and the others remaining. He helped Lina to her feet, brushing off the dust. She seemed to be unhurt and said so.

"Such a fuss," she told them. "I'm embarrassed about crying. I didn't even fall very hard."

Boston looked around. "Well, of any place to tumble, you picked the best one." Then he turned to Erik. "Think, she can ride, doc?"

"Are you a doctor?" Lina asked Erik.

"Gynecologist," he replied, then looked very concerned. "You're not pregnant, are you?"

"Don't worry," she told him. "My son's almost two. Nothing in the oven right now." Giving them all a smile, she took her bike from Carlos and hopped on. The four of them followed. The remaining way down still had steep pitches and sharp turns. Except for Erik shooting out ahead, the rest of them stayed together, carefully taking the turns, constantly checking speed.

The road finally bottomed out just as it came upon a narrow river bridge. In the shade of the only roadside tree, Bert and Caitlin were waiting with the husband, Raymond, as skinny as a jockey but taller, seemingly made for biking. He was very solicitous of his wife, apologizing for having descended the whole way before realizing she was no longer trailing. She assured him that she understood, telling the group how her husband was a demon on downhills as well as very fit and fast on uphills.

Stopped where they were in the bottom of the draw, the increasing heat of the day was readily noticeable. The now eight of them started up the short climb on the other side of the bridge. Raymond hung back with his wife Lina, until she told him to go ride with the leaders as she was keeping pace with Bethy and Carlos.

The roadway went through several small creek valleys before it turned northward. Boston took a turn at front then peeled off to the back of the draft line where Caitlin seemed struggling to maintain contact. "How's it going?" Boston asked her.

"Fine," she answered, "working hard. It's hot out there."

"Catch on," Boston told her and she fell in line as he pushed to keep up with Bert while Erik and Raymond exchanged leads. Ahead, a road sign marked the junction in one direction to Livermore and in the other to Patterson on Highway 5, beyond which was a small café on a little knoll. Racing up to the front, Boston yelled to Erik to turn up the driveway entrance before he faded back where he found Caitlin lagging behind. Boston followed her gliding into the building's small parking lot where a few motorcycles were parked in front of windows that held neon signs advertising beer inside.

—

Settled around picnic table in the shade of a valley oak tree, the group was almost done munching on an array of chicken sandwiches, fries, potato chips and soft drinks, all of which they agreed was better than what any upcoming rest stop could offer.

In spite of her fall, Lina seemed fine. She was taller than Caitlin, stouter with muscular arms and shoulders, and was a few years older than Bethy. Her tumble was nothing, she told the group as she was more concerned about her loss of conditioning, having given birth not long ago. "I have a two-year-old, by c-section, so I'm just getting back into biking."

Boston glanced to Caitlin, whose face was blank, eyes hidden by her dark shades. Since he had learned about Caitlin's child, Bethy had never mentioned it again. Caitlin had never said anything either to the group. He could not recall seeing a picture of a baby whenever he went to Caitlin's apartment Saturday mornings to retrieve her, but then he had never ventured further than her living room whenever she bustled about getting ready.

"We're training for the Death Ride," Boston announced.

"So are we," Lina told him. "We've rented a cabin in Markleeville. Actually, our friends have cancelled. So we have lots of room, don't we, Raymond?"

"Plenty," he said. "You all can stay there with us if you want. In fact, we need people to share the four-day rent. Couldn't get it just for the weekend."

"We'll take it," Boston said, looking around the group, seeing their agreement.

Lina went to say that they were looking for people to train with. They lived in Belmont. When she heard that the group was Palo Alto based, she mentioned that Raymond was a Stanford professor. Admitting that she had been looking for somebody to tire out her husband who was much too strong for her, she wanted to know everyone's names again.

Bert had kept his sunglasses on throughout the whole lunch, watching and listening to her. Five years ago, when he was just getting divorced, he had met a Lina Rodriguez at a singles event. After a couple dinners, they slept together and then he never called her back. "Bert Leunberger," he told her when it was his turn, then reluctantly added, "I believe we've met."

She studied him for a moment. Her eyes narrowed as she recognized him. "The shrink?" she asked wryly. The table hushed. "Didn't know you biked?"

"I didn't. Not back then. Then, I moved to Hawaii for a while."

"Where he robbed banks," Boston tossed in. "Kind of the Butch Cassidy of Honolulu." Lina still glared at him. Bert sat there speechless for once.

"All four are probably criminals," Bethy added. "But they do know how to bike. For myself, I'm worried sick about doing the Death Ride."

Lina kept a long silence. Finally she said, "My Caesarean had complications that wiped me out for half a year."

"Mine was natural," Caitlin spoke up, causing all heads in the group to turn towards her. Bethy bit her lip while Boston studied the young, stoic face. "Like you, I also have a two-year-old," she announced. "Mandy lives with her father in San Diego. We never married. I hardly ever see her." It was new information to everyone but Bethy and Boston. Bert sat stunned.

"That has to be hard," Lina sympathized.

"More than I ever dreamed," Caitlin replied. "Ready to roll?" Picking up her helmet, she stood, her faced turned to the side as the bottom of her sunglasses caught a tear.

—

Irina and Katherine lay inside the private indoor tub, sitting across from one another with the still water just below their necks. "Erik is so focused on the Death Ride," Irina began. "He now rides his stationary bike at night after dinner. We don't do anything together except sleep. I mean, really sleep." She paused. "How's Boston?"

Katherine bunched her shoulders. "He's pretty much useless on weekends and he's been very busy at his work. Actually, I don't think his business is going that well. I've tried to schedule a vacation later on in the year, but he doesn't want to discuss it. My best shot at getting his attention is Friday night when at least he's excited about Saturday's biking." She paused. "I don't think he wanted the two girls to join the group at first, but now they're full fledged members. Actually, they seem kind of fun. I wish there was another hot tub get together."

"That'd be fun," Irina agreed. "All I do is see clients, feed Erik and the two boys and read in bed until lights out. This is no life." She gazed over at Katherine. "Did you know that they teach massage classes here?"

"No," Katherine replied. "I use to get them about once a month. I love them."

"Want to take a class together?"

Katherine looked away. "Classes like that aren't my thing. I wouldn't mind if Boston learned how to give massages, the right way that is, not the husband way."

"I wouldn't even mind the husband way these days," Irina replied, standing up with the waterline just above her waist. "Giving a massage is the last thing in the world that he would want to do, not after staring at women all day. I wish he had a hobby like playing the clarinet something that would keep him at home, put him in touch with his own hands. I'd listen to the clarinet. It would be very soothing." Irina dropped to her knees, letting the water come up to her chin as her blonde hair floated on the surface.

"Is he musical?" Katherine asked.

"He listens to Icelandic music. It's just noise to me," the Russian woman answered before submerging.

Chapter 17

Calaveras Road

Calaveras Reservoir is part of the Hetch Hetchy Water system with the entire drainage shed owned by the City of San Francisco. Calaveras Road was built high on the western slopes of the reservoir and extends through the City of Milpitas.

The nearby 2594-foot tall peak was once called Cerro de las Calaveras, later named Monument Peak as it lies on the boundary between Alameda and Santa Clara Counties, marking the point dividing the linear eastern line from the creek-following western border.

A "parage de las Calaveras" or "place of skulls" was mentioned as early as 1809 as being located in the hills east of San Jose, apparently denoting a spot where local Indians kept skulls and skeletons.

April ride, part 2

The century ride into Livermore from the junction café in the San Antonio Valley started with a short climb on hot, exposed slopes where the riders were soon strung out as the road meandered sometimes shaded alongside a creek, trending downhill. Bert was eager to know more about Caitlin's history but she seemed to be tiring and was hanging back with Lina Rodriguez Delzio, whom Bert was eager to avoid, at least for the time being. He had no need to get in between the two young mothers. Instead, he stayed close to Erik, Boston and Raymond, Lina's husband as the four of them boiled along in the heat.

After briefly pausing at the next official rest stop alongside a treeless, shallow meadow-creek, the four pushed on again as temperatures continued to climb during the final drop into Livermore, where they waited to reconvene with the others. Caitlin and Lina arrived in silence, followed sometime later by Carlos and Bethy. From Livermore, the route was flat and into a hot headwind. By the time they reached the next rest stop in a Pleasanton city park, it was late in the afternoon and nearing a hundred degrees.

As each of them pulled into the final official rest stop, they found little food left with only warm water in the yellow plastic coolers. Getting what they could and opening their own gel packets, the group spread out on the grass to eat and rest. With a face red from the heat, Caitlin's expression conveyed to everyone that she didn't want to talk about the daughter she had mentioned hours ago back at the café. Lina took care not to mention her caesarean again. Bethy sat sweating next to Carlos while Boston and the others checked their route maps, discussing what the rest of the distance was like.

No cooler and not much refreshed, the group resumed their westerly direction, staying together into the hot headwind before turning south at the Sunol junction toward Calaveras Reservoir. The road undulated in the fading sunlight before it reached the shade of the last climb. In front, Boston pulled over for a rest at the bottom of the next climb. "How's everyone doing?"

Younger than the other men by around ten years, Raymond seemed the freshest whereas the other four looked plainly beat. Lina was sweaty but seemed ok. Bethy looked worn and Caitlin appeared exceptionally flushed. They had come over ninety miles with another long ten to go.

As the group restarted, Bert, Raymond and Caitlin rode out ahead. Erik and Boston stayed with Lina while Carlos shepherded Bethy. The climb, slightly cooler in the shade, was still slow as they were all exhausted. Erik, admittedly an Icelander who wilted in heat, seemed to be really sagging. Cresting finally, Boston was happy to see a broad expanse of reservoir, believing the end would be a simple ride around the west shore.

Instead, the road went in and out along the hillside, following various creek cuts. At every culvert crossing, the road dipped and then climbed steeply up again. Finally, his threesome came upon Caitlin, helmet off, sitting on the shoulder with Raymond standing alongside. As they stopped, Raymond explained that Caitlin had thrown up a couple of times. Bert had gone ahead to get his truck.

"How do you feel?" Boston asked her.

"I'm fine," she said. "A little light headed. I just can't ride anymore."

"You want some more water?" Lina asked.

"No, thanks. I have plenty. It's just too hot for me to keep on my bike."

While Raymond stood by, Lina reminded him that they were going to be late for the babysitter, then cut herself short remembering that the young blonde woman didn't have care of her own child.

"Hey, it's ok," Caitlin said, gazing up at her. "You have your family situation and I've got mine. It's ok."

"Sometime can we talk about it?" Lina asked her.

"Sure. Sometime. Go, don't be late for your sitter," Caitlin replied. After giving Bert a parting scowl, Lina left with Raymond.

Soon arriving and seeing her friend on the ground, Bethy jumped off her bike and went to her in a panic. Explaining that she overheated and threw up twice, Caitlin stated that she was fine, then chuckled over the apparent contradiction.

"Maybe you're part Icelandic," Erik joked lightly. "We never do well in the heat."

Caitlin sighed, saying to Bethy, "I've never whimped out before."

"I know," Bethy comforted her. "It was too hot and you rode too hard earlier."

Finally, Bert's Chevy Silverado truck arrived. Picking up the two women and their bikes, he sped off, leaving the three men to continue biking around the reservoir's west side.

Bert drove to the Milpitas Starbucks and got his two female passengers and himself ice cold coffee drinks. Sitting in the small restaurant, replenishing, Caitlin immediately felt better. Seeing that, Bert stated, "That was quite a little secret you revealed."

Caitlin responded sharply, "Do you want to analyze me?"

Bert began, "Well, it wouldn't be ethical . . ." but Bethy immediately cut him off. "Of course, not," she stated. "We're your friends."

With Caitlin saying nothing, Bert saw the other three men biking across the parking lot shoulder to shoulder. "It's the Earps," Bert announced. Both women were silent.

Meanwhile, Boston, Erik and Carlos entered through the glass doors and walked over to their table. "Hello, Wyatt," Bert called out.

"Hi, Doc," Boston countered, without missing a beat. "How's your patient?"

"Recovering in the OK corral." Bert smiled at the two women, who showed no response to his Tombstone patter.

"Hamilton's a big mountain," Carlos said. "Sometimes the effort that it takes doesn't hit you until later."

"It wasn't the mountain," Bert told him. "It was the heat."

"Not for anyone else," Caitlin said meekly, turning to her friend. "I whimped out. You guys made it no problem."

"I just wasn't going fast enough to get sick," Bethy countered.

"We'll have more mountains," said Boston, "and more hot days." Stating that Erik had to leave, he asked Caitlin again if she was all right, which she repeated she was. Carlos also had to depart, explaining that one of his daughters was joining him for dinner. That said, the three men left Bert and the two women still nursing their cold drinks.

Once on the highway, Boston admitted to Erik that he had been told months ago about Caitlin's daughter. "Single women seem to have such complicated lives," Boston surmised.

"Undoubtedly made so by men," Erik responded. "My uncle in Reykjavik once gave me his philosophy that all women were the same woman, just in different forms. Of course in Iceland, it's literally true. Everyone's related to everyone in that country."

"So they're all waves of the same ocean?"

"Something like that."

"Think Katherine and Irina would agree with all that?"

"Irina can't stand my uncle."

Boston laughed. "And the hills we bike, all part of the same mountain? What's that say about us?"

"Someday you have to come to Iceland."

—

It was already getting dark as Bert drove the two women to Donald Drive and Bethy's house, where Caitlin had spent Friday night and was staying tonight as well. After taking their bicycles off his truck, Bert rolled Caitlin's bike to the backyard for her.

"I think a hot tub would feel really great. Don't you, Bethy?" Caitlin asked, following Bethy who was pushing her own bike.

"I do," Bethy said. "I might just melt away. But are you sure?"

"Yes, and I could sure use a beer. Bert, will you stay?" she asked him as he set her bike against the rear house wall.

During the return drive, meeting up with Lina again had been on his mind. He realized that he had not handled their split at all well. In fact, he had just cut her out without any communication and that was now bothering him. "You'll join us, won't you?" Caitlin asked him again.

Fifty years old, divorced, he had no place to go but his dark apartment. "You guys get in the tub," Bert told them, going into the kitchen. "I'll get the beer."

He went inside as Caitlin sat down on a bench to take off her bike shoes. "You really want that beer, sweetie?" Bethy asked her. "Definitely," Caitlin replied. Bethy shrugged and sat down next to Caitlin to undress as well.

They were on their way to the tub when Bert returned to the outside bench to take off his own clothes. Just as Lina had pointed out, she had been a conquest and then he had dumped her to move onto others, the sum total of which was now what? He was about to get into a hot tub with two young women about half his age. Had he told some of his cronies about such a situation, they would undoubtedly be envious, but it wasn't exactly mixed-company dinner conversation, was it?

A single light was shining on the hot tub when Bert approached with a six-pack. The two women were already in the water, which wasn't bubbling, with Caitlin sitting, leaning back against Bethy as Bethy rubbed her shoulders and neck. "Mmm, that feels good," Caitlin murmured, taking the beer handed her by Bert.

"Do you want the jets on?" he asked, still outside the tub, sipping from his bottle.

"No, it's nice and quiet without it," Caitlin replied, shutting her eyes, taking a long gulp on her beer, as Bert entered the water.

Bert said nothing, nursing his beer, watching Bethy, her beer alongside the tub, working on the younger woman's shoulders. "It's so peaceful now," Caitlin said after awhile. "I was so weak today."

"You ride too hard sometimes," Bethy replied, gently massaging while Caitlin continued to drink. Bert watched the two women in silence, illuminated slightly by the twilight with stars now appearing overhead.

Finally Caitlin rested her beer on the tub edge. "I often think I was too weak with my daughter," she remarked, opening her eyes, gazing at Bert. "Got a second beer?"

"Go easy with this one," said Bert, handing her another beer while still on his first.

"Now he tells me to go easy." She hurried onto the other beer. "It's a little too late to go easy. I've a two-year old daughter who I gave away to her asshole father."

Bethy dropped her head forward. "We have a guest, sweetie."

"He's not a guest," Caitlin said, looking to Bethy. "He's somebody who'd like to fuck me."

"Don't be rude," Bethy lightly scolded.

"Bethy's my friend," Caitlin told Bert. "We also sleep together," she said, dreamily, her eyes still shut, taking another big drink. "Naked." She slumped against her Bethy.

"We're good friends," Bethy explained. "That's all. Maybe it's time to get out. Want some dinner?" she asked Bert.

"I'd love something, anything," Bert responded, finishing his first beer and reaching for a second. "But I think our friend is ready to fall asleep." Caitlin said nothing, still slouched against Bethy.

"Com'on, sweetie," Bethy told her, then looked to Bert. "Can't take the heat, can't hold her beer. We better help her." Together, they lifted Caitlin out of the water. Bethy dried her and herself off with nearby towels, as did Bert. They walked Caitlin inside the house to Bethy's bedroom. Pulling back the covers, they curled her on one side of the queen-bed and covered her back up. Head resting on a pillow, Caitlin mumbled a faint thank you then closed her eyes once more.

Grabbing a robe for herself, Bethy offered another to Bert. "It doesn't fit," he told her. "I'll stick with the towel." He went outside to collect the beers, whether empty or full, while she went to the kitchen and began to boil water for the spaghetti.

"When she stays over, we do sleep together," she told Bert, sitting down across from him as the water heated. "Just like Caitlin said. But we don't do anything."

"Not my business," he replied.

"It is your business," she said. "She likes you. Sleeping together naked is a Caitlin thing, not a lesbian thing."

"Doesn't matter to me," he volunteered.

"Matters to me," she told him. "This deal with her daughter has been very hard on her and I know she's wanted to share it with you for months. She just didn't know how until that other woman mentioned her son, who, of course, just happened to be the same age. It's really her job to fill you in, but that's awfully difficult for her."

Sitting down, Bethy continued explaining that Mandy's dad was Caitlin's college biking coach. They broke up, actually never were really together, at least apparently not as much as Caitlin thought. She still calls him her ex-boyfriend but Bethy doubted that he ever even felt that committed to her. He was also seeing this other woman, who already had his baby. When he found out Caitlin was knocked up, he married the other woman and told Caitlin that it would be better for his daughter—Caitlin's daughter—to grow up with a sibling, a step-sibling. He lets Caitlin see Mandy anytime she wants, which Bethy regarded as the only thing to his credit.

When Bert asked about Caitlin's family, Bethy told him that her father was quite old when Caitlin was born and died when she was in junior high. Her mother passed away while Caitlin was in college. Caitlin has hardly any money. Bethy told him that she admires the way that Caitlin handles a very tough situation, stating that she rarely breaks down like she did tonight.

"Wasn't much of a break down," Bert replied, then volunteered, "I've never pushed for any sex."

"She told me she blew you in the hot tub," Bethy stated, delayed to see his expression, then added, "but also that it was her idea. That's no surprise." Then she asked, "How old are your kids again?"

"In their mid-twenties. Does that make me too old?"

"Does it make her too young?" Bethy questioned. "Don't ask me. She likes you. So do I, for that matter. You're good for her. She's never had a stable male friend before, established. She told me that you seemed to enjoy her hot tub treat but you didn't pressure her to repeat it. What she really likes is that you guys are giving her the Death Ride training and she can count on you every weekend."

"And then?' he asked. "What about after the Death Ride?"

"And then I don't know," she answered. "Got any ideas?"

"No, just working and biking right now, staying in touch with my kids. I think the water's boiling," he told her.

"Well," she said, getting up, "it's not like I have any game plan for my own life." Then she asked, "Are you any good as a psychoanalyst?"

I often wonder that myself, he thought.

—

After dinner, Boston told Katherine about meeting the Delzio's and arranging to stay at the cabin they rented in Markleeville for the ride. Katherine's first thought, which she kept to herself, was that Boston had found another way to bring one more woman into the riding group, albeit this new rider was married.

She was also somewhat perturbed that Boston had not bothered to find out in what department the woman's husband taught at Stanford, but then Boston had never been a stickler for details. Boston having rescued a woman in distress was all that Katherine needed to know about this adventure.

Her day consisted of lounging around a spa with Irina, enclosed within a chlorine-odored room with piped-in flute music. Had Boston been there instead, the setting would have been romantic, just as it always seemed to be when she had been there with other men in her past.

Lying in bed alongside Boston with their books, she blurted out, "At least you could have found out what her husband teaches. Mark's an English professor, you know." Instead of arguing, Boston put down his paperback and got her to put down hers as they became intimate, leading both to fall quickly asleep afterwards.

Katherine awoke soon after, listening to her husband's light snoring. She was aware that his biking circle was enlarging once more and again with people, especially women, whom she did not know. When she and Mark biked, it was always just them. It has been that way too with her and Boston their first year together. In her drowsiness, she envisioned several scenes of him biking away until she finally fell asleep with him gone down an empty road.

Chapter 18

Mt. Diablo

The peak was once known as Cerro Alto de los Bolbones, or Tall Mountain of the Bolbone Indians. Mariano Vallejo reported a story about an 1806 fight between soldiers of the San Francisco Presidio and local Indians at the foot of the mountain although Dr. John Marsh said the fight occurred near a thicket, or "monte," near Concord, which was the town where Marsh lived. The "diablo" or "devil" got attached to the monte either due to an unusually wild dress of one of the Indians, or how the Indians fought or else how troublesome the thorny thicket was.

In any case, "monte" did not mean "mountain." The "diablo del monte" was mapped within the area of the mountain, later misinterpreted by non-Spanish speaking explorers to represent the entire mountain.

On the easterly side of Mt. Diablo is Marsh Creek, formerly shown on maps as Arroyo de los Poblanos, which may have been another spelling of Bolbones. On the banks of the creek, closer to the delta, was where settler John Marsh, a Harvard graduate, built his home, having in 1837 acquired Rancho Los Meganos, or Ranch of the Sand Dunes, named for the numerous dry mound-shaped hillocks in the area. Six-foot-two and well over two-hundred pounds, he had studied under an Army doctor on the Sioux frontier and drifted west after his wife died in childbirth, entering Southern California at age thirty-six and presenting his Harvard Latin-worded undergraduate diploma to the local authorities as proof of his medical certificate.

Known as a fierce individual who charged high fees, Marsh was a central figure in California's early history, including getting early information on the gold rush from a messenger traveling through Marsh's property on his way to inform the American military governor in Monterey of the discovery. In 1856,

123

Marsh was fatally ambushed on what is now Pacheco Boulevard in Martinez. His murderers never publicly identified.

May ride, part 1

Bert Luenberger and Raymond Delzio reached the Mt. Diablo Ranger Station at the Summit Road fork first, with Erik Erikksson and Caitlin Carter right behind them. The five of them weren't racing uphill, at least not yet. Farther down the South Gate Road, Boston Reed biked alongside Lina Delzio with Carlos Cordova and Bethy Kono closely trailing.

This was the Delzio's first opportunity in four weekends since Mt. Hamilton to join the other six. Riding beside him on South Gate, Lina related to Boston that she had met Raymond four years ago. Raymond had been a casual mountain biker, whom Lina converted to road biking. He was a college professor and herself a soils engineer, so their meeting was pure chance, she told him. Boston asked what was his subject, which wasn't exactly germane to her story but it was a detail he could give Katherine. Lina told him that Raymond taught English but he did not ask her about possibly knowing Mark Kirk, Katherine's second husband, as Lina continued with her story, telling him that friends set them up as she was closing in on thirty and Raymond was just past it.

Delivering Zack had been very hard on her. The caesarean was unexpected when it suddenly was discovered the baby was in stress. After giving birth, she then hemorrhaged a lot internally. She admitted to Boston that she was jealous of her husband's good health and fitness as she had suffered so much. On top of that, she did not really know what she felt about being a mother except that she loved Zack totally. If Raymond stayed biking at her side, she felt bad for holding him back. If he biked way ahead, she got angry for his leaving her. It was not fair, she knew. All she wanted to do at this point was prove to herself that she could do the Death Ride, which in her mind meant that having both a husband and a baby was a good thing.

She did not say anything to Boston about having known Bert, which included having slept with him for one night. Over the three weeks that they couldn't ride with the group, she had debated whether or not to cancel doing the Death Ride with Boston's group. However at this point, Raymond already had them signed up to share the cabin and she could hardly mention having slept with Bert as an excuse to sever ties. But it disturbed her to know that within their group was a man who had sex with her, all with her invitation to do her that night as pleased him. Why hadn't he called her afterwards?

The South Gate climb was only a few miles. The leading four stopped at the little ranger kiosk to let the other four catch up, which they soon did. While everyone rested for a few minutes, Lina kept eyeing Bert. All she wanted him to do was explain why her never called her. Instead, Bert was clearly avoiding her and was obviously solicitous of the young blonde girl. When the group started up again Lina told Boston by all means to go ahead as the others sped off. If he had stayed again with her, she was going to spill everything about her experience with Bert.

Bert, Caitlin, Erik and Raymond were already ahead of Boston. The continuous hillside curves cut off his view of them most of the time. Whenever he saw them, they were always pulling away, with Caitlin at the back of the line but apparently well recovered from her Mt. Hamilton meltdown four weeks before.

Raymond had been all over Mt. Diablo previously on a mountain bike, including the top, whereas the other three not at all. Ahead was a large, red rock pillar that he recognized as the point near which a sharp switchback turned to the left. Bert was setting a strong pace with Erik trailing. Caitlin fell behind as the three reached a large parking lot from which a narrow one-way lane that took off steeply. Charging up, Bert stood in his pedals, fighting to keep momentum up the 20% grade. In the middle, Erik went by and then Raymond passed him, giving him only a slight nod. Bert had no acceleration left—it was all he could to finish the few hundred feet more where he stopped while the other two were done and circling.

On level ground, virtually crawling up, Caitlin barely made it without stopping. Right behind her, Boston popped over the crest, also huffing. They joined the others slowly spinning in their recovery mode.

Lina soon appeared, walking her bike to the top. "Couldn't do it," she gasped to Raymond as he came by and stopped. "Almost, but couldn't make those last hundred feet. Anybody else walk?" Raymond answered by shaking his head. "I didn't think so," she said.

The rest of the group coasted slowly to the stone building at the end of the lot, joined shortly by Raymond and Lina. As they waited, Carlos arrived, strong as ever, stopping on top to watch the road below. Bethy finally made the crest, pushing her bike.

"I had nothing left," she sighed. "I thought I was at the end and then I didn't see anybody, only this shitty one-way road that went straight up. After about fifty feet, I got off and walked the whole thing. Sorry."

"The top isn't fair," Carlos told her. "It's just as steep as Orbit, if not steeper."

"Well, I walked that one, too," Bethy shrugged. Standing for a little while, she eventually got on her bike to rode to the stone-veneered building where the group waited. Taking a break, they all trudged up the outside staircase to the rooftop deck and a small, enclosed observation room, surrounded with windows. In the distance to the east, they could barely discern the snowy peaks near Lake Tahoe. Mt. Hamilton with its white domes was visible to the south while the bay spread broadly to the west, bordered on the northern edge by pyramid-shaped Mt. Tamalpais.

"Supposedly you can see more land surface from here," began Boston, "than from any other place on earth excepting from Mt. Kilimanjaro."

Studying the snowy mountains to the east, Caitlin asked, "What are those?"

"That's Desolation Wilderness. Markleeville's south of there," Boston replied, pointing to the horizon where the earth met the sky in a hazy blend that was impossible to tell what was mountain or cloud or shadow. Being May, the Sierra was still partially snow covered during that short, quiet pause between ski resorts closing and backpack trails opening. It felt strange to Boston and he sensed also for the rest of the group to be able to see the land where their ordeal in two months was to take place. About a hundred and fifty miles away from where they stood, the Death Ride roads waited with Ebbetts and Monitor Passes most likely still closed, snow melt sliding across the asphalt, little creeks and streams gushing. All this training here, thought Boston, to culminate there in a mysterious place he was faintly observing for the first time without even being able to distinguish it.

—

At Boston's direction for the descent, they took the Ranger Station fork to the right, following North Gate Road into Walnut Creek and a paved pathway alongside an irrigation ditch. The ride now was casual, almost carefree along the level route, with a steady stream flowing by. Reaching Ygnacio Valley Road, they biked up and over the crest, descending into the town of Clayton, at the northerly base of the gigantic mountain. The group took a break at a small sandwich and coffee shop.

"What's next?" Lina asked Boston.

"Morgan Territory Road, which supposedly will take us back toward Blackhawk."

"Morgan Territory?" asked Bert. "What do they mean by 'Territory?' Have we biked outside California?"

"Maybe," Raymond added, "we're way past anywhere I've ever biked."

"That's typical Boston," Bert said.

"I've never been back here either," Boston said, "and I have no idea who Morgan was."

"Easy. He was pirate," Bert said to blank stares. "Captain Morgan?"

"Him, I've heard of," Caitlin replied. "In fact, I wouldn't mind a little tonight. You have to join us for dinner, Carlos. Don't leave us at Bert's mercy."

"Maybe," Carlos answered, looking to Bethy, who had mentioned the possibility earlier in the ride.

"So, how did you get the name Boston?" Lina asked the group leader.

"Damn good question," Bert added, looking to Lina, surprising her. "I've often wondered that myself."

Her return look told him that she still wondered why he had never called her after sleeping with her.

"My parents attended Harvard," Boston replied. "They were both from the West Coast but really enjoyed Boston. They weren't college sweethearts. In fact, they didn't even know each other. My dad was graduating from law school when my mom entered as a freshman."

"What's his name? Detroit?" Bert joked.

"You know," Boston took over. "I've always wondered about Bert, like short for Robert or Bertram but I'm starting to think Humbert Humbert, as in 'light of my life, fire of my loins.'"

"What's that from?" Caitlin asked.

"*Lolita*," Carlos said. "Yep, that's pretty much Bert."

"Carlos, impressive," Bethy noted.

"Never read it but I saw the Jeremy Irons movie," Caitlin continued, turning to Bert. "Is Humbert your role model?"

"No, but I liked the James Mason version better."

Lina couldn't stand it anymore. "Why didn't you call me, you shit head?" she blurted. That stopped the group chatter.

Bert blinked at her. "I figured you deserved better than me."

"Don't give me that psycho-bullshit," she returned icily, "even if it is true." Looking around the group, she turned to her husband. "I'm sorry. We went on a few dates. I thought we were hitting it off and he was going to call me. As it turns out, I'm glad he didn't," she stated, then her voice rose again. "But he still should have."

The group was silent. "I also preferred James Mason," Boston said finally.

"Excuse me?" Lina asked.

"Bert reminds me much more of James Mason," Boston replied with a smile. "A little more despicable and a little older than Irons." The group waited for Lina's reaction.

She fumed a little more. "You should have called me."

"I know," Bert told her. "I'm sorry."

As they started getting back on their bikes and with Lina out ahead, Caitlin asked him, "Bert, did you really sleep with that woman and not call her?"

"Wyatt," cried Bert toward Boston, "get us out of Dodge!"

—

Dennis Crowe joined Katherine and Irina for coffee at Katherine's house. When asked about Ophelia, Dennis explained that she was in Washington State to be with one of her daughters, who was pregnant with what would be Ophelia's first grandchild. Knowing the due date, she had wrapped up her teaching early this semester.

When asked what was new with them, Katherine responded that Irina was taking massage classes and volunteered that she was pretty good.

"I'm just learning," Irina stated. "Actually, they only had an intermediate class. We meet once a month."

"Do you like it?"

"I love it. Besides the instructor, I'm the only other woman."

"Plus it's in the nude," Katherine chimed in.

"That's something," Dennis stated, raising an eyebrow.

"You know I'm not shy," Irina responded, "com'on, you remember us all in the hot tub at your place?"

"Of course, I remember. Do you massage Katherine in the nude?"

"Me or her?" Irina asked.

"Both?" Dennis grinned.

"Can't pull the wool over his eyes," Katherine laughed. "Dennis use to give pretty good massages, as I remember, what few he did. Maybe I got three, six of them at the most."

"I didn't know shit from shinola regarding massages," Dennis replied, grinning at her. "But I loved getting my hands on you." Then he turned to Irina, "So, how many in your class?"

"Four," Irina replied. "At first I thought they were all gay. But one of them is at least bisexual I'm sure."

"Feel like trying your skills on someone new?"

"Sure."

"You behave now," Katherine told him. "Ophelia's coming back, isn't she?"

"Some day," Dennis replied, thinking that it was a funny to hear Katherine remind him. "You're married to the Icelander, aren't you?" he asked her.

"He's not into massage," Irina answered. "When would you like one? Remember, I'm just a beginner."

Dennis turned to Katherine before answering. "How about in the afternoon? This morning I've got some errands to run."

"I've a table set up in my studio, formerly the garage."

Katherine interrupted, speaking to Irina, "Don't forget about our dinner tonight. With our biking husbands."

"How can I forget with five bikes hanging from the studio ceiling?" Irina shrugged.

Chapter 19

Morgan Territory

Jeremiah Morgan was a Cherokee from the Indian lands in Alabama who came to California in 1849. Seven years later, while grizzly bear hunting, he claimed all the land he could see on the backside of Mt. Diablo, which territory was then unsurveyed. Winding up with 10,000 acres, Morgan had seventeen children for which he left his estate. Generations later, his descendents dedicated Morgan Territory Regional Park, centered midway on the road bearing his name.

May ride, part 2

They left the Clayton coffee shop and headed out toward Marsh Creek Road, continuing into the afternoon heat through a narrow hillside gap, then descending to the right fork marking Morgan Territory Road. The gigantic Mt. Diablo to the west blocked any offshore airflow. At first, the road merely rolled past ranches, then narrowed slightly, crossing a creek and very soon dove into pure wilderness as it followed the ascending drainage basin.

The road was now shaded and the flowing water sounded inviting. Caitlin held back while Erik and Boston pressed to the front and began to pull ahead. Being on the group's first long ride since Mt. Hamilton and just as hot as then, Caitlin was determined not to falter this time. Bert stayed alongside, talking to her, checking her condition. Lina and Bethy followed, welcoming the current tree canopy, joined by Raymond and Carlos.

It was a long climb with a section of steep tight s-turns, sometimes withering in the heat, others in deadened shade. Boston and Erik stayed side by side as they reached a regional park parking lot with nearby unshaded picnic benches and a drinking faucet but no canopy for cooked cyclists.

Caitlin and Bert crested next, both soaked with sweat, each with their helmet dangling off the handlebars. Letting out a big exhale, Caitlin smiled and Bert gave a thumb's up as Boston waved them over. After a long interval, Lina appeared, drenched, accompanied by Raymond and, not far behind, Bethy and Carlos. Slightly fanned by a wisp of breeze but without shade, the group collected over the tables, commiserating about the long, hot climb.

"I have no idea where we are," Raymond volunteered, "or how to get back to where we started this morning."

"Me neither," Lina agreed. "Clayton was small but it at least was somewhere. There's nothing here. But thank you, honey, for riding with me," she told her husband.

It seemed to Bert that the heat had taken the starch out of her anger, but he wasn't about to open up any conversation. Instead, he went to the faucet and let the water run until it was cold before filling his plastic bottle.

"The beauty of it is that Boston has found this road that we've never heard of," Erik announced. "Morgan Territory—it's like Northwest Territories, some uncharted region. We don't know what to expect so we have to learn to pace ourselves. The Death Ride will be the same: A journey into the unknown."

"This reminds me of the Cantabrian Mountains in Asturias," Carlos offered. "When I visit my mother, I sometimes take my bike on the mountain roads, little roads that I've never been on and I don't know what they're like or where they're going."

"I had to keep climbing," Bethy started. "If I turned around, I'd never find my way back."

"I thought we'd never get out of that damn valley," Bert said.

"You were getting a little rosy there, big guy," Caitlin told him. Bert shook his head no but he had felt hot and exhausted. She continued, "I feel better now and much better than I did on the Mt. Hamilton ride. Going slower really helps."

The group kept talking and chatting. Boston introduced a new thought, "Mt. Hamilton was named after a minister, and Diablo is the devil. Carlos, what do you make of that?"

"Why was he climbing mountains instead of ministering?"

"You are a contrary son-of-a-gun," Bert stated. "Maybe he wanted to get closer to God. You're from a Catholic country so you tell me."

"For me, there's more of God on top of Mt. Diablo than in any church I've ever attended," Carlos replied. "Cathedrals are for the sick and old people, just like in the middle ages. Ministers should minister, bikers bike."

"St. John the Apostle," Bert replied, "our defender of the faith." Carlos said nothing, merely gazing over the drying hills until it was time to leave.

The road south suffered a little uphill past ridgetop houses before carving down a hillside open onto a huge slope already cooked brown with the arrival already of the dry season. Surprisingly alone in front, Boston started forcing his descent speed. Almost to the bottom, suddenly Carlos shot by. Seeing no sharp turns ahead, Boston took out after him, bouncing barely under control in and out of unexpected dips, still able to maintain a set distance behind, even when a car approached, visible in and out of the road bends ahead. After it zipped by, he pushed harder and harder as the curves lessened.

Full speed, blood pounding, legs drained, Boston focused solely on Carlos. Any reluctance due to his crash three months ago on Sierra Road was abandoned as he sensed the gap between them shortening. It just felt like pure adrenaline or testosterone or both but he was determined to not let the opportunity slip away to catch the group's best downhiller. The road turned into a single straightaway, terminating with a stop sign far ahead. As he gained more ground, Boston accelerated, drawing even closer until he had powered into a draft behind the Spaniard, held it just to recover whatever he could, then swooped by with legs tightening to take the lead. Closing in on the intersection, they both began braking hard.

"We haven't done that in awhile," Boston muttered, coughing deep from his lungs.

"You looked too confident all by yourself in front," Carlos replied. "Thought you might have needed a little competition."

"You're all heart," Boston replied. "Next time, stay back there with your girlfriend."

"She's not my girlfriend," Carlos said, seriously.

"Just kidding," Boston told him as the others began arriving. "Where are we?" he asked, seeing their group surrounded by dried, rolling hills with no sign of anything except salt licks for cattle with the road bordered by barbed wire.

No one was really sure. Heading west being the only reasonable option, they rode into a strong, hot headwind. Having gone sixty miles already, they were a weary bunch, trying to maintain a draft, changing leaders frequently, breaking in and out of smaller clusters, lunging their way through the hot headwind.

Finally the first marks of civilization appeared with farmhouses, then some rural businesses and finally the tract housing edge of development. Soon they were at Blackhawk with its gated community and museum-style residences.

—

The women went to Starbucks to order iced drinks while the men began loading the bikes for the drive back. Carlos had ridden with Boston in his Honda Odyssey while Erik drove along in his Toyota Highlander. Bert brought the two women in his Silverado truck. "So, Carlos," Bert called out from his car, "come join us for dinner tonight? No use asking you married guys."

Carlos was holding his bike up for Boston to put on his rack. "I don't know," he replied, tired.

"Com'on, man," Bert said, "what else are you doing?" Carlos didn't answer him. "Look," Bert continued, "you spend all this time with Bethy biking, at least give her an little evening company."

Carlos finally turned to him, letting Boston deal with his bike. "You just want me to distract Bethy so you have Caitlin for yourself."

Bert responded with a laugh, "Well, what's wrong with that?"

"For one thing, you're fifty and she's half of that."

"So?"

"So she's already been through a lot without being led on by you."

"Who said anything about leading her on? It's only a dinner. Plus, Bethy likes you."

"She's still married."

"Separated," Bert corrected him.

"Listen, Bert," Carlos began again, stepping toward him, "stay out my life. If you want to get in my face, let's get started right now."

"I only asked you to join us for dinner, you Spanish son-of-a-bitch," Bert replied, also stepping toward him.

Abandoning the bikes, Boston quickly moved between him. "Fellas," he started, "we're all hot, tired. Bert, you asked and I think you got your answer so just leave it at that." Bert and Carlos glared at each other, neither backing away. "I'll finish loading the bikes. Carlos, you and Erik help the girls with the coffee and then let's get out of here."

Erik headed toward Starbucks along with Carlos, passing by Raymond who had watched the whole scene from his own car.

"What's with that asshole?" Bert said, when they had gone.

"What's with you?" Boston replied. "You know he's uptight right now. His divorce is still less than a year old."

"He spends all this biking time with her. Obviously she must like him somewhat, even though he's stubborn as a mule. Maybe I'll just have to knock some sense into his head."

"I wouldn't try that if I were you. Carlos was apparently quite a boxer in Spain, something like our golden gloves."

"I've had a couple street fights in my day. That's a little different than boxing rules."

"So has Carlos," Boston told him. "In fact, that was why he left Asturias for Madrid. Seems like he put a guy in the hospital. I wouldn't trigger him if I were you."

"Far be it from me to get bloody just trying to get our friend to have a little female companionship," Bert replied, finishing tying off the bikes.

"Maybe he has as much as he can handle," Boston replied, leaning against his car, waiting for the coffee, which arrived shortly.

After Starbucks drinks were passed around, Bethy asked Carlos if he would join them for dinner. Just in case, she told him that they would be at Chevy's around 7:30 pm. Carlos stared at Bert, who only shrugged in disdain, indicating that this time he could care less. Bethy told Carlos that she hoped so as she got in Bert's truck.

—

On the drive back, Boston asked Carlos, "Don't get upset if I ask, but what's the story?"

"Bert thinks he's such the ladies man," Carlos answered. "When I was single in Madrid, I knew a lot of young women like Caitlin, who had no idea about the older men they met."

"Ok," Boston replied. "But leaving Bert and Caitlin out of it if you can, don't you like Bethy? You're always hanging back with her."

Carlos stayed tense. "Yes but, the divorce has been very hard on my daughters. If I start going out with somebody thirty-years-old, my wife is going to try to prove to them that all along I wanted the divorce just to date girls much too young for me."

"You're oldest daughter's barely twenty-one, right? They probably think thirty's pretty old. Bert can be an asshole, I agree, but—and don't hold it against me—he does have a point in this case. But it's your life."

"You don't think forty-five and thirty are too far apart?"

"Of course not," Boston said. "There's something else here that you're not letting on."

Taking a deep breath, Carlos was silent for a moment. Then he began telling Boston about his growing up in Spain, how Spanish women were held in the highest esteem. The fight he had gotten into was over a slur that an older man had made about his sister. Even though Carlos had fought in his sister's honor, knocking the man unconscious, he knew there was something truthful about what the man had said and it made him suspicious of all Spanish women.

His punishment was to leave Asturias and so he had gone to Madrid. He met lots of women there and they presented themselves as available to him, which confused him, he told Boston, and it was a problem for him. Because of that, he never established a relationship. Then Gertrude came along and he felt relieved of his anxiety. She was German, blonde and outgoing, the opposite of the Spanish women he knew. As a result, he had no compunction about sleeping with Gertrude. In hindsight, because of the sex, he was blind to her temper, which was strong enough to finally ruin their marriage.

"Just your luck that Bethy has dark hair and olive skin, just like Mediterranean girls," Boston empathized with him.

"I think I'm more mixed up than ever," Carlos replied. "At least biking, I don't have to think about any thing else."

"But you did join her in the hot tub that one afternoon," Boston added.

Carlos' face showed consternation. "I did."

—

After returning to his apartment to shower and change, Bert picked up the two women again to go to Chevy's. At about a quarter to eight, they were sitting with a pitcher of margaritas and unopened menus when Carlos suddenly appeared and joined them, delighting the women and surprising Bert, who quickly poured him a glass.

After dinner Bethy invited Carlos back to her house for a nightcap with Bert, their driver, and Caitlin, who was spending the night. Carlos declined and she let it go seeing that he was resolute.

As they all left the restaurant, Bethy asked Caitlin and Bert to wait by his truck while she walked with Carlos to his car, parked on the other side of the lot. Once there, she stood facing him. "I'm so glad you came by tonight," she told him.

"Me, too."

"I don't know if I would keep doing these rides if you didn't look out for me. I was really thankful to see you waiting for me today."

"You don't need me," he told her. "You're strong and you're getting better every time out."

"Hopefully," she replied. "Today was really hard and I do need you." She gazed up at him, his face lit by a distant light pole, his eyes watching hers as she sought something else to say. Staying silent, he then glanced over her head to where Bert's truck was.

"I have to go," she whispered. Standing on her toes, she gave him a quick peck on the cheek, then left, turning once to give him a little wave that he returned before getting in his car.

During the short return to Donald Drive, Caitlin suggested a hot tub soak, to which Bert readily agreed while Bethy merely nodded. Inside the door, Bert went to the kitchen while Caitlin ran off down the hall to the bathroom. "Gotta go, too," Bethy added, also disappearing around the hallway.

A cold six-pack under his arm, Bert waited still in the kitchen as both returned. "You know what?" Bethy began. "I'm going to bed instead."

"Not joining us?" Bert asked. "How about one beer at least?"

"The margaritas were plenty for me," Bethy replied, "especially after seventy miles in the heat." Thanking him again for dinner, she left the room once more.

"Looks like it's just you and me, sport," Caitlin smiled at him.

"Looks that way."

"Will you help me with my dress?" she asked, spinning around. Still holding the beer in one hand, he unzipped her with the other, noticing that she wasn't wearing a bra. As she let the dress fall, he then saw that she wasn't wearing anything else either. Facing him again, she asked him, "How about a beer and I'll meet you in the tub?" Handing her a bottle, he watched her depart out the patio door before he undressed to join her at the darkened tub

Their conversation was light-hearted. In low tones, they discussed what they agreed was a rather strange relationship between Bethy and Carlos. Caitlin stated that she liked Carlos but he seemed under a strain, unlike Bert, whose easy-going manner she appreciated.

"That's sort of a compliment," Bert told her

"You're still too much of a wise-ass," she replied, "too sarcastic. But you don't seem to have any problem with women. Or, I should say with me."

"Why would I have a problem with you?" he asked.

"For one thing, you're old enough to be my . . ." her voice trailed off. "You're twice my age. Many men couldn't handle that."

"Not many women either," Bert said. "That hasn't prevented our friendship."

She bit her lip slightly, then told him, "I don't think I can take this hot tub anymore."

"Last time we had to help you to bed."

"Maybe this time, too," she replied, as she went to the steps once more. Reaching for his beer, Bert stayed. "Are you just going to sit there by yourself?" she asked, hands on hips.

"For a moment," he said, sipping his beer and gazing at her. "Talk about a sight for sore eyes plus sore everything else."

"Everything?" she replied, "Well, at least come say goodnight before you leave." Spinning around, she headed back to the house, dripping water all the way across the lawn.

Blew that one, he thought to himself when he finally got out of the tub to return the unopened beer to the refrigerator. A towel was waiting for him in the kitchen. Debating whether or not to get dressed, he decided to keep the towel wrapped as he went looking for her to say goodbye. He continued down the hall to the master bedroom, where a small light was on, the door cracked open. Expecting this to be Bethy's room, he was surprised when Caitlin called his name.

Inside the room, she lay alone on the bed, propped up against the pillow, the sheet open. "Where's Bethy?" Bert asked.

"She's in another bedroom," Caitlin replied. "She said we could have this one."

That's interesting, mused Bert. "What exactly are 'we' doing?" Bert asked.

"We're screwing," Caitlin replied, opening her arms up to him. "That is, we will be once you get into bed."

"And then?" he asked.

"And then, if it's any good, we'll keep doing it," she smiled.

"You know I have a shit-heel reputation," he said.

"Plus you're way too old for me. Now, get into bed." Dropping his towel, he slid onto the bed next to her, pulling the sheet up to chest high. "Are you going to be good to me, Bert?" she asked, nestling up to him.

"How so?"

"Treat me right and don't let me fall in love with you," she answered, gazing into his face. "Isn't that what every guy wants to hear? Sex without commitment?"

Putting his arm under the sheet on her waist, he responded, "Sounds like you've had that already."

"Only I didn't know it at the time," she answered, rolling onto her back and turning out the bedside lamp.

—

Across town in Menlo Park, Katherine and Boston were finishing their dinner with Irina and Erik. With the wine all gone, they were now drinking decaf coffee and discussing Markleeville travel plans for the second week in July.

"When this is all over," Katherine began, "let's do some other weekend trips that don't involve biking, even if we have to go to Iceland for Erik. Any cathedrals like in Europe?" Katherine asked.

"We were just discussing cathedrals today," Boston interjected. Katherine gave him a double take. Then he explained how mountaintops were the cathedrals for bikers.

"There's a famous one in Reykjavik," Erik spoke "It's like a giant mountain spire in the center of town. Irina and I've been there many years ago." He looked to his wife but she seemed distracted with her own thoughts. "Hallgrimskirkja it's called," he continued. "From the observation deck you can see all of the capital plus the surrounding mountains."

"It was our honeymoon," Irina contributed, sipping her coffee while leaving Iceland far behind in her mind and contemplating instead her afternoon massage with Dennis Crowe. For a fifty-year-old man, he was still thin and sinewy, the result of still performing physical tasks, such as moving around his doors. His body also had its share of bumps and sore points, also the residue of continual labor.

She had covered him with the skimpiest of towels, barely hiding his bottom as he first lay on his stomach while she oiled and rubbed his legs. When he eventually rolled over, the towel slipped off while he just lay there unconcerned with his eyes shut. As she had already seen him naked in his pool, she didn't retrieve it. Instead, her hands traveled as far up his thighs as she allowed them to. Dennis seemed perfectly at ease, unflinching. It was all she could do to keep from reaching upwards.

Then she was aware that Erik was talking to her, stating that he was wiped out from the day's biking and was ready to leave the restaurant. Her mind came back into the dinner conversation as she said goodnight to Boston and to Katherine, to whom she gave a little wink that was not reciprocated.

Chapter 20

Page Mill Road

The *Mayfield and Pescadero Toll Road* was built in 1866 by William Page to serve his sawmill located on the headwaters of Pescadero Creek, west of Skyline now encompassed within Portola State Park.

His lumber yard was located at the bottom of his road in Mayfield on what is now El Camino Real then called Main Street, along which the town of Mayfield began with the 1853 opening of Uncle Jim's Cabin, a stage stop and tavern.

In 1867, after being treed by a grizzly bear at his sawmill in the redwoods, Page sold half interest in his business to Alexander Peers, letting Peers run the mill while Page operated the yard. That same year a train station was built in Mayfield at the end of California Avenue, then Lincoln Avenue, along with the Mayfield Hotel being constructed to serve passengers on the new line. The opening of a brewery a year later ensured that Mayfield was a lively place, which suited Stanford students who began attending the University's inauguration in 1891. Ten years later, the University pressured Mayfield to close its saloons, which led to the town's decline and its eventual annexation by the more sedate and alcohol-banned Palo Alto.

When Interstate 280 was built, a multi-lane connector cut off a short stretch of the original Page Mill Road that follows Matadero Creek. Along the bypassed road is an isolated brick tower resembling a gothic castle turret, named Frenchman's Tower, recalling a time when a non-English European foreigner living in the area was unusual.

The purpose of the tower remains unknown as was the background surrounding the wealthy immigrant identifying himself only as Peter Coutts, who in 1874 purchased the Rancho del Matadero, or Ranch of the Meat Slaughtering

Field, later one of the properties acquired by former-Governor Leland Stanford when the Frenchman sold out, departing as abruptly and mysteriously as he had arrived.

The toll road was later purchased into the public domain, named for its original purpose, which was the route Page's mill.

June ride

Memorial Day weekend went by before Raymond and Lina Delzio were available to ride again with the group. Boston Reed waited for them to arrive at his house from where they would bike to join the others.

The couple was overdue. Katherine wanted to meet them but had to leave for an appointment. Still waiting for them alone, he got a call from Erik, who said he couldn't ride today because his derailleur was broken and he was getting it fixed. When the doorbell rang, opening the door, he only saw Lina.

"Our sitter cancelled at the last minute," she said. "Sorry I'm late. Raymond's staying home with Zack our son. Besides, I told Raymond that I needed the training and he didn't. I don't believe in this business of the mom getting stuck with all the kid duties," she told him, excited.

While he was helping her get set up, the other four in their group came riding down Charleston Road. The late morning was heavily overcast—not unusual for early June—as the six headed out Charleston to Arastradero and over a short hill to Page Mill Road, which the group had ridden several times over the past few months.

The road began with a mile or so of fairly level roadway. With few cars out so early in the morning, they were able to ride in pairs and converse. Caitlin and Bert biked together, trailing the other four. Only Bethy knew that Bert had spent last Friday night at Caitlin's apartment, which wasn't the first time they had spent a night together since the Mt. Diablo ride sleepover at Bethy's.

By the way the two behaved toward one another, Boston figured that their relationship was blossoming, evidenced by the affection that had gone back and forth during the previous Saturday ride. This morning they seemed unusually content to hang back, talking between themselves. Lina noticed the same thing. "Are those two a couple?" she asked Boston, who only responded that they biked together.

Carlos had observed their slow start as well, noticing their growing closeness, which only emphasized to him in contrast that he and Bethy still acted the same toward each other as when they started riding together. The past weekend he had thought about phoning her to get together on the Monday holiday but was so busy the day before on Sunday with his daughters that it got to be too late to call. Spending Memorial Day alone, he rode several hills behind his Cupertino apartment instead.

The group stayed connected through the first climbs. With the sky still clouded, the road steepened as Bert and Caitlin caught up and passed everyone on the narrow incline past Foothills Park.

Twisting through a series of steep curves, the road then dropped before it began a mile-and-a-half section of ten to fifteen percent grade. Now in mid-season form and at a comfortable pace, Boston pushed up the difficult stretch, with Lina working hard to closely trail him. Still miles from the top, he saw Bert and Caitlin waiting, off their bikes and leaning against a railing gate across a dirt access road. Stopping, Boston parked his bike there and took out a gel snack from his jersey pocket.

Lina arrived a few moments later, joining them at the gate, her jacket off and dripping sweat. "Boy," she said, "that part always gets me." After taking a big drink of water, she said, "Now I've got to pee."

"Me, too," said Caitlin. "Follow me." She led Lina under the railing gate and walked about five feet before halting. Caitlin peered at Bert. "We don't want to waste any effort traipsing into the bush, right, honey?" Bert just smiled and shook his head in agreement. "These boys aren't much for modesty," Caitlin smiled and lowered her bike shorts. "Especially when it comes to us girls."

"Well, giving birth took all the shyness out of me," Lina responded, squatting down alongside Caitlin.

When finished, Caitlin told Lina, "You have a very small caesarean scar."

"You're shaven," Lina commented.

Caitlin nodded. "Ever since my daughter was born." The two women stood together and lowered the front of their shorts, checking each other out.

"It's my way of always remembering the whole experience," Caitlin told her, her voice a little shaky. "Not that I would ever forget. I don't have her and I don't have him."

Boston and Bert meanwhile observed the whole episode. "I think you've created a monster with your rule," Boston told Bert.

"These girls are as crazy as we are," Bert replied, shaking his head. Leaning his bike against the fence, he walked behind a roadside oak.

Letting her spandex waistband snap back, Caitlin ducked under the gate, looking in Bert's direction. "Hey, where are you going? What about your rule?"

"Yeah," called out Lina. "Don't be shy on my account. I've already seen it, remember don't you?" There was more than a little attitude in her voice, which did not seem to please Caitlin. Ignoring them, Bert let his stream fly behind the tree.

Meanwhile, Carlos and Bethy had arrived. Everyone drank from their bottles. When the group was ready, Caitlin left first with Bert behind her. Working hard, Boston caught them at the base of the next big climb. The three snaked along, then sped down a dip before charging up a short, steep slope, on top of which it was wordlessly assumed that the sprint to Skyline Boulevard was on.

Descending under the trees, they shot out onto a shaded level section with sharp turns, now wetter than ever from trees dripping fog making it slick and dangerous. Caitlin faded while Boston battled Bert for a short while, then overtook him as they rounded the turn with the stop sign in sight.

Boston stood on his pedals, confidently outrunning Bert down the remaining distance as they both turned onto the highway before slowing to a stop.

"Do you think she misses him?" Bert asked suddenly.

"Who?"

"Her baby's father?"

Before Boston could answer, if he had an answer, Caitlin biked up behind them, breathing heavily. "Ok, who was the big dog this time?" she asked.

"The rugger," Bert grumbled. "When he smells the goal line, he's gone." Bert nodded to Boston indicating they could discuss it another time.

The other three arrived, also turning and stopping on the highway edge. A cold, glistening breeze blew strongly from the ocean. Gathering everyone, Boston explained that there were two ways to bike to Skylonda, eight miles to the north on Skyline. They could continue down to the town of La Honda and come up Highway 84, taking well over an hour including a big climb, or go north directly, taking less than a half hour and mostly downhill. Even though rain was threatening, Caitlin was all for taking the longer route, but she was the only one.

"We might get dumped on going further west," Bert told her. "Plus I'm beat."

Caitlin shook her head. "What's the matter, baby? Bad night's sleep."

Bert smiled at her allusion to their late night romp between the sheets at her apartment. "Hard work week," he lied. "Nothing that some Zotts burgers can't cure."

"We still can hot tub afterwards, can't we?" Caitlin questioned.

"Hot tub?" Lina asked.

Boston interrupted. "Let's go before it rains. Skyline to Skylonda."

"Marshal Earp has spoken," Bert pronounced.

Only a couple motorcycles passed them also headed north to 84, too damp for the usual rocketeers to be blasting up and down the highway on their motorcycles. The group also took it easy descending until they were past the most downhill dripline, where the good downhillers in the group cut loose upon reaching dry pavement, leaving the more cautious ones behind.

Following the Loop, they reassembled at the corner of Portola and Alpine Roads. "Last one buys?" Bert suggested.

"Unfair," Bethy cried out.

"Not if we give you a head start," Boston added. "Lina, also."

Lina protested, "I don't want a head start."

"Nothing personal," Boston told her. "You can race Bethy for kicks. Otherwise, you're both beaten before you start."

"Story of my life."

As it turned out, Bethy and Lina were given too much of a lead. Caitlin jumped the start with the guys but they caught her anyway. It didn't matter as Carlos' chain came off. Everyone ordered food whereas last-arriving Carlos went to buy beer.

He was still inside while the others waited at the outside tables as a man walked over to them, standing there. "Well, well," he said to Bethy, "you didn't waste any time in attracting some flies."

He was about five-ten, a little portly, about forty, Boston judged, Asian ethnicity with a sarcastic little smile. "Henry, don't be an asshole," Bethy said.

"Aren't you going to introduce me to your boyfriends?" he asked.

"Guys," she said, "this is my jerk ex-husband."

"Still married, honey-pie," he reminded her, glancing at Bert and Boston. Soon, Carlos arrived, carrying two large pitchers and several cups. "Look at this one," Henry continued. "He has beer to share. Do you share your women, too?"

Bert was first to speak up, "What's the matter, buddy? Somebody piss in your beer?"

"Don't get into it with him," Bethy said. "He's drunk."

"I've had some beer, yes, but I'm not drunk," he replied, turning to her. "I just thought maybe you'd be feeling bad about the separation. Instead, I see you partying with these cowboys, or maybe this is just the warm-up."

"Can't find anybody to drink with?" Boston asked him.

"Yeah," he replied, "so I thought I'd come drink with the guys banging my wife. I don't bike but at least we have that in common."

"Leave, Henry," Bethy quickly said, "just go."

"You're right. I'm outnumbered three to one."

Bert snorted a chuckle, "You'd even be out-numbered one-to-one."

"Let me buy you a drink inside," Carlos said, matter-of-factly.

"I don't need a drink from you."

"Man-to-man. Come with me and I'll buy you a drink." Carlos put his cup down and stood up straight-shouldered beyond arm's distance.

"What for?"

"Man-to-man. Let's go have a drink." Carlos nodded toward Bethy. "She doesn't want you here and you're bothering my friends."

"She's still my wife," Henry responded.

"Sure, com'on."

"What if I don't want to?"

"It'd be better if you did," Carlos told him, staring at him. Boston and Bert waited for something to happen and which, if so, they both were ready to intervene.

Henry glanced once at Bethy. "Screw it," he said to her. Then he looked to Carlos, "Buy me a damn drink if it means that much to you. I'm not guaranteeing that I'll drink it with you."

"Up to you," Carlos replied as Henry followed him out of the picnic area and through the fence opening to the back of the roadhouse.

"What's going to happen?" Bethy asked the other two guys.

"I think Carlos is going to have a little heart to heart with him," Boston answered but he had no idea what would actually occur.

"That was really cool how our St. John the Apostle handled that," Bert said. "I was getting ready to punch out his lights right here."

"So was I," Caitlin added. "Sorry, Bethy, I don't know when it went wrong but Henry's gotten even worse even since I've known him."

"Well, he's always liked you," Bethy said.

"Only in the hot tub. Otherwise, he's been a prick to me, too."

"What's this hot tub business I keep hearing about?" Lina asked. "Sounds pretty risqué. I can kind of see that man's point."

"Meaning what exactly?" Bert spoke up, gruffly.

"Meaning I'm starting to understand why you ran out on me. Looks like you have a nice set up with these two pom-pom girls." Then Lina turned to Caitlin. "Don't give in too easily to this one, sweetie, or he may skip on you."

Caitlin's focus became very intense. Then she began to speak in very measured words. "I may look like a cheerleader to you, but I've had my share of tough times. Let me tell you something. He fucked you once. If he had liked it, he would have kept fucking you. Now he's fucking me, more than once, got it?" Lina just stared back at her, not answering. "And if you ever get out of line with me again, I'll rip out your arms and beat you to death with them. Is that clear enough for you?"

Lina continued her stare, both girls intent on one another, sitting across the table from each other. "All right," Lina said finally. "I've made my point. You've made yours. I'm over it."

I'll have to remind Bert to never mess with Caitlin, Boston thought to himself. But Bert had already understood the same thing. Things eased up ever more when Lina refilled Caitlin's cup.

Carlos soon returned, empty-handed. Getting up from the table, Bethy went to him. "What happened with Henry?"

"Nothing," Carlos said.

"Nothing?"

"No, I told him that I'd just gotten divorced myself and that I felt pretty lousy about it."

"That's it?" Bert asked.

"That was it. I handed him a bottle of beer and stood there as he drank it," Carlos answered. "I think our hamburgers are ready."

Soon they were all at the table eating, talking. Boston surveyed the scene. The Icelander was not present nor was Lina's husband but otherwise there were six of them, all signed on to do the Death Ride, less than a month away. Stopping at Rossotti's had once been an integral part of the Saturday rides when it was just he and the other men. The women had added a whole new set of complexities, not without its awkward moments, such as had just occurred and had seemingly passed as Caitlin and Lina chatted away.

As he listened to them and Bethy, Boston realized that biking in an all-male foursome, he had missed a feminine side. Since Katherine had stopped riding, he had lost the perspective of the opposite sex and their take on the difficult climbs and swirling descents.

The outdoor picnic tables loaded with beer and burgers set before the biking group was worlds away from his engineering business. His partner was not actively trying to sell their company within the month. Boston could not see beyond the possible sale. To be relieved of their financial hole would be a blessing. His work and his biking all seemed to be coalescing with the upcoming date in Markleeville.

Meanwhile, he gazed across the table and saw Bert give him a sigh of relief, obviously pleased that Caitlin and Lina had made peace.

—

Katherine and Irina sat for lunch in San Francisco after looking at a possible design project in Pacific Heights where Katherine needed her structural engineer's opinion of some possibilities on a remodel. The restaurant was a small French bistro in one of those little neighborhoods near Golden Gate Park. The day was quite cool in their part of town, not unusual for June.

With wine poured and their entrees ordered, the two reconnected for the first time in several weeks. Katherine's workload had gotten busy during June and she had not been able to have coffee with Irina for several weeks. Irina mentioned that she had completed her massage course but she did not ever plan be trained to get professionally certified. It pleased her enough to have the knowledge and skill. When asked by Katherine what she planned to do with this newly found talent, Irina mentioned that there was always Dennis.

That did not surprise Katherine. "So, what's new on that front?" she asked.

Irina replied that she had not had enough wine yet to talk about it. That wasn't good enough for Katherine, so Irina took a big gulp. She told Katherine how they had really hit it off, how Dennis had this fantastic body and then she capped it with, "He wants to sleep with me."

That did not surprise Katherine either. "You're married, remember," Katherine told her.

"So were you."

"Yes, but I'm a bitch. You're a mom."

"Sure," Irina replied, "but the boys are almost off to college. They spend most of their time out of the house any more. My mom days are pretty much behind me." Irina drank another sip. "You know, deep down I'm a Cossack. I came to America thinking to conquer, to use my mathematical education to do my own thing, like they say. Instead, I married Erik and got pregnant. When he used to be so busy, I told myself it was his career. But the career has gone on forever. He is self-contained. He doesn't need me. I need to look after myself. And to do that, I need somebody. Just like you did. And Dennis is a fine man."

Katherine leaned forward across the table. "Dennis can be a fine man," she began, "plus a great lover. But you'll never have a life with him."

"I don't want a life with him," Irina returned. "He wants to sleep with me. Do you know how much that means to me?"

"Do you want to sleep with him?" Katherine questioned her. "Wait, don't answer that. It's a dumb question."

"I already have and it was wonderful."

"Christ," Katherine sputtered. She took a big gulp from her wine.

"Are you upset?" Irina asked. "We are your two best friends, outside of Boston of course. You must have thought this might happen, didn't you?"

"You've really slept with him?"

"More than once," Irina brightened. "He's a very good lover, but I don't have to tell you that."

"We had our moments," Katherine said, but in the restaurant such moments all seemed to fade away. That little shit, she thought. I talked with him only last week, or maybe two weeks ago and he never mentioned it.

As their food began to arrive, she felt that the little memory-space she had devoted to her affair with Dennis was now squashed, gone. It made her feel old. She felt the only way she could get that secret place in her mind back was to sleep with Dennis once more, behind Irina's back.

"I won't leave Erik," Irina said, "at least not in the future. But I won't stop seeing Dennis either. He can do whatever he wants with me, turn me inside out. It just feels so wonderful."

—

It was still cool and overcast as the group returned on Arastradero. Carlos turned south at Foothill Boulevard, clearly disappointing Bethy. Once he was gone, she questioned out loud if the Rossotti's encounter with her estranged husband had freaked him out.

Bert addressed a different question to Boston, "Do you think Carlos really just let him go? No threats?"

"Carlos doesn't have to say much," Boston replied.

Lina wanted to leave for Belmont right away so Boston accompanied her back to his home where her car was parked while the other three turned onto Donald Drive toward Bethy's.

After putting her bike away on the car's rack, Lina said to Boston, "That Caitlin really put it to me, didn't she? I don't mind. I guess I had to get my shot in, even if it wasn't right."

"I don't think you're the first one that Bert has let down, if that's any consolation."

"It's not," Lina responded with a slight smile, getting into her car. "He wasn't really my type anyway. I just wanted the damn phone call afterwards. At least now, I feel I've gotten some closure. Tell Bert not to ditch that one, no matter how much younger she is." With that, Lina was gone.

Meanwhile, Bethy told Caitlin and Bert that they were welcome to use her hot tub but she was going to pass. The two stayed on the street to make up their minds as Bethy took her bike around back.

"Let's do the Skyline century tomorrow," Caitlin told him, referring to an organized hundred-miler taking place the next day, Sunday.

"You really want to?" Bert asked, reluctantly.

"We hardly rode today."

"Did you ask the others?"

"No," she told him, "just you and me. Keep it simple."

It seemed to him that she was going to ride it anyway, with or without him. "All right," he said. "Want to hot tub?"

"No," she said, "A hot tub will waste me for tomorrow. Think I'll just go home and rest up." Then she looked sideways at him. "That ok with you? No naked girls today."

Bert smiled, saying nothing. Having just spent last night with her, he wondered if she was sending him a message. But then she asked, "What are you doing later?"

"Later, like tonight?"

"Like tonight," she smiled.

"Want to get some dinner?"

"I'll cook," she said, then added, "if you stay over, we can get started early tomorrow morning. The ride only begins a half-mile away. But we have to get to bed early," she told him, "not like last night."

"No problem,"

After Caitlin went inside to tell Bethy goodbye, they biked down the street to her apartment where Bert has parked his car from the previous night. "If we're biking tomorrow," Bert told her as they arrived, "I might as well leave my bike in your apartment. I'll be back around 8, ok?"

She agreed and they both rode up the elevator together. "You really went to bat for me, for us today," he stated.

"You can't hurt women like you did her," Caitlin replied. "It'll always come back."

"How am I doing with you? So far?"

"So far, so good," she smiled as the elevator door opened. Dropping off his bike, he gathered up his previous night's clothes, returned to his truck and left the apartment house. Two nights in a row, he mulled. With no more commitment than a biking obligation the following day, that was fine with him.

Chapter 21

Fremont Peak

An American army officer Lt. Colonel John C. Fremont, while officially on a wagon-road route survey of California accompanied by a force of some sixty well-armed frontiersmen, raised the American flag over his makeshift fortification on the upper slopes of Gavilan Peak. Below in the town of San Juan Bautista, Mexican forces gathered, seeking to expel the intruders from Alta California. The flag was hoisted up a pine tree on March 6, 1846, ten years to the date after the fall of the Alamo in Texas and three months before other American rowdies would seize General Mariano Vallejo in Sonoma, raising their own flag embroidered with a grizzly bear and declaring California to be a sovereign republic.

Actually, Vallejo and several other Mexican Californios were all in favor of the United States administering their province, having gotten little support from Mexico except for a few unsuitable governors and waves of Mexican prison-expelled soldiers.

When the wind snapped off the pine-tree-top secured flagpole, Fremont and his band headed down the peak's slope facing away from town south to the San Joaquin Valley from where they circled northward to Oregon before coming back in time to influence the Sonoma revolt.

Lt. Colonel Fremont had a lifetime of both bucking the establishment and also being its standard bearer. Born in Savannah, Georgia, possibly illegitimately, he eloped at age twenty-eight with the seventeen-year-old daughter of a prominent Missouri Senator. Thomas Hart Benton later accepted his ambitious son-in-law and supported Fremont as the leader of a Great Basin survey expedition, guided by Kit Carson, whom Fremont met on a Missouri River steamboat in 1842.

Leading his California force in 1846 while Mexico went to war with the United States, Fremont was appointed Military Governor of California by the departing head of US Naval forces in the future state. However, in this capacity, he disobeyed the orders of his commanding general, who arrived late in southern California outraged enough to successfully court-martial the junior officer. Pardoned by President Polk, Fremont speculated unsuccessfully on a transcontinental railroad route but became wealthy during the gold rush of 1848 with the discovery of precious metal on his San Joaquin Valley ranch.

A most prominent citizen in the new state, Fremont was elected one of California's initial pair of senators, serving the shorter two-year term, and then became the new Republican Party's first presidential candidate in 1856, losing the election to the Democrats but establishing the party as a viable political force.

Four years later, he conceded the party's nomination at the Chicago convention to Illinois ex-congressman Abraham Lincoln. Commissioned as a Major General during the Civil War, he was made Military Governor of Missouri by Lincoln and then removed because of unapproved unilateral actions, including emancipating the state's slaves, which was too controversial for an administration still seeking popular support from borderline states for the on-going war. Rebuffed, he resigned from the army.

After making another unsuccessful attempt at gaining nomination over Lincoln in 1864, Fremont faded from national politics. His ranch was meanwhile overrun with more mining claims than he could defeat. Broke from pursuing the railroad venture and other failed mining interests, he was appointed Military Governor of the Arizona Territory at age sixty-five, serving only three years of his five-year term under constant criticism of spending too much time in the East, finally resigning in 1881, the same year that the OK Corral gunfight occurred in October in Tombstone.

His last years were spent living in Los Angeles, supported by his wife's writings, before dying in a New York hotel on an east coast trip at age seventy-seven. Gavilan (sometimes Gabilan), or Hawk, Peak was renamed in his honor, although there's a movement to return it to its original title honoring the birds of prey still riding its drafts.

Fremont's former San Joaquin Valley ranch had been named Mariposas, or Butterflies.

July ride

Having done fairly lengthy, strenuous rides all June around the mid-Peninsula, Boston Reed picked a short, hard climb for the last Saturday before Markleeville. Located over an hour's drive to the south near San Juan Bautista, the three-thousand-foot tall Fremont Peak tops the range between the cities of Hollister and Salinas, in a totally different surrounding from the local hills where they had been riding. Boston had never done the mountain before, but it seemed to match well on paper in distance and height gained with four of the five Death Ride climbs.

Boston rode with Erik in the Icelander's Toyota Highlander. Noticing that Carlos was starting to fall a little out of the group, he suggested that Carlos be picked up by Bert along with the two women while Raymond and Lina were driving themselves. It then surprised him when Katherine suggested that she and Irina join the group for lunch, never having met the new couple.

On the drive so San Juan Bautista, Erik talked about next weekend's Markleeville ride, discussing various strategies for food as well as clothing options, which Boston thought was getting a little overly detailed but he had to admit that the Icelander was certainly into the Death Ride mindset.

They arrived first out of the group to San Juan Bautista, driving past the whitewashed old mission buildings, scattering some roaming chickens and parking in the shade of a large pepper tree. Getting their bikes out of the back of Erik's Highlander, they spotted Raymond's Nissan Pathfinder coming down the small street. Once parked behind Erik's car, Raymond explained that Lina had caught a cold along with their two-year-old son Zack so they both were home. "She's already worried to death about the ride," he continued, "and for sure didn't want to make herself worse."

With no sign yet of Bert, the three decided to take a warm up loop through town, also seeking a possible lunch spot to rendezvous with the two wives at noon. Except for the occasional crowing of a rooster, the town was pretty quiet. "It's like something out of Steinbeck," Raymond noted as they were slowly biking. "We're close to Salinas aren't we? There's a Steinbeck museum there."

"Do you teach him?" Boston asked.

"No, although he did attend Stanford."

"So who do you teach?"

"My field is mostly Southern writers. Last quarter I taught a class on Flannery O'Connor. Ever hear of her? *Everything that Rises Must Converge* was one of her stories."

Boston replied not. ""I read a lot of Steinbeck in school. Who's your favorite writer?"

"Faulkner."

Meanwhile, biking past rustic storefronts, they spotted a Mexican restaurant that looked suitable for lunch. Returning to the car where Erik's cell phone was located, they saw Bert drive up with Caitlin, Carlos and Bethy. Erik phoned the name of the proposed lunch spot to Irina while the others unloaded the bikes.

Everyone seemed relaxed this morning. Today was additional training for climbing, not distance, as the mountaintop was only twelve miles away. Before heading off to the peak, the whole group biked down the rural main street, past plastered walls, enclosing cactus gardens.

Leaving town at the stoplight intersection at Highway 156, they crossed onto an old time concrete highway, which forked with the right side going the back way into Salinas and to the left toward the peak. Following a narrowing valley, they passed by a little neighborhood of old homes then soon small ranches. After the long car ride, the group started out slowly.

"So Carlos," called out Boston, "who's your favorite writer?"

"Everybody thinks I should like Hemingway because he wrote about Spain. But I don't care for his style."

"What about Faulkner?" Raymond asked.

"I don't care for him. My favorite is Mark Twain."

"*Huckleberry Finn.* I get to sneak in Twain every now and then in the syllabus because he's technically also a Southern writer.

"What are you teaching next quarter?" Boston asked.

"Faulkner's *Go Down Moses.* I'm actually writing a paper on it this summer. As soon as the Death Ride's over, I'll have to bear down." He waited as no one responded. "That's a pun. He wrote *The Bear.*"

"Did he write *A Streetcar Named Desire?*" Caitlin asked.

"Tennessee Williams," Bethy answered. "'I've always relied upon the kindness of strangers.'"

"What the heck are you guys talking about?" Bert asked.

"Raymond's a Stanford English professor," Boston reminded him.

"I liked Faulkner when I was in college," Bethy joined in. "*The Sound and the Fury.*"

"Anybody read *Lust for Life?*" Caitlin asked.

"That should be my autobiography," Bert noted. "Thought I'd say it before anyone else did."

"I only saw the move," Caitlin said. "Kirk Douglas."

"I went and bought *Lolita,*" Bert told them, "after everyone gave me a hard time."

"The movie?"

"No, the book," he told her. "Didn't get further than the first chapter. That girl was not even half-Caitlin's age."

"Suddenly I feel like an old lady," Caitlin sighed. "Maybe I should toss out my plaid mini-skirt and knee socks."

"Don't you dare," Bert chided her as he gave Boston a wink.

The literary discussion ended as the route wove past oak trees and now larger ranches with custom homes set tucked away in slopes and on hilltops. With the road beginning to undulate over small rises, soon they were at the foot of the first significant climb.

"What else did O'Connor write?" Erik asked Raymond.

"The Violent Bear It Away."

"That'd be Carlos' autobiography," Bert stated, suddenly forcing an uphill pace, followed closely by Caitlin and Raymond. The ascending route curved around tree-shaded hillsides until finally breaking out of the woods for a big climb ahead. With Erik alongside, Boston saw Raymond far ahead, pulling away, followed several bike lengths behind by Caitlin with Bert even trailing her. Meanwhile, Carlos came up from behind, explaining that Bethy told him to leave and let her go at her own speed.

The three of them continued around the view-obscuring bend curving right and finally up a steep pitch to where they saw Bert standing with Caitlin, who had her helmet off, breathing heavily, standing in sunlight without a breeze. "You ok?" Boston asked as the three of them halted.

"Yeah," she replied, gasping. "I just got out of breath." She stood up straight, hands folded behind her head, taking deep breaths. "I was trying to keep up with Bert and Raymond."

Bert was breathing heavily himself. "I was running out of gas myself. That professor just took off."

Finally arriving and seeing her friend distressed, Bethy quickly got off her bike. Caitlin reassured her that she felt fine. Reminding them that the Death Ride only a week away, Boston stated it wouldn't matter toward anyone's conditioning to turn back down the hill. However, Caitlin wanted to continue. "Sorry, Bert," she said softly. "I'll do better at Markleeville."

"No worries. It's all a question of pace," he smiled.

Once she was sufficiently recovered, they biked along a pine-treed ridgeline, overhanging a broad, flat plain of green farming fields. The roadway now rippled in and out of shade until they reached a large parking lot where Raymond waited, curious about the delay for which Caitlin apologized.

The parking lot was at the base of the peak itself, a rocky crag covered with antennae, connected by a gated off service road circling up the slope toward the backside of the peak. Bethy and Caitlin stayed while the others slipped past the rail gate and headed up a road that began steep and got steeper. The end of the road terminated in gravel with some metal trailers and a No Trespassing sign. The view was of Salinas in the foreground and Monterey Bay in the distance. The group stopped, all sweating with the climb and heat, augmented by the reflection off the metallic buildings. Only a narrow, rocky hiking trail continued from road's end to the peak, rising slightly above them. "This must have been Steinbeck's view that he wrote about in *Travels with Charley*," Raymond told them. "He came up here to see his hometown one last time. He and his standard poodle Charley."

Caitlin reached the group, huffing and puffing. She barely rumbled through the gravel and up to where they stood. "What a view! Almost worth it!"

"Thought you were wasted," Bert said.

"I am and it's all your fault," she told Raymond.

"So Lina tells me," he responded with a smile.

Bethy was eating a gel snack at the parking lot when they returned. They all started back together, casually rolling through the shaded level area and then onto the ridge. Boston stayed back with Bethy as Carlos joined the fastest of the downhillers. After the steep drops, which included a few tight turns, they came upon the others stopped on the other side of the road. Erik was standing on the left-hand shoulder in front of a wood rail fence, brushing sand and weeds off his jersey and shorts, laughing. Seeing the three arrived, he began to explain. "I was chasing after Carlos," he said, "and I missed the curve. Luckily, there were no cars coming. But my shirt was working perfectly." He lifted up his open long-sleeved shirt, which was his inventive technique of creating drafts against the body. "I could feel cool air circulating all around me," he added, brushing grit off his stomach. "Although it wouldn't be so great hitting dirt instead of sand."

"Or pavement," Boston advised.

"Yeah, I was lucky. I can't believe one week before Death Ride and I dumped it. Is my bike all right?"

Bert examined his bike and said it looked ok. Erik got back on and the group started down the road, which leveled out ahead with few curves. Any residual caution from Erik's spill quickly began to dissipate as the pace increased. Without verbalizing it, the male riders began to speed up, each simultaneously realizing that this would be the final charge before the next weekend's ordeal at Markleeville.

Boston broke from the group and Carlos immediately went with him, quickly followed by the others, including Erik. Draft leads were changed several times over the next couple miles before whatever remained for the final sprint. Closing on the highway, Raymond shot up to the front past Boston but ultimately, with the Highway 156 stoplight nearing, Erik outsprinted everyone.

Boston trailed the young college professor who was unable to overtake Erik. It had been over a month since Boston had beaten Erik in one of these races and now, having gone all out, he realized he was now only the third fastest in the expanded group. He had lost an edge and was no longer the dominant sprinter of the bunch.

It was a second front where Boston felt something had slipped with the first being his company. His partner had found a likely prospect to buy them out of their company. It seemed likely that he might have a whole new employer situation by the end of the month. Striving to be first for this little run into town was insignificant compared to his company's plight. Still, contending for these little sprint victories meant something to him. Winding up the business was not so defined.

Bert and Carlos pulled up to the stoplight, not far behind the first three but not close to the final burst. Still feeling the effects of her momentary exhaustion, Caitlin had refrained from this last dash and accompanied Bethy instead. The light changed and they all biked across.

Biking the main street, Raymond announced that he was not staying for lunch, wanting to get back home where his wife and son were stuck with colds. "Come say hi to my wife," Boston told him. "You must know my wife's second husband Mark Kirk."

"Chairman of the Department. But he was already divorced when I joined Stanford. I didn't know anything about his ex-wife. Small world. She's coming to Markleeville, isn't she?" Raymond asked and Boston nodded that she was. "I'll meet her then. I feel guilty enough as it is." He turned off the main street toward his car.

Parking their bikes just inside the courtyard entrance to the restaurant, they found Katherine and Irina already seated at a small table, drinking sangria. Caitlin and Bethy were re-introduced to Erik's wife, whom had met just once before. They seemed just as slight to Irina as she had remembered them. Then she noticed Erik was covered with foxtails. Telling her about his fall, Erik assured her that he was fine, even as she started cleaning off his shirt.

"Where are Raymond and Lina?" Katherine asked, looking around.

"Lina couldn't make it," Boston told her. "She's home with a cold babysitting their son, who's also sick. Raymond left."

"Darn," she said, "I wanted to meet him. Mark says he's one of the top professors in the department."

"Well, you'll just have to wait until Markleeville."

"How does today compare with the Death Ride?" Irina asked, seated and still brushing the back of her husband's shirt.

"Similar," Boston began, "except only about five times longer plus each pass is at another five thousand feet higher in elevation."

"Today was a piece of cake," Bert told him. "Next week the whole enchilada."

"Speaking of enchiladas," Erik began, opening a menu, "what looks good here?"

"Any Mexican restaurants in Iceland?" Caitlin asked.

"Yes, couple great ones and with enough hot sauce to melt the whole island back under the Atlantic."

"What about in Madrid?" Bethy inquired of Carlos.

"Not when I was there twenty-years ago."

Requesting the pitcher of sangria, Boston filled everyone's glass. "Here's to Fremont Peak, John Steinbeck and his poodle."

"*Grapes of Wrath*," Erik volunteered.

"*Tortilla Flat*," Katherine added.

"We don't say that around here," Boston told her.

Katherine dipped her head down, "Tortilla? It's a Mexican restaurant for goodness sake."

"No, the other word."

"Flat?"

Boston put his finger to his lips as a hush sign as the other three men nodded.

"Like in tires," Caitlin explained. "Big deal. You guys still get them all the time."

"Ok, but we still don't use the f-word," Bert said.

"Erik uses it," Irina announced.

"Not that f-word," Erik told her, silently mouthing "flat" to her.

"Big tough bikers," Caitlin laughed. "Superstitious over a word." The group smiled but still, nobody said the word.

"*Of Mice and Men*," Bethy smiled. "Who will be one or the other when it counts?"

"Of Markleeville," Boston toasted, raising his glass of sangria on a very warm midday in an outdoor Mexican restaurant on the first Saturday in July in the town of San Juan Bautista at the foot of their last pre-Death Ride peak, once named Gavilan, Spanish for the hawks circling in its updrafts.

Boston watched Katherine as she chatted with the group. Soon he would have to tell his wife that his partner Larry Dunne had found a possible buyer for their engineering firm. Larry had told him not to expect much in the way of price given the debts they had incurred. The sale might finalize the upcoming week, which would resolve the issue, for better or worse.

Realizing that he should have warned her much earlier about the company's sale. But, then again, having been professionally established when they met, they had not lived through a career disruption affecting one of them and had no history of how they would handle this as a couple. Were they truly a couple?

If the sale did not happen until after the Death Ride, that would be fine with him. He had been training for this ultimate ride for almost eight months. The group around the sangria was in good spirits. There were no more mountains to ride up in preparation. For now, Markleeville was Boston's only horizon and this was his group.

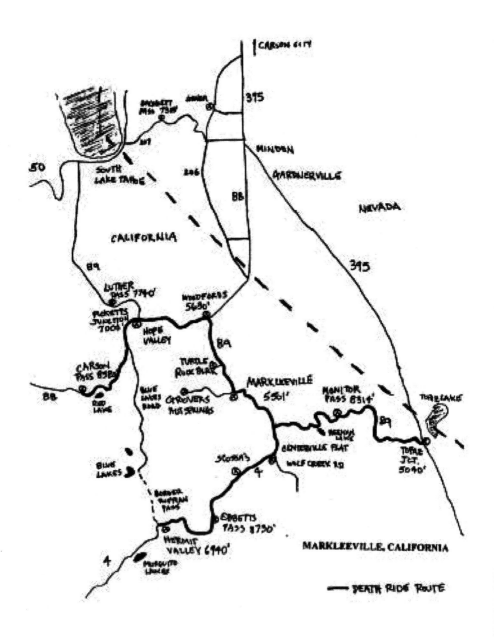

MARKLEEVILLE, CALIFORNIA

—— DEATH RIDE ROUTE

PART 2
The Death Ride

The Death Ride is the name of an organized bike ride that takes place in Alpine County, California and is the fundraiser for all the capital improvements within the county scheduled for the following year. Alpine County is the least populated county in California, located adjacent to the Nevada border just south of Lake Tahoe, near the hinge of the angled line of California's boundary.

The ride begins in Markleeville, the county seat of Alpine County, and used to be called the Markleeville Death Ride, which let people know where to find it, or rather where to look for it as finding Markleeville is a whole other matter.

The prime establishment in town is the Wolf Creek Restaurant and Bar, formerly called the Cutthroat Saloon, named for a type of trout once found frequently in the nearby streams, the most prominent being the East Fork of the Carson River. The famed scout, Kit Carson, led John C. Fremont and his band of toughs through the area in 1844, on their way to seeing what Mexican California was all about.

The Cutthroat Saloon was then what could be called a biker bar, not for the bicyclists but for motorcyclists who liked to roam the backroads, often with ladies, many enticed to remove their upper body support garment in order that such could be hung from the rafters. Back then the bar was part of the Alpine Hotel, which also served breakfast in a greasy spoon linoleum atmosphere. Renamed the Wolf Creek after a tributary of the Carson, its dangling bras are all gone now. The annual wave of highly trained and motivated bicyclists may have tamed the rowdier aspects of the town, or maybe the times have just evolved with real estate values being driven up by retiring baby boomers. Neither group has much use for a boisterous bar scene—the bikers too worried about the ride while the second home homeowners and retirees are just looking for a place to have a quiet drink and dinner out. The fishing is not what it used to be and hunting has largely gone out of style. But every year during the second week of July, the population of the county quadruples for the Death Ride.

The Death Ride is so named for the hardship it imposes on its participants. It's a one-day ride, which covers 129 miles of distance and five mountain passes averaging 3,000 vertical feet each, generally from 5500 feet above to 8500 feet above sea level. The distance, the overall climb, the altitude and often the mid-summer heat all contribute to the challenge.

The route was created by a group of South Lake Tahoe riders, taking advantage of the nearby high elevation roads for their brutal training. Such group included Robert LeMond who took along his son Greg, who eventually turned pro and was the first American to win the Tour de France, doing so in 1986 at age twenty-five. The first open Death Ride was sponsored by a bike club in 1981. The following year the Alpine County Chamber of Commerce took it over, organizing volunteers to handle the 350 riders. In two years, the number of riders doubled. By 1989, there were over 2000 riders. A decade later there would be 3000. By then, the county was closing the lightly traveled highways to automobiles for the first 90 miles.

The county officially named the ride the Tour of the California Alps but the only "alps" in the state are the Trinity Alps, far to the north west of Mt. Shasta. Also, a "tour" usually denotes a multiple day event, like the Tour de France. In reality, the county already had an enticing promotional name compared to the other hard one-day.

What hardcore biker wants to suffer the excruciating ordeal only to return home with a jersey flaunting a travel poster-sounding California Alps? The original sobriquet of "Death Ride" remains.

Chapter 22

Alpine County

Alpine County was created in 1864, assembled from adjoining counties due to the silver mining boom in order to accommodate the growing population, which was then 11,000, more than five times the desert coastal village of Los Angeles. The population more than doubled within the next ten years but then the boom ended and, in 1875, the county seat was moved out of the snowy forests to Markleeville, which, at a lower elevation, was more accessible to the Carson River Valley.

Now the least populated county in the state according to the 2000 census, with 1208 residents in a state of 34.5 million, it is also a county without a stoplight, bank, movie theater, dentist office or supermarket. Markleeville is a county seat just the same as Los Angeles, San Francisco, San Diego and Sacramento, but with a population of 197, including 92 households.

It does have two ski resorts, one at Bear Valley and the other at Kirkwood, plus a State Park at Grovers Hot Springs, named for Alvin M. Grover, a county assessor who homesteaded the valley where the springs are located.

Wednesday

Sitting in the passenger's seat of the Toyota Highlander, Boston Reed realized how much of Highway 4 he had forgotten. It was all new to Erik Erikksson, who was driving. With Markleeville at 5500 feet, Boston and Erik both wanted to get to altitude as soon as possible. The two had left early this Wednesday morning. Their wives could not see the sense in arriving so early, plus Katherine had several appointments later in the day. They would be driving up tomorrow Thursday in Katherine's car, the same day that Bert was

159

bringing Caitlin and Bethy along with Carlos. Raymond and Lina couldn't make it until Friday,

Freeway traffic had been mired until they reached two-lane Highway 4 out of Stockton. Shannon, Boston's first wife, lived in Stockton, where she was born and raised. He never talked about her, rarely thought about her but she was never far from his mind. They were friendly by phone, limited to discussions of their now adult daughter Serina. Passing by Stockton reminded Boston of their most fun outings, which were eastward to the Sierra, where they backpacked and skied, activities which Katherine had never adopted.

Shannon was tall, thin, blonde and as athletic as the outdoors she loved. She had remarried a housing developer and had two young sons. Her interior decorating business was a moderate success, much more so than it had been when they were together. As far as Boston knew, she was well off, far better than when they both had been young professionals. None of his biking friends knew anything about her, only that a person named Shannon was his ex-wife. The biking group had sensed his first marriage was not an allowed topic of discussion, which was fine with Boston.

But the two-lane road screamed her name in his mind as they passed by orchards and vineyards. Shannon lived in his past when they both were married too young for each other: college graduates intent on love and careers. Their favorite activity together was adventuring in the Sierra, away from the stresses that intensified in their small apartment and impoverished lifestyle. As their workloads increased, the number of ski days and hiking trips diminished.

While his young wife bounced around various occupations, Boston fell in love with another young, married civil engineer in the same office. Nothing intimate happened for the first few years they worked together. At the end of the day, they began meeting for drinks. One evening their passion intensified while they were parked in a car. That led to a motel room at the next opportunity. But then she moved away as her husband took a job in Phoenix.

Boston suspected that Shannon sensed something was going on with him. A year later Serina was born and the couple enjoyed several years of happiness, especially on vacations in the mountains. He never told Shannon about his infidelity, never told anyone. As far as he knew, only the now middle-aged Phoenix woman was the only other person aware of their affair. Whether she was still married, had kids and worked as a civil engineer, or not, was a question he did not pursue. She was gone. The mountains remained and he was returning with far more significance than Erik, driving his Highlander, could have guessed, which was how Boston wanted it.

A little hamlet called Farmington was the last outpost of central California before the road rose with the first foothill. Through summer dry savannah, they approached a series of hills. Erik had never heard of Copperopolis, suddenly appearing at the base of a desolate, sunny hilltop. The bleak, volcanic landscape reminded him of parts of Iceland. This countryside was totally different from forested Lake Tahoe, where he and his family often vacationed when they explored California.

Bouncing through the jigsaw terrain that followed, they emerged, crossing Highway 49 at Angels Camp, suddenly deep into gold rush and jumping frog country. Continuing to Murphys, Boston told Erik to turn off the highway to the main street. With limestone block buildings and cool-shaded streets, the town seemed like a French village to Erik, reminiscent of his own few travels in Europe. The newly wed Shannon Martin Reed had been charmed by Murphys, especially the shamrock painted in the center of the street, on which she stood one night, claiming that it channeled her Irish heritage.

From Murphys, the road climbed steeply to higher plateau lined with pine trees and red earth covered with pungent ferns. Cruising through little mountain settlements, some busier than others, they passed Big Trees State Park, continuing past elevation signs all the way to Bear Valley at 7000 feet. Boston had to check out how the ski area looked in the summer, directing Erik to the turnoff that ran a mile to the deserted parking lot and buildings. The ski resort, so full of snow and enthusiasm in the winter, looked forlorn in the hot sun, dirt wheel tracks cutting through the fields of miner's lettuce. Gaps in trees that had been mowed down for the chair lifts seemed unnatural and unaesthetic when now snowless. Across the deep river canyon, the pyramid-shaped Mokelumne Peak majestically dominated. Having spent several moments on top of the ski ridges, staring at the peak, stark white in the winter, it singularly made him feel at ease with his memory of the area, including weekends with Shannon and, later, them both teaching his daughter Serina to ski.

The road past Bear Valley to Lake Alpine had been only open in summer and fall. Riding over it for the first time in years, Boston was amazed at all the activity on the lake and around various cabins. Past the lake's end, the road severely twisted, almost agonizingly curving and carving through the heavy forest, past rocky heights and brutal peaks, to a little oasis of ponds called Mosquito Lakes, all of which he now recalled. From there, the bottom of the road dropped away to what was identified by a road sign as Hermit Valley before the climb began toward Ebbetts Pass.

It was only six miles to the pass, winding along a mountainside slope with a deep valley on the right. The view was spectacular, hushing their conversation as the Highlander climbed up to the 8600-foot summit, with the road narrowed by pine trees. Slightly down the other side was a Pacific Crest Trail parking lot, which was as far as Boston had ever been, having sequestered vehicles there for past backpacking trips in his pre-biking life. Knowing that beyond was one of the five Death Ride passes, they continued slowly in Civil War battlefield-type reverence, knowing that was the highest and toughest climb on Saturday's ride.

Descending the eastern side of Ebbetts Pass, still called Highway 4 although far from being a highway, the whole geography changed, from pine trees to open slopes with yellow and gray soils; misshapen dark brown lava-outcrop curtains on ridges; a death drop slope on the left, and two gigantic mountains on the right.

Through a series of steep pitches, the road seemed to descend forever. With the car in second gear, they both kept pointing out sights to each other. Farther downhill, the road crossed the drainage one more time as the eastern vista grew into a huge river valley. In and out of trees, they soon were driving along a rushing river, pooling around rocks, wide with either rapids or deep fishing holes. The slopes were dry and the weather hot, with a warm breeze flowing up the river canyon. They passed the turn-off to Monitor Pass, another severe Death Ride climb.

Eager to see what that road looked like, Boston was also excited about the rest of the drive into Markleeville, deciding that Monitor could be checked out another day. Following the river, the road led to a bridge, historically marked as a hangman's site, then curved up and over a ridge, leaving behind downstream fields of irrigated green cattle grass, and into Markleeville, the seat of Alpine County, evidenced by a granite-block civic building on the right.

There were a few buildings on both sides of the street, the Wolf Creek Restaurant & Bar on one corner, Creekside Lodge on the other, J Marklee Toll Station, some more buildings and then, just like that, they had driven through town. Erik turned around at a wide shoulder. Back at the Wolf Creek, he made a right on Montgomery Street, according to the directions he'd gotten from Raymond, and after one block was out of the downtown, going past scattered residences on open hills.

The road led toward Grovers Hot Springs. Before that end-point, their directions called for a turn-off onto Pleasant Valley Road into a mountain subdivision called Marklee Village. Making a left-turn as instructed and turning again onto Timber Lane, Erik drove up to their rented house, a rustic, wood-sided large two-story home where the front door key awaited under the mat.

Inside, the house was decorated with a California western theme, combining gold mining decorations along with some ski posters and pictures of Lake Tahoe. Upstairs contained three bedrooms plus the master bedroom with its own bath. Erik conceded Boston the only downstairs bedroom, which Boston figured Katherine would appreciate. It had a glass door onto a deck, which faced the rear of the property, which sloped downhill to a little ravine with nothing but trees and brush on the opposite hillside.

The decking looked somewhat worn but there were wooden chairs and padded lounges scattered about, partially shaded from the afternoon sun by the second story above. On one side was a large hot tub, currently turned off and protected by a cover.

"Irina will love that," Erik commented.

"So will Katherine," Boston said. "Of course, so will Bethy and Caitlin."

"Think our wives will get along with them?"

"Probably better than with us," Boston replied. What was really on his mind was the imminent sale of the company. His partner Larry Dana had been hopeful on Monday of concluding the details but nothing had been finalized yet as of Wednesday, Boston's scheduled departure date.

Larry had pushed him out the door Tuesday night. As Larry was the company's founder and also more involved with it's financial problems, Boston deferred to his judgment. "No use throwing away a year's worth of training," he had told Boston.

The negotiations seemed far from the mountains surrounding Markleeville but it wasn't something that Boston could put off his mind either. Only a few years ago, he had looked forward to being sole proprietor of the engineering firm. Soon it would all be gone.

—

That morning Katherine was frantic on several levels. First, she had to finalize some last minute plan submittals. But beyond that, with Boston out of town, this was a time that she could meet with Dennis Crowe, now back on her mind after a couple years hiatus. When she reached him by cell phone that morning, he stated he was on his way over to Irina's. Searching a few moments for a way to approach what she wanted to say, Katherine just got to the point. "Are you fucking her, Dennis?"

There was a long pause on the other end. "Just because you and I were lovers once—," he began.

"Tell me," Katherine demanded, pressing him to tell her what she already knew from Irina.

"Yes, we've slept together," he answered.

"I need to see you today," she told him. "Can you come by here this afternoon?"

He replied that he was going to be busy at his shop the rest of the day. When Katherine asked if she could swing by his place, he asked what it was all about. She only said that she needed to talk with him, to which he gave a lukewarm response but that was enough for her to consider it open. Hanging up, she went back to finishing her house plan set.

She dreaded the idea of being stuck in Markleeville, having to sacrifice three days of work plus some weekend drawing time for Boston's biking adventure up in some forsaken part of Nevada, which was the only word she heard when the Sierra Nevada was mentioned. Born in Santa Barbara and having attended college in San Luis Obispo, she had always considered herself a child of the coast. Her first wedded home was in San Diego and, though her second one wound up being in Palo Alto, which at least was close to San Francisco and its fabulous bay. She wanted the Mediterranean, Scandinavia, the Caribbean, South America. With Boston's daughter off in college, they had the whole world to tour.

That was her overall future plan. But for the immediate present, her main interest was a return to the Crowe's Nest at the end of the day.

—

After putting away suitcases and some groceries, Boston suggested they take a short test ride, maybe check out Grovers Hot Springs up the road while getting a sense of the higher altitude as well. Erik agreed and off they went.

The road to Grovers meandered a short distance until breaking out into a large, rounded valley with a huge meadow in the middle. Ahead was a wood-fenced compound with several buildings beyond. Biking up to it, he discovered that Grovers Hot Springs was actually two concrete lined pools. The square swimming pool was full of very active, very young kids, some teenagers and a few adults. The other was a shallow rectangular pool, stained an unsanitary-looking iodine color, apparently quite hot, with most adults sitting passively on an underwater shelf lining the perimeter. Inside a narrow gate, a teenage boy in a kiosk collected payment of a few dollars.

It was about as far an image from what Boston had pictured as a scenic Sierra hot springs. He and Erik biked back to their cabin, without having learned much about the altitude effect. Getting late in the day, they changed clothes and drove into Markleeville, if nothing else to see what they had missed.

Approaching town and within sight of the highway, Boston turned right onto Laramie Street. After crossing the creek and passing a few homes, he was within sight of the highway once more. This time he turned left, crossed the creek once more, and drove to the Wolf Creek Restaurant & Bar.

Being slightly early for dinner, they went into the empty bar for a couple of beers. The bartender was tall with jet-black hair, square-shouldered in a tank top. From the Ukraine, her name was Tanya. Boston ordered two Sierra Nevada Pale Ales, which seemed appropriate in the setting. The bar was tastefully decorated with pine paneling outline with green trim, which Boston considered pretty upscale for the remote setting.

The bartender Tanya asked what brought them to Markleeville, to which Boston replied the Death Ride. She had never heard of it but then, she'd only been working in town since May. Boston explained the whole ride to her. She asked why they had come up so early and were they just by themselves. Boston explained the altitude adjustment concern and that others would be arriving tomorrow.

Tanya related that she had immigrated with a girlfriend, who was working at the Pigeon Coop outside Carson City. She made a lot more money than Tanya did, but Tanya said she could never work at a place like that. Boston got the picture but Erik asked what kind of a place and Tanya, looking surprised, said it was a bordello. From her pants pocket, she then produced a business card for the place, which she gave to Erik, telling him to quickly put it away because the bar's owner had warned her not to hand them out.

With only them in the bar, Erik wanted to know more about the Pigeon Coop. Tanya had known lots of prostitutes in Kiev but there were no bordellos just off the highway like in Nevada. She was not particularly pleased her roommate worked there, but at least they could afford a nice apartment in Carson City.

Tanya then asked Erik what he did for a living. When Erik replied he was a gynecologist, she gave a hearty laugh.

—

The sun was over the ocean when Katherine drove into Dennis' place on Pomponio Ridge Road. It was a warm evening and he was sitting outside next to his workshop, wearing dark sunglasses facing the western expanse of valleys and sky. He stayed in his chair, unfazed by her appearance, as she parked and approached, taking the chair next to him.

"My friend Irina's pretty happy with you," Katherine began.

"She's a nice lady," Dennis replied. "Of course, she'd have to be nice to be your friend. Nice people generally have nice friends."

"You're a little stoned, aren't you?" she asked. He replied that he was and wanted to know if she wanted to smoke another joint with him. Instead, she asked if he had any wine. Reaching behind his chair, he pulled up a bottle and two glasses, one of which had residue already.

"Were you expecting me?" she asked.

"Of course," he replied, pouring her glass. "You were pretty clear that you had something on your mind."

"I do, but right now I've had an exhausting day and I'm hot and sweaty. That pool of yours looks pretty inviting. Any reason not to take a dip?"

"If you're asking if anyone else is coming by, no they're not. It's just us, just like the old days," he told her.

"Good," she replied, standing. "I'm going to get in the pool and I want you to join me." Taking a deep breath, he rose from the chair, picked up the wine bottle, took his glass and followed her to the lap pool.

In a moment, her clothes were off and she was in the water. Dennis took considerably longer to undress but eventually he climbed down the few rungs of the ladder. Wading through the hot water, he reached over to a chair and his shirt, took a joint out of his pocket along with a lighter and got it started. After taking a small draw, he offered it to Katherine.

She had been watching him the whole time, observing his body more than she had nine months ago when Boston and his group had biked up. She thought he had aged considerably since they had been lovers in this same pool over five years ago. He used to get stoned in the pool also then, as did she. This time she turned down his offer to have a hit. He took another one instead as she drank from her wine glass.

Exhaling a large smoke cloud, he asked, "What's on your mind, Katherine?"

Leaning back against the pool, her chin resting on the water, she asked him, "Did you fuck Irina today?"

"That's really none of your business, is it?" he replied. With his fingers, he smothered the end of the joint and put it down, then sunk down to his neck, gazing at her.

"I don't care if you did or you didn't," she told him. "What I want to know is, are you still my lover when it counts?" She was slumped with her arms out to the side, resting on the pool edge, a purposefully submissive and suggestive stance, which she figured would not be lost on Dennis.

"We haven't made love in years," he replied, eyeing her. "When does it count?"

Rising with her upper body now out of the water she took a couple strides toward him, causing him to also stand. Her arms wrapped around his neck as she pulled her body into his, pressing her breasts against his chest and, underwater, her hips against his. "Are you still my lover?" she repeated, avoiding his question.

"Always," he responded. Bending his head down, he kissed her full on the mouth, just as he had in their past. She could taste the marijuana remnant in his mouth, which brought back another memory. With one hand, she ran her fingers lightly through his gray chest hair. Sinking back down, he spread out his knees, giving her a platform to sit facing him across his thighs. It was a familiar position they had used in the past.

But instead, she released her embrace and returned to her spot on the opposite wall, sipping from her wine glass once more. Instead of looking at him, she turned to the view. "You have a wonderful spot here, Dennis."

Reaching for his glass of wine, he replied, "You always did like it."

"I love it," she said. She sipped her wine more slowly now, knowing that when the glass was empty, she would head back to Palo Alto, which she did.

—

Boston and Erik sat down to dinner. Their server was a female high school student, whose father used to ride in the Death Ride but had quit such a hard ride once he turned forty, which amused the two men, as both were in their mid-forties.

After she took their order, Boston asked Erik if there were any so-called bordellos in Iceland. Erik replied that in Iceland prostitution was recently legalized but not pimping or houses of ill repute. In the nineties, women worked in nightclubs as barmaids and offered sex on the side, which was pretty much officially tolerated. But before that, he confessed that there were prostitution houses. Boston tried to quiz him some more but Erik didn't want to talk about it, at least not in the restaurant.

By the time they finished dinner, it was partially dark but the night was still warm. Returning to their cabin, they each got a bottle of beer and sat out on the deck, across from the covered hot tub. Boston recognized that had Irina and Katherine accompanied them today to Markleeville, they all could have been soaking inside.

Instead the two men in deck chairs sat with their beers, viewing the open hillside across the way. "Funny how that Russian bartender used the word 'bordello'," Boston began. "Sounds Italian."

"I would have said 'brothel'."

"I think out here they're just called whorehouses. That's pretty cut and dried isn't it."

Erik just sat stone-faced. Finally, he asked, "Ever been inside a brothel?" Boston replied no but wasn't sure that Erik even heard him. Instead, Erik started telling him his background. He was raised by his American stepfather after his own father had been killed in an industrial accident when Erik was around five, an only child and old enough to remember his real father. After his mother married, they moved to the United States.

His mother thought that, being an only child, he should keep in contact with his Icelandic relatives. When he was ten, they all went back to Iceland. When he was fourteen, he went by himself. That was the summer his uncle, on his father's side, took him to a brothel outside of Reykjavik. In Iceland back then, that was considered doing a young boy a favor, making a man out of him.

He met several women lounging around inside the brothel, all wearing the thinnest of fabrics. His uncle favored a woman from Latvia. His uncle was a big man and the Latvian woman was also big, much bigger than Erik at that age. He thought she was one of the older women, but, reflecting, she was probably all of thirty. She had straight blonde hair except below the belt, which was quite dark and thick. Like any young boy, he was very curious about women's privates. In one quick lesson, he discovered more than he wanted to know and more than he could deal with. The woman and his uncle exchanged mutual apologies. On the drive home, his uncle told him not to worry about it but that he had gotten a good education about brothels. Next time when he went, his uncle told him, it would go much better. He also told him that he was now a man and next time he visited one, when he was a little older, he could go by himself.

Of course, Erik told Boston, he had never been to one since but that visit did jar within him a fascination about women. "I didn't lose my virginity until much later," Erik told him. "It was my senior year in college, in the spring, with a girl who was also graduating. Then I went to medical school and became celibate again until I met Irina."

"Who just happens to be Russian," Boston commented.

"You know, I often wonder about that. Of course, Irina's from Moscow, not Latvia. I know that visit triggered something in me. It I'd been successful that first visit, who knows what might have happened?" Then he asked, "Is it late?"

"Not really," Boston replied.

"At this altitude, this last beer is all I can handle," Erik told him as he got up, saying goodnight, leaving Boston alone with the increasing appearance of stars.

—

Katherine had been gone about a half-hour when, from upstairs, Dennis heard another car enter his driveway below. Dressed only in a robe, he walked out from his kitchen onto the second story deck and saw a Honda Accord parking below. Several people he knew owned the popular model, but it was Irina who got out of this one, her car.

Soon she was trouncing up the steps, knocking on his door. Expressing his surprise at seeing her, Dennis asked her what was up. She cheerfully produced a bottle of massage oil from her purse, stating that she felt bad about not being able to give him a session this morning. "No phone call?" he asked. "What's up really?"

"Ok, fine," she stated, then asked him, "What smells so good?" He was cooking veal and offered her dinner if, during the course of it, she would level with him. To that, she agreed, then asked him, "You look awfully relaxed."

"I've just gotten out of my pool," he informed her. "And I've smoked a little grass, had a some wine and was just getting ready to crash."

"Am I intruding?" she asked, knowing that she was.

He knew it, too. "Not at all. Our time did get cut short this morning. Care for a glass of wine?" He got her a new glass but poured from the same bottle, with which he filled Katherine's glass a short time ago. Then he returned to cooking the veal, which was done shortly.

With just veal and a couple glasses of red wine, dinner was over pretty quickly. Refilling her glass, he asked her again what was on her mind. "How about a dip in your pool?" she asked him instead. "The night's warm and the sky's filling up with stars. It's so clear up here. Besides, you're already dressed for it."

"That's a possibility," he replied. "But first, talk to me."

Taking a sip, she began, first explaining that her two boys were spending the night at friends' houses and Erik was away at Markleeville. As neither they nor her husband ever called when away, she had the night out for herself. Drawing a breath, she let Dennis know that this little affair they had been having was at a critical point for her. Having quickie sex in her garage-studio had run its course for her, but it also was preventing her from deciding how much she really cared for him.

To that, he gave her a rather surprised look. Okay, she admitted, maybe they both knew they weren't well suited for each other. What she really wanted to find out was how much she cared for her husband.

"You want to stay with me tonight in order to discover if you still love your husband. Is that it?"

"Pretty much," Irina answered.

"And if your husband finds out by accident that you spent the night here?"

"Then maybe he'll pay more attention to me," she stated, taking another sip. "Let me ask you something?" He told her to go ahead. "I thought I saw Katherine's car coming down while I was driving up."

Now it was Dennis taking a sip. "You probably did. She was here a half hour ago." Irina asked him what did she want. "To know if I still love her," he admitted, not knowing any reason why he shouldn't be truthful. "I told her I did. That was apparently enough for her and she left."

"Are you seeing her?" Irina asked, her face studying him.

"No," he replied. "She didn't seem to want that, only to know if I loved her still."

"Interesting," Irina said. "Katherine's a very intriguing person. Can we just go in your pool and forget the massage. I'm beat. Got an extra robe?"

"Sure," he replied. "Help yourself. It's in the bedroom. Might as well undress there, too."

As she left the room, he took the short stub of the joint out of his pocket and relit it, before following her.

Chapter 23

Woodfords

In 1847 a year prior to the discovery of gold on the American River, Mormon entrepreneur Sam Brannan positioned two men at the bottom of the West Fork of the Carson River Canyon next to a hillside spring to start his new trading post. The post failed and in 1849, Daniel Woodford built a hotel on the spot, naming it "Sign of the Elephant" in honor of the rugged journey endured by the cross-country gold seekers he was accommodating.

With the gold rush over a couple years later, John Carey built a sawmill opposite the hotel and soon the area was known as Carey's Mill. The short lived Pony Express created a remount station next to the hotel in April, 1860 to cross Carson Pass but was rerouted a month later to Luther Pass as a cutover to the American River Canyon leading toward Sacramento, before folding in October, 1861. In 1869 Carey was bought out by Woodford and the settlement grew in his name.

Thursday

Waking up Thursday morning, Boston was surprised at how quiet everything was around the cabin, realizing that the city noise was completely gone. With a few cobwebs in his head from the previous night's beers, he wandered into the empty kitchen and began making a cereal breakfast as he waited for Erik to get up. Today, he figured was their last opportunity for a moderate ride, more than the short out-and-back to the hot springs but much less than their normal Saturday ventures.

Once underway at Markleeville, they turned left and unexpectedly discovered that the road climbed. Following alongside a dry gulley, they reached the entrance to Turtle Rock Park, the official headquarters, start and finish of Saturday's ride. Thursday morning crews were busy setting up around a one-story main building, next to which small tents were being set for different booths for various manufacturers and organizations.

Continuing fast down a long hill, they were soon at the Highway 88 junction called Woodfords, which was a general store surrounded by a few cabins. Their choice was now to either ride left up the Highway 88 canyon toward Carson Pass, or continue right on 88 into Nevada and the wide-open valley. "We'll get to do that canyon soon enough but we won't get to bike to Nevada again this trip," Boston declared. That was fine with Erik and they were soon rolling on the highway edge at almost forty miles per hour toward the valley floor, where the highway bisected huge fields of green grass, containing alternating herds of black cows and white sheep. To the right in the far distance were dry, distant mountains while closer on their left was the steep Sierra eastern escarpment, full of shining granite, sparse trees and deep gulleys, still with snow clinging inside.

Fast but not racing, they exchanged leads into a slight headwind until they reached a blue "Welcome to Nevada" sign. At that point, they had only gone around ten miles and Boston was ready to turn around, knowing that it was uphill back to Markleeville. Taking in panoramic scenery, Erik spotted cars ascending a steep road up the mountains on their left and asked about it. Boston identified it as Daggett Pass, which was one of the original Death Ride passes and that it led to South Lake Tahoe.

Erik wanted to try it but Boston stated that the climb would be a lot more than he wanted to do so close to the big ride. Instead he suggested that they go back, get Erik's car and scout Carson Pass. "No need for us both to go back," Erik told him. "If you don't mind getting the car, I'd like to keep riding, maybe check out that Daggett road. What else do we have to do today?" Boston knew that the state capital Carson City was about the same distance north as it was back to their cabin. Agreeing to get the car, he cautioned Erik not to go chasing up Daggett Pass but to instead take the easier route to the capital city, conserving energy for Saturday's ride. He suggested that they meet in front of the capitol building, wherever it might be.

Boston's bike ride back toward Woodfords had plenty of elevation gain and a little headwind. The direction into California, with the tall wall of peaks on his right, retraced Kit Carson's original expedition route with Fremont Turning off to Markleeville, he imagined what it might feel like at the end of Saturday, tackling the few remaining hills returning to the Turtle Rock Park start. After cresting at the park's entrance, he enjoyed the long descent back to Markleeville, tucking into a streamline posture, not pedaling, feeling the wind, and eyeing the bikers that were coming the other direction, also checking out the conditions.

Quickly changing clothes once inside the house, Boston cell-phoned his office, speaking with his partner Larry Dunne and getting the daily update. Larry told him that the sale might be concluded by the end of the week, then reminded Boston to have fun but to not get hurt, which was always his partner's concern, both professionally and personally.

Boston appreciated having his partner there to share the business duties and concerns. Larry had never really understood Boston's passion for bicycling but did recognize the younger man's need to do it. Boston's partner used to fly a private plane when they first went into business together. Having been on the other end of cautionary concerns for years, Larry never pressured Boston to give up his sport, but Boston could always detect the concern in his voice as to what a serious injury would mean to the business. Of course, with the sale pending, Boston realized that such worries would soon be moot, just one of many changes soon to come.

When the phone call ended, Boston was transported back from his office two hundred miles away and to the Markleeville cabin where he started up Erik's Highlander for the drive to Carson City.

—

Irina arrived at Katherine's house, but later than planned after a frantic trip down from Dennis' to pick up a friend who had volunteered to stay at the house over the weekend, ostensibly to feed their dogs and really to stand sentry over the two boys. Irina parked her Accord in the driveway and put her suitcase next to Katherine's Expedition.

A couple more hours' delay had allowed Katherine to complete her work and deliver it to the blueprinter for copies to be made. Now she felt at ease, even if it was in the middle of an extremely hot day as they headed out. One thing about going to the mountains was that it would be cooler at the higher elevations.

Irina must have been thinking the same thing, as she asked Katherine if there would be glaciers where they were headed.

"I don't know what's up there," Katherine answered, still annoyed at their destination. "Boston said Lake Tahoe is close by but don't expect anything like the Italian Alps." Katherine had never been there but she was prone to mention Italy, a place she longed to see. With a long drive in front of them, she wondered how soon Irina would bring up the subject of Dennis Crowe. Katherine realized she had tolerated her better when Irina was the ignored wife of that Icelandic gynecologist, who was pleasant enough but a cold fish, as far as Katherine was concerned. As Dennis' lover, Irina presented a whole new dimension.

Meanwhile, finally settled in the Expedition's large front seat, Irina wondered if Katherine had recognized her Accord from the previous night when they passed each other on Page Mill Road. She didn't see any indication of Katherine's awareness of their autos meeting up, but then Irina knew that her friend never revealed her private thoughts until ready to do so. To talk about something, Irina inquired as to what Katherine knew about sights along the route.

Katherine told her that Boston had said to not take Highway 4 as he had done, but to go through Stockton and take Highway 88. All Katherine could think of was that Boston's ex-wife Shannon lived in Stockton. To create some sort of conversation, Katherine devoted the beginning of the long drive with her take on Boston's first marriage and wife.

—

Erik was not there when Boston arrived in front of the capitol building, over two hours after they had parted company. It was hot in the early afternoon and Boston was concerned. As he waited in the shade, his cell phone rang with Erik asking if Boston would pick him up. He gave Boston directions to a gas station on a side road off Highway 50, east of Carson City.

Boston found the road and Erik, sitting in the shade alongside the building. A road sign stated that the Pigeon Coop was a half-mile ahead. Both his tires were flat. Erik told Boston that he thought he had run over some broken beer bottle glass. With the heat and running late, he had decided he had better call.

"What are you doing out here?" Boston asked.

"It's really a great place up ahead," Erik reported as he loaded his bike onto Boston's rack. "They have a little bar where I'll buy you a beer."

"You went to the Pigeon Coop?" Boston asked to which Erik said yes and that he must have run over the glass on his return to the highway. Boston declined the beer offer and turned back toward Carson City.

"I didn't think they'd be open," Erik stated, welcoming a cold stream from the air conditioner. "That was pretty naïve on my part. It was totally different from my experience thirty years ago in Iceland." Boston didn't know quite what to say. "Tanya's friend works there, but in the evening so I didn't see her," he continued. "There were about a half dozen girls, counting at least the ones in the bar, all different types. I don't know how many more were working, if any. I never saw any customers."

Erik paused long enough that Boston had to ask him what happened thirty years ago. "It was amazing," Erik continued. "I was fourteen when I was in that Reykjavik brothel, scared to death of these women. Now I'm forty-four and it felt today like I was in a room with my patients, actually younger than most of my patients. Of course, they thought I was dressed pretty weird. Actually, they liked my bicycle shorts. Spandex is dangerous to wear into a brothel."

"A whorehouse," Boston corrected.

"I like 'brothel.' Anyway I told them I couldn't stay. Then I said I was a gynecologist. What a mistake that was." Erik laughed, but didn't elaborate. "You know, I've been carrying this weight on my back for thirty years."

"How so?"

"It all started back in Reykjavik," Erik mused, gazing out the window, staring at the Sierra and seeing Iceland. "Long story."

—

Boston and Erik had only been back a short time when Bert's Silverado truck pulled into the driveway and out spilled Caitlin, Bethy and Carlos. The newly arrived foursome was excited to link up with familiar faces in a totally new environment. They had traveled along Highway 88 instead of the longer Highway 4 route that Erik and Boston had taken. Carson Pass, Bert said, was spectacular, especially cresting over and seeing next Saturday's bike ride descent. Spotting the hot tub, Caitlin went to it, putting her hand inside. "Feels perfect," she said. "I'm ready. God, it was hot driving up."

"It was about 105 in Stockton," Bert reported. "We got a late start."

"Not my fault," Caitlin cried out, stripping off her top. "Anybody else getting in?" she asked.

"I want to unload my stuff first," Bethy replied.

"And all the bikes," Bert added.

"Damn," said Caitlin, putting her tank top back on. "But then we hot tub, right?"

Nobody answered. "Where do we sleep?" Bert asked.

Boston answered that there were still two untaken bedrooms upstairs. Caitlin announced that she and Bethy were staying in a one-bed room. That led to Bert and Carlos depositing their suitcases in the other room, also with just a king bed.

"What about Raymond and Lina?" Bethy asked.

"They'll just have to make do," Boston replied. As everyone was returning downstairs, he suggested the possibility to doing a short bike ride to Grovers Hot Springs.

Eager to go, Caitlin asked what the hot springs was like. Boston's dismal description of the public pool did not sound promising. As nobody had any swimsuits plus there was a perfectly good hot tub right on their own deck, the group declined to go out riding. The afternoon was also well over ninety degrees.

Caitlin stripped down first and climbed into the hot tub, soon followed by Bert and Bethy. They called out to Carlos but he stayed in the kitchen talking with Boston. Erik, who had gone upstairs, now came down, wrapped in only a towel. The three sitting in the tub were amazed as previously diffident Erik tossed off the towel and climbed in with them.

"If Erik can go in there, why not you?" Boston asked Carlos while both watched through the kitchen window.

Carlos answered that he had just spent the last few hours in the back seat with Bethy. When Boston asked him to explain, he elaborated that he did not like the pressure to be always paired with her. If she were really his girlfriend, he would have driven her up himself instead of riding in the backseat while Bert flirted up front with Caitlin. And tonight, Carlos continued, he just knew that Bert was going to find a way to switch beds with Bethy. Then what was he supposed to do?

"I don't really understand the problem," Boston told him. "You like her, don't you?"

"Haven't you been listening to what I've been telling you?" Carlos replied, frustrated. Boston asked him to go over whatever it was again. "I have a problem with nice women like Bethy, who reminds me of home. Call it my Spanish curse. With Gertrude, I had no problem. Bethy is like a Spanish girl for me."

"Gertrude should have been your problem. As your friend, I hope you don't mind me saying that."

"I know you're right. Bethy is more my temperament." But he stayed where he was in the kitchen.

The group in the tub called out for both of them to join them. Boston's cell phone rang. He wondered if it was his partner Larry but instead Katherine called to explain that the car had a problem that could be fixed but not until tomorrow morning. They were broken down in Stockton, where it looked like they would have to spend the night. She went onto say before Boston brought it up, that she knew Shannon lived in Stockton and if they got really stuck, she would call her but for now the repair shop gave them a ride to a nice hotel with a nice restaurant nearby and they were fine.

Going out onto the deck, Boston let everyone know what was happening. Having started to relax with the tub's female company, Erik looked dismayed.

"Nothing you can do about it," Bert told him although Erik didn't appear convinced. "Boston, no reason for you to stay out either. Get in here."

Boston agreed to but first disappeared into the house to call his partner. As Larry was out, he only left a voice mail asking to be called tonight with anything new. Re-entering the kitchen, Boston saw Carlos was gone. Back outside, Boston undressed, tossed his clothes aside and climbed into the hot tub, seeking a place in the already tight squeeze.

"Why don't you sit on my lap?" Bert asked, then quickly clarified that he was addressing Caitlin.

"Maybe Boston should sit on mine," she returned, sticking her tongue at Bert.

As modestly as possible, Boston wedged in between Caitlin and Erik, sitting thigh to thigh with both of them.

Carlos emerged from the house holding a phone book. "There's a Basque restaurant in Gardnerville. Is that close by?" Boston replied that Gardnerville was about midway to Carson City. "You guys want to go there for dinner?" Carlos asked. The group all nodded yes and he returned inside the house, where he stayed for the rest of the afternoon.

—

In a little over a half-hour later, the six of them traveled in Bert's Silverado on Highway 88 to Nevada, where Bert eventually turned right toward Gardnerville. Driving first past ranches, then smaller ranch homes and finally suburban houses, they met with Highway 395 and found the JT Bar and Restaurant.

Inside the bar was busy, even for a Thursday night. The tall, dark-haired hostess allowed them to sit outside as they had requested on the side patio, partially shaded by evergreens to the west. She explained how the dinner would be served family style with the main course being lamb.

Boston asked if she was Basque, which she replied she was, and then Bert volunteered that the guy next to him was from Spain. She asked from what part and Carlos replied Asturias. "Asturias," her eyes widened. "I attended Universidad Oviedo."

"My town was close by," Carlos told her. "I came to the United States over twenty years ago."

"I've been here almost a year. Do you live around here?"

Answering they were all from the San Francisco Bay Area, Carlos told her that they were in town to attempt the Death Ride, which she had never heard of and she asked if the whole group was doing it. The hostess was amazed to learn that the other two women planned on riding it. She introduced herself as Carla and giggled at the coincidence when Carlos stated his similar-sounding name.

As the meal progressed, Carla became a frequent visitor, making sure they plenty of everything, including the clarets of red wine. Pressing Carlos for more information about himself, she extracted how he came to America, his three kids, his divorce, his work, and so forth, most of which was more than the rest of the table had ever gotten from the normally taciturn forty-five-year-old Carlos Cordova.

There was more food being served than they all wanted to eat. Having watched their weights over the last month, the bikers tried to limit their intake. The same was true with the copious amounts of red wine, of which Bert, their driver, reluctantly had to pass on several rounds.

Meanwhile, Carla was all enthusiastic about Carlos' living near San Francisco, which she told him she dearly wanted to visit. "I love Nevada," she said to the table during their serving of ice cream dessert. "But I want to see California, the real California." Then she asked him, "Are you free tonight?"

"No," Carlos replied, embarrassed. "We have to go back to Markleeville."

"If you want to stay, I can give you a ride back. I'm only working another hour and I even might be able to get off earlier." Carlos shook his head. Pouting her lips, she said, "Please, I'm dying to talk with someone from Asturias."

Carlos looked to Bethy, who told him, "Go ahead. You don't get to connect with Spain very often, much less your Asturias. Why else did we come to a Basque restaurant?"

"Right, thank you," Carla responded, putting her arm around Carlos' arm. "When were you last in Spain?" When Carlos told her over twenty years ago, she said there was so much she had to tell him. To Boston's surprise, Carlos decided to stay. Carla sent one of the busboys to get the check, not wanting to let Carlos out of her sight. After they paid, she then thanked and hurried everyone along.

Watching the group leave, Carlos reminded them that he would be back later and to leave the door unlocked. "Don't worry," called out his roommate Bert on his way out to the truck, "I won't wait up."

In the car, back on Highway 88 returning home, from the backseat in Bert's truck, Bethy asked, "What did she mean the 'real' California?"

"She meant the 'real' Carlos," Bert piped up. Caitlin elbowed him in the side and he shut up for the rest of the return drive, which was silent except for comments about the scenery as the car slipped through the evening shade provided by the Sierra crest while the distant Nevada mountains to the east still caught the last reddish sunlight.

Disembarking at the cabin, Bert took Bethy aside and mentioned that since Carlos was returning later, he would like to switch places with her, with Caitlin's permission, which he already gotten. Already having anticipated such request, Bethy conceded and gathered up her suitcase out of the bedroom she might have shared with Caitlin, moving it into the bedroom Bert might have shared with Carlos. Changing into a long t-shirt, she got into bed, staring out the open window, waiting to hear the sound of a car dropping off Carlos, still waiting when her body finally surrendered to sleep.

Chapter 24

Carson River

The East Fork of the Carson River is fed by several creeks, the largest of which are Silver Creek, Wolf Creek and Silver King Creek. Following the final eastern segment of Highway 4, the East Fork then flows along Highway 89 before turning eastward under Hangman's Bridge just south of Markleeville, meeting with the also eastward flowing West Fork in Minden, Nevada.

The headwaters of the West Fork of the Carson River begin at Lost Lakes and flow through Faith Valley into Hope Valley along Highway 88 and into Nevada. The combined branches of Carson River continue northward, staying east of state capital Carson City to Lake Lahotan, once a much larger ancient inland sea and now a reservoir, emptying its flow empties into the Carson Sink, near the town of Fallon, south of the Humboldt Sink to the north.

The distance between the drinkable sections of the Carson River to the south and the Humboldt River to the north was known as 40 Mile Desert to the covered wagon parties enduring their last dry stretch on the Carson Pass trail before having to tackle the formidable Sierra Nevada range.

Friday, part 1

Friday morning and Bert Leunberger woke up with Caitlin Carter's head upon his chest. It was barely light and totally quiet outside, unlike his East Palo Alto apartment adjacent to a bustling street. Though they had spent the night together, there had been no sex. Caitlin had told him, "Not tonight." He sensed that what had seemed so privately exciting in her apartment might have lost its mystique in the crowded house. He knew that she was also sensitive to Bethy's obvious disappointment in Carlos. Though he appreciated that, he had not anticipated that their lovemaking might be shutout on this trip. Lying next to her, he wondered if their intimacy was reaching the end, just as finally reaching the Death Ride event signaled the end of their bike training.

When Bethy Kono woke up in the bedroom across the hall, she reached over and touched the empty side of the bed. It was Bert's fault, she felt. Carlos probably never would have volunteered to that Basque woman that he was from Spain. All these weeks before Markleeville, she had thought it might work out that they would get to bed together in the rental cabin with its neutrality. She had hoped that Carlos' indifference riding up in the car could be overcome if they converse alone without the hindrance of being with the group.

Lightly dozing, Erik Erikksson envisioned disconnected images of the Pigeon Coop, jumbled with flashes of the Reykjavik brothel, then the hot tub at their cabin with the two young women. When Irina walked onto the deck in his dream, he woke up.

Boston Reed awoke wondering if Katherine's car was going to be fixed. Before ringing her, he first phoned his partner's cell phone number. Answering from his house, Larry reported that the details were almost finalized. The engineering firm seeking to acquire them would take over all their debt as well as their accounts. They wanted one of them to stay on for at least a month's transition, at salary. How much money they were willing to pay was still subject to discussion. Larry added that, as far as he was concerned, Boston could be the transition partner.

With that in mind, Boston decided to wait until calling his wife, not wanting to disturb her quite so early in the morning.

—

Their Best Western Stockton Inn room was almost pitch dark when Katherine Kirk opened her eyes. Her head throbbed and her mouth was dry. She was also aware of being covered with massage oil and totally naked underneath the single sheet. Slowly rolling out of the queen bed, she barely drew open the middle of the heavy curtains, enough to allow a knife blade of light into the room, landing on Irina Erikksson, lying on her hip with tussled blonde hair nesting on the pillow.

Gazing at the red numbers of a bedside digital clock, Katherine saw that it was a little after nine. She remembered and regretted calling Boston's ex-wife Shannon to meet for coffee at ten o'clock at a Starbucks a short walk from the motel. It had seemed a good idea at the time, after a couple margaritas, allowing her a chance to be sociable and also avoid a taxi ride to the garage when the car was being fixed.

Snoring slightly, Irina looked as if she might need help awakening. Katherine shook her gently to wake up, which the Russian woman did, turning over with a groan, then sitting up, her large breasts spilling over the top of the sheets. She rubbed the tops of her arms, checking the amount of massage oil left over. "I was hoping the massages last night might have blocked any hangover," Irina stated. "No such luck."

"Me neither," Katherine added. In an alcohol haze, she remembered that they each rubbed each other from head to toe, front to back. Irina had gone first, giving a very engaging rubdown without boundaries. Some of Irina's handwork had the stamp of Dennis' moves, as Katherine recalled thinking at the time.

When it came her turn to do the hands-on, Katherine began more reserved but Irina seemed to be enjoying her touch, giving compliments that went to her head, along with the margaritas they had consumed. If she could have remembered more or been less hung-over, she was sure she would have been embarrassed by some of what went on.

"Are you naked?" Irina asked, shielding her eyes against the glaring backdrop of the open curtain behind where Katherine stood.

"Like yourself, remember?" Katherine replied. "Anyway, we have coffee at ten. You want the first shower?"

Still a little punchy, Irina lifted up the sheet, groggily examining below, then yawned. "By the time I got to the bathroom, you could probably be done. Please go ahead."

Into the motel bathroom, Katherine started the shower water. The last thing she wanted to do with stumble into Shannon at Starbucks looking like as disheveled as she felt.

—

Carlos Cordova had awoken early, disappointed that last night had not gone well, frustrated that when they got into bed together, he had been too nervous to maintain arousal, at least not longer enough to force on a condom. Carla Berruta had been kind enough to suggest that they both had probably too much wine. In truth, he head did feel a little thick but he considered his failure to be just another example of his curse with Spanish females. It upset him as he waited, sitting in a chair in Carla's studio apartment, watching her getting ready to drive him back to Markleeville. Having slept naked with him, she wore a simple white bra and bikini bottoms, as she put on lipstick, combed her hair and so forth.

Before putting on the rest of her clothes, she called him over. Draping her arms around his neck, she told him how wonderful she thought he was and how much fun she had last night talking with him. Even if they had too much wine, it was the best night she had spent in Nevada, she told him, hugging him. As she did so, he felt himself pressing against her. Dropping his hands to the small of her back, he kissed her. Quickly, she was back on the bed and he was on top of her with his pants off. She reached for the open packet of condoms and tossed it to him. This time he quickly managed. It was not elegant but they successfully made love in short order.

Afterwards, instead of heading right away to Markleeville, Carla drove them both to a little diner at Carlos' insistence, where he bought breakfast.

—

Friday morning and the five-person biking group, minus Carlos, was finally all riding all together again, turning onto the road toward Markleeville. Boston was only interested in a short ride one day before the Death Ride and thought it would be good to show everyone what the highway was like along the river, at least before the turnoff toward Monitor Pass, where the ride's first climb would begin tomorrow.

Carlos' absence was not a topic of conversation. Bethy had alternated between appearing disconsolate and ambivalent while crunching her cereal. Starting out on the ride, she hung back as usual. Ignoring Caitlin's companionship, she kept behind the group as they descended the short distance into town.

Turning right, they crossed the town bridge over Markleeville Creek and then began a short climb over the ridge toward the Carson River. At that point in Carlos' absence, Erik fell back to accompany Bethy, which she neither welcomed nor objected.

Soon, they reached where Highway 89 turned to Monitor Pass, where they circled around the intersection before heading back downhill along the rushing river. In unspoken deference to Bethy, the group stayed together instead of stringing out at top speeds. They took it easy going up the ridge, and into town, across the bridge over Markleeville Creek before turning at the Wolf Creek back to their cabin.

After everyone quickly changed, they traveled in Bert's Silverado on the highway north the few miles to Turtle Rock Park to report in for the Death Ride. The pre-race event was crowded with a cluster of tents, manned by various manufacturers of bicycles, apparel, sports foods and publications. Many men and women riders wandered through the exhibits, while dressed in baseball caps, t-shirts, shorts and sandals, showing off a lot of skinny, tanned arms and legs, definitely not a beginner crowd. Still, even these apparent veterans discussed doubt as to what would happen tomorrow, especially if it were as hot tomorrow as today.

In one corner of the asphalt, shaded by an oak tree, was a large map of the routes that was a subject of deep study by surrounding bikers, which soon included Boston and Erik. "Can't waste time," advised a guy, who had overheard them, tall and wearing a straw Panama hat. "Start early, zip through the rest stops and you'll be fine," he told them in a slow drawl. "Don't let yourselves stall out at the lunch stop." Pointing to the map, he showed them where it was. "By the time riders get here, they've already done four passes," he continued. "It's about twenty-miles from there back through Markleeville to Carson Pass. Many people decide to bag it right here. They're exhausted so they just got into the lunch line and waited. The riders going all the way using grab something, stuff it in mouths, get water enough to make Woodfords, and party on."

"So how many times have you ridden it?" Boston asked him.

"Four. It would have been five but last year I broke my collarbone after hitting a pothole. Just happened to be looking the wrong way at the wrong time. You've heard about two kinds of riders? Well, I'm the second kind," he informed them, then moved on.

"What's the first kind?' Erik asked Boston.

"That's the bikers who haven't broken their collarbone yet."

Boston soon rounded up the group and they returned to the cabin, where he was glad to see Katherine's Expedition parked in front. Going inside to greet her and Irina, the group also found Carlos, cleaning Bethy's bike.

—

Joining Carlos, Bert set about cleaning his bike and Caitlin's. Carlos gave no indication of how his evening went with the Basque woman or why he didn't return all morning. Bert didn't press him for any details but stayed available out of curiosity, in case Carlos wanted to elaborate.

Boston prepared a snack with Katherine and Irina in the kitchen as he listened to the details of the car problem and also, to his surprise, the breakfast with his ex-wife Shannon.

Worried about degreaser fluid possibly get into and loosening his spoke posts, Erik left his bike alone. Sitting for a while in the kitchen next to Irina, he debated whether or not to get in the hot tub, not necessarily wanting more heat on already a hot day. On the other hand, he thought, how fatiguing could it be? He asked Irina to join him and she told him in a moment, being a little worn from the heat and the drive, as well as her late night with Katherine.

Bethy resented Carlos working on her bike, even if it dearly needed cleaning. Caitlin sensed her tension and suggested that they both get in the hot tub together, which was already in shade provided by the house. With only Erik alone in the water, she quickly undressed. Still preoccupied, Bethy slowly took off her clothes and quietly entered the water.

Erik observed her hesitation. "Worried about tomorrow's ride?"

Bethy suddenly was aware that she'd temporarily forgotten the ride. "I'm scared to death."

"Maybe that's why they call it the Death Ride," Erik joked. At least, Caitlin laughed, sitting across from him.

Meanwhile, Irina peered out the kitchen doorway and saw the threesome in the hot tub. "Bloody hell," she muttered.

"What?" Katherine asked, scanning her house plans for something terribly wrong.

"My husband's in the hot tub with those two girls. Alone with both of them," Irina said, putting down her sandwich and heading out the kitchen door. The three in the water stopped their chatter as she began to strip, tossing each item of clothing across the chair where the girls had dropped their clothes. Then she carefully entered the tub pausing on the first underwater step. "It's really hot," she said, staring directly at her husband. Forty-years-old, tall, bosomy and blonde, she towered above the waterline. Wading the short distance, she slowly sat down next to him, causing Bethy to slide over. With the water reaching her shoulders, she draped an arm around his neck, murmuring, "Ahh, that feels good."

Observing all this, Katherine then turned to Boston. "So what do you want to do for the rest of the afternoon?" she asked him.

"I'd still like to go see Carson Pass. Want to go for a drive?"

She agreed. When he asked if they should invite any others, she told him that she just wanted it to be them. They left in her Expedition, leaving Bert and Carlos, still working in the garage on their bikes.

When Bert was finished, he suggested to Carlos that they both join the others in the hot tub. Only partway done with his own bike, Carlos told him to go ahead without him.

As Bert was undressing on the deck, Bethy announced she was getting out. Toweling off, she went into the garage. Finding the Spaniard still cleaning his bike she asked in a clipped tone, "So, what is it, Carlos?"

He gazed up at her, not answering. She continued, "I mean, when we ride together you're always alongside me. But anything other than biking, you ignore me. Then last night, first chance you get, you go off with a total stranger. You don't come back. Ok, fine. You're not attached to me. We don't even date, in fact. Just let me ride my bike and stay away from me." As she turned away from him, the towel slipped down. "God, I don't even have any clothes on," she bemoaned, picking it up and leaving the garage.

Carlos stopped what he was doing. He tried searching for the words to tell her that sleeping with the Spanish woman had just undone something he'd carried around for thirty years. He wanted to also add that he had not been with another woman since getting married and he was unsure of himself. There were so many reasons he had not approached Bethy physically before. Knowing that she was fifteen years younger than himself was another.

Mostly, he wanted to say that, in spite of all that, he probably screwed up in going off with Carla. But admitting mistakes reminded him of all the apologizing that Gertrude had constantly made him do. Still conflicted over his tryst this morning with the Basque woman, he went up the stairs anyway. After looking first in his room, he found Bethy in Caitlin's room, sitting on the bed in a long t-shirt, staring out the window.

"I'm trying," he began then stopped.

"Not hard enough," she replied, turning away from him.

Caitlin suddenly bounded through the bedroom doorway, holding her own clothes up to her chest. "Oops," she said, seeing them together.

Embarrassed, Carlos said, "No, I'm going." He quickly left the room, darted in and out of his own room and then swiftly went down the stairs without another word.

After seeing him go, Caitlin asked. "Want to talk?" she asked Bethy.

"He's a son-of-a-bitch," Bethy said softly. Gazing out the window, she saw Carlos riding away on his road bike.

—

Behind the master bedroom doors, Irina lay on top of sheets next to her husband Erik, waking from a slight nap. Both were face up in the luminous afternoon sunlight lazily drifting into the room. It seemed to her that being in the hot tub with those other young women would have gotten him excited, enough so to want sex for the first time in months.

"I think those two girls must have turned you on," he mentioned, staring up at the blank ceiling.

"What makes you say that?" she wondered rolling onto her hip, a hint of sweat in the narrow gap between her breasts. Her night with Katherine was still a fog and Erik's comment had caught her off-guard.

"There was a lot of femininity in that tub."

"Other women don't get me excited," she objected, flashing again on the image of massaging Katherine in the Stockton motel room. "You enjoyed being naked with them."

"Not that much."

"Something must excite you," she stated, falling onto her back once more.

He pondered. "I'm nervous about Saturday's ride." He didn't admit that he had also been thinking about the Pigeon Coop all day

"We need to take vacations," she responded.

"Iceland," he stated. "I've never biked there."

She rolled all the way over onto her other hip, facing away from him. As far as she could tell, he stayed on his back, fantasizing about Iceland into the ceiling.

He gazed at her bare back, studying the vertebrae knuckles in her spine and the random pattern of a handful of moles.

—

Bert had joined Caitlin as Bethy had left for the bedroom next door. On her stomach, head turned toward him as he lay face up on his back with his eyes shut, Caitlin thought that he couldn't have fallen asleep this fast after sex. She spoke to see if he was awake. "You and Bethy do the same work but never discuss it with each other."

Eyes still shut, he lazily answered, "We're not supposed to talk about our clients, so there's not much to say to each other."

"Do you ever psychoanalyze me?"

"Why would I?"

"For what I did to my daughter."

"For her, not to her, you mean. Sounds like a reasonable choice given the circumstances, hard on you, of course, but you put her in a family situation with her biological father."

"Her biological father, as you call him, was my lover. At least, I thought he was. In the end, he didn't want me. Can I talk about him to you?"

"Not professionally," he responded, eyes opening and watching her. "Say what you want to."

"Not now," she answered. "I just wanted to know if I wanted to that I could."

"What's going on?" he asked softly.

Sliding over so that she rested half of her chest on his, she tussled his hair with her hand. "Do you think we've made love too often?"

Pausing, he replied, "I notice we didn't last night." Seeing her frown as his non-answer, he added, "No, not at all."

"You like making love to me, don't you?"

"Yes."

"I know," she sighed. Sliding off his chest, she returned her head on her pillow, still gazing at him before turning her head to the side. Bert continued looked at the back of her blonde head, noticing the pattern of her hair resting downward as if for the first time. Carefully, gently, he began to stroke her hair. "That's nice," she cooed. Then she droned, "I thought he was going to be my life-time lover but he only wound up my daughter's biological father."

—

Boston and Katherine drove along Highway 88, to the Carson Pass summit, just past a huge, impressive rock wall, blasted out to make the roadway. Once around the corner, he spotted a summit sign. A hundred yards away he pulled into a paved parking lot with several portapotties waiting for the tomorrow's ride. Stopping the car, he told Katherine that this was where the fifth pass sticker would be given, identifying those who had completed all the ride's major climbs before returning to Turtle Rock.

"That Carson Pass looks pretty hard," Katherine stated. "If you're totally exhausted before you start up it, you don't have to do the whole thing."

"Every rugby season I played always ended in injury," he began.

"You've told me many times. What's your point?"

"Point being I never quit on a season voluntarily."

"Counter point is that you always went too long and got yourself hurt."

He paused, gazing about the hillsides, taking a deep breath. Finally, he stated, "The company's for sale. It might happen today."

At first she was silent, not quite startled but waiting to see if he would offer more detail. When he didn't add anything else, she started, "I'm glad. I'm glad you're getting out and I'm glad you've finally told me. This past year you've been killing yourself at work."

"I plan to keep working," he replied. "I just don't know how or who for. If Larry can finalize the deal, there'll be a month or so for me and then I'm on my own."

"Are you worried?"

He shook his head. "I guess I'm mostly relieved."

"Me, too. You're a little crazy, you know."

"How so?"

"Selling your company while doing the Death Ride all in the same weekend," she smiled, wrapping her arm around him. "Let's have some fun."

"Fun?"

"Back seat type. Park over there," she said, pointing to the far end of the asphalt.

"Why not back at the house?"

"I like it here, just us, up on a mountain pass, sort of like an automobile mile high club. What's the matter? You can bike up here with single women but you can't have spontaneous sex with your own wife?"

He thought about asking if they were too old for this but he did as told, parking the Expedition. After he cracked down all the windows, both went out the front doors and opened the rear side doors, climbing into the back seat where they stripped below the waist before laying down together on a back seat that was such a tight squeeze that it was funny. As Boston had his doubts, Katherine turned her head to the side. "I hear something."

He looked up through the tinted windows to see a pick-up truck stopped alongside their vehicle. Reaching forward over front seat, Boston turned the car key to accessory, then lowered his side window. "Can I help you?"

The driver, young and bearded, didn't seem surprised that the question came from a man sitting in the back seat. "Where do you want these tents set up?"

"We're not with the ride organizers."

"Where do you think I should set them up?" he persisted. Katherine laughed and Boston shushed her. Glancing around, he saw that they were parked in probably the best spot. He pointed across the lot to another open area.

"Got time to give me a hand?"

Boston turned to Katherine who nodded her head, still laughing. "Sure," he said, then put the window back up. Putting back on their pants, both got out and helped set up two lightweight tent tops for a half hour.

As they were finally done and leaving, Katherine told him, "That was fun, though not the fun I had in mind. Maybe we've gotten past backseat encounters."

"It would have been tricky," he replied, "but where there's a will."

"Yeah, yeah," she said nonchalantly. "Just remember, you can call the ride off at anytime tomorrow. You may have the will but the body may not have the way."

"Don't worry," he assured her, "I'll be back here tomorrow riding my bike."

Back on the highway, he let the car drift downhill in second gear, getting a feel for the Carson Pass eastside descent. Their vehicle glided past a low rock-cement wall on the right, with the mountain slopes on their left and no bikers on the road, which did not surprise Boston with the start almost twelve hours away. Even in second, the car went fast, which meant the climb would be long and steep.

Katherine noticed the same thing. I hope you get your victory, she thought. In light of what he just told her, she realized that his year-long detachment had been more than just due to the pending bike ride.

—

When Boston and Katherine returned to the cabin, Carlos was back from Turtle Rock Park with his own registration packet. Eager to eat so that they could get to bed early, Boston suggested to the group that they leave soon for dinner. When asked what he had in mind, he informed them that there was a low-cost spaghetti feed for all riders at Turtle Rock, where they'd been earlier in the day. At that point, Katherine announced that she had not driven two hundred miles for a paper plate of spaghetti. Not wanting a long drive, Boston proposed the Wolf Creek Restaurant and Bar, which was acceptable to the group.

Katherine and Irina first went to the bath in Katherine's room. "We almost made love this afternoon," Irina confided to Katherine as they both looked into the mirror. "But he's too wrapped up in this ride. What did you guys do on your drive?"

"We were getting ready to fuck in a parking lot but somebody came by needing our help to set up tents. So we did that instead."

"Gee, that's disappointing," Irina commented, stepping inside the narrow water closet.

"You know, the fact that Boston went along with the idea really turned me on," Katherine responded as she followed. "I don't know if I could actually manage it in a backseat anymore. So, maybe it was just as well we didn't find out we were too old for car sex. However, we're so close to Lake Tahoe," Katherine added. "That's where the romantic setting is, not here."

A short while later, the group divided into Katherine's Expedition and Bert's Silverado. When Carlos went to get into Bert's truck, he found Caitlin already in the back seat and so he got in the front passenger side. Nobody said a word about this new arrangement but, obviously, Bethy was still upset with him.

Although 6 pm was early for dinner, the Wolf Creek's dining room was almost full, including other bike riding types who had also forgone the spaghetti offering. The same high school age waitress from two nights ago was there again. Two tables were slid together for their group of eight.

Sitting next to their table, Erwin, who introduced himself as from suburbs north of Chicago, gray-haired and about sixty-years-old, short and wiry, sitting next to a dark-red-haired doe-eyed woman almost half his age, whom he introduced as Lyudmila. Erwin spoke of how he was looking forward to this first Death Ride tomorrow and was anxious because he only had freeway overpasses for training hills where he lived, plus it was often too cold to bike in the winter. Lyudmila did not speak.

"So, how do you train?" Bert asked.

"Spin classes at the health club," he replied. "I'm wasted after an hour, guaranteed."

"The Death Ride will be at least ten hours," Bert informed him, "guaranteed."

"Oh, I've been doing some long rides recently," Erwin replied. "Do you girls bike, too?"

"These two do," Katherine answered. "We're just along for the waters." Erwin and Melanie looked at each other. "Well, maybe we were misinformed," Katherine added, looking at Boston, grinning as he ordered a bottle from the table's wine list.

"I hear Lake Tahoe's nice," Irina stated without response from anyone. Then she whispered to Katherine that Lyudmila was a *prostitutka*.

—

After dinner, the woman all ordered decaffeinated coffee. Boston cellphoned Larry and learned that there was a Saturday morning meeting to wrap up the final details. Keeping that information to himself, he suggested that the four men go to the bar for one last pre-ride toast. When Caitlin asked, Bert explained it was a Four Horseman kind of thing, part of their training vow. Katherine waved them on.

The bar was empty except for the bartender Tanya and two men in their forties, dressed in motorcycle leather. The Four Horsemen all ordered Diet Cokes to the snickering of the two motorcyclists in the corner. In a low voice, Erik tried to tell Tanya without being overheard that he'd visited the Pigeon Coop.

The bigger of the two motorcyclists belted out to Tanya that she and her Russian friend ought to set up shop in Markleeville. Humored, Tanya, who spoke to him by name, asked if Frank would sponsor them, reminding him that they both were Ukrainian, not Russian. In a loud voice, Frank continued that these four might make pretty good customers, unless they couldn't get it up from sitting on those tiny bike seats all the time. In a drunken tone, he asked the group if that were true.

Tanya told Frank to knock it off. Even Frank's friend tapped him on the shoulder. He might have except at that point the four women entered the bar. With a new audience, Frank asked the women collectively if their road biking had made their boyfriends sterile and wouldn't they like some new meat.

Caitlin responded first, giving the finger as she proclaimed, "Sit on it and rotate, motherfucker." That shut up Frank, at least for a moment, while his friend chuckled. Boston paid the drink tab and the eight of them left. However, the two motorcyclists followed.

"You got some balls, lady," Frank hollered at Caitlin, once he got outside. "Why don't you ride a real bike with me?" Caitlin ignored him so he turned to Bethy, telling her, "Why don't you treat your little pooper to some real comfort? Check out my Harley?" he laughed, tapping one of two motorcycles parked in front of the bar.

"You guys go ahead," Carlos told the four women. "I want to talk with him."

Bethy hesitated but Caitlin took her by the arm to the Silverado. Katherine and Irina waited by the Expedition.

"What's up bike boy?" Frank said to Carlos. "Don't get your bike panties in a knot."

"You shouldn't talk to him that way," Boston warned.

"What of it?" Frank asked, thumping Carlos in the chest. In an instant, Carlos flicked out his hand and the heavy motorcyclist was on the ground.

When he started to get up, Carlos bent down, slapping him until the cyclist's face was red while demanding an apology.

Boston stood ready in case the friend attacked Carlos, but the friend just stood there amused. "You better, apologize Frank," he stated. Carlos stopped the slaps but still ordered the apology. "He's just drunk, is all," he friend said. "He didn't mean anything by it."

"I'm sorry, I'm sorry," Frank finally admitted, still lying on the pavement. Carlos asked him if he'd had enough. "Hell, yes," he replied. "I'm sorry. Let me buy you a drink, mister."

Carlos stood up slowly while Frank stayed down as Boston replied with a smile, "Can't. Got a big ride tomorrow."

The group left in the two vehicles. Bert was absolutely incredulous and kept praising Carlos for what had just occurred. From the back seat of Bert's truck, Bethy sourly asked Carlos in front if he had treated her husband Henry that way when he'd been so rude at Rossotti's back in June.

"No, I only bought him a beer is all."

"Caitlin, honey," Bert started, "where did your trash mouth come from?"

"I just got pissed that he called you sterile."

"Actually, I am, though by getting snipped, not from biking. But I think he meant to say 'impotent.' Which I'm not," he quickly added.

"I know, honey," she said, nudging Bethy.

Bethy returned a polite smile, then stared at the back of Carlos' head, thinking that he was plenty physical, though just not with her.

Chapter 25

Pleasant Valley

Marklee Village is a custom lot subdivision located on the outskirts of Markleeville off Grover Hot Springs Road, situated around Pleasant Valley Road, which follows Pleasant Valley Creek, the drainage of which is separated from Charity and Faith Valleys by a ridge that includes 9417-foot tall Markleeville Peak.

Pleasant Valley provided another route from Markleeville to Silver City through a canyon that was once the site of Raymond City, mapped back in 1865 beside Raymond Canyon Creek named from Rossiter W. Raymond, a mineral examiner. Nearby 10,011-foot tall Raymond Peak has nothing taller between it and Mt. Lassen at 10,457-feet tall to the north.

Friday, part 2

Raymond and Lina still had not shown by the time the group returned to the cabin in Marklee Village. After more enthusiastic discussion of the bar incident, Boston suggested that they all get everything ready tonight because tomorrow they would have to get up between 4 and 4:30 to be ready to leave the cabin around 5 am.

They each began preparing their biking essentials for the morning: pinning numbers on shirts, putting energy gel packets in saddle pouches, preparing dehydrated electrolyte powders and so on. When done, Boston assembled everyone in the kitchen and read a printout about the course, advising that:

The first Monitor Pass summit came at 15 miles and would again be reached after a ten-mile descent and return climb, coming at mile 35.

Twenty miles later, the Ebbetts Pass summit at mile 55, and then again fifteen miles later at mile 70.

Finally, after first turning at Woodfords and then stopping at Picketts, Carson Pass came at mile 110 before returning to Turtle Rock Park to finish at mile 129.

The ride started and finished at Turtle Rock Park, elevation 5501-feet above sea level. All of the passes were in the mid-8000-foot range, from Monitor Pass, twice at 8314-feet, to Ebbetts Pass, twice at 8730-feet. The last pass, Carson, was at 8580-feet.

There were also important cut-off times, he told them, of which the two most critical were on the final way to Carson Pass. All bikers had to leave Woodfords, at mile 95, by 4 pm. From Woodfords to the bottom of Carson Pass, called Picketts Junction, was only six miles, which Boston felt should take no more than an hour even as a slow uphill. You could rest at Picketts as long as you left by 5:15.

Bert began, "If we leave around 5 am, that's twelve hours to make a hundred miles to Picketts by 5 pm. What's that, 8 miles per hour? That includes the descents. Should be plenty of time left over for food stops. I heard the fastest riders do all 129 miles in nine hours, but they hardly stop and when they do, it's not for long."

"Exciting, right?" Caitlin chimed in. "I've never felt this nervous when team riding in college."

"I'll just be happy when it's over," Bethy said.

"I'm so happy I'm not riding tomorrow," Katherine called out from a living room couch. Sitting across from her, Irina agreed, asking what the two of them could do while the others were biking. Katherine answered that she heard of a lot of stores in Carson City that carry Indian jewelry, which she definitely wanted to see.

"Aren't you going to cheer us?" Boston asked from the kitchen.

"The roads are closed you said."

"Only in the morning on Monitor and Ebbetts. Markleeville will be open all day. We'll be passing back through town on our way to Carson Pass." Katherine asked when and he replied that they should be biking into Markleeville around 1 pm. Also, he suggested that, if they were running late then the two could meet them on top of Carson at around 3 or 4 pm when they would be completing the fifth and final pass.

Katherine did not commit to either place or time. Instead, she wondered aloud where Raymond and Lina were going to sleep as all the bedrooms were taken. As they had to pay a full share for four days rental to stay one night, should they be stuck on the floor? Boston tried calling them on his cell phone without any luck.

He proclaimed that either they were coming or they weren't, but in any case, they'd have to settle for sleeping in the living room. Addressing the group, he stated, "We've had our dinner. Carlos beat the shit out of a drunken motorcyclist." The group cheered. "We got the bikes ready, our gear ready. Our training is all behind us. All we have to do is wake up in a few hours and ride. So, I guess this is goodnight, ladies and gentlemen. See you in the morning."

"A few hours?" gulped Bethy. Then she whispered to Caitlin, "Can we stay together tonight?"

Bert overheard. "Don't get me wrong. I like Carlos but I don't want to sleep with him before Death Ride."

Bethy did not want to make a fuss in front of the group. Caitlin took her aside, "I promised Bert that we would at least be together the night of the ride. You've ridden with Carlos all year. You two should be together also. Besides, he defended your honor this evening, even if that guy did have a point about bike seats," Caitlin smiled.

"What about him being with the Spanish woman?" Bethy asked, her face unhappy.

"I don't think that was a big deal. He's here now, isn't he?"

The two women were the last up stairs. Going into the bedroom, Bethy found Carlos sitting on the bed. "Staying tonight or going out again?"

"Are you mad at me?"

"What am I doing?" she began, as she started to undress with her back to him. "I'm not a real biker. My husband and I have split up. I should be getting my life together." Putting on a t-shirt, she stepped out of her shorts, wearing only bikini bottoms underneath. Starting toward the door, she left for the bathroom.

When she returned, Carlos was already in bed, lying under just a sheet. She flicked off the light and slid in next to him. "I'm not mad at you," she said matter-of-factly, giving a big sigh. "I don't know what I am."

"I never meant to get married," he stated, staring up at the ceiling. "I didn't come to California to marry Gertrude. I had my plane ticket to return to Spain before she told me she was pregnant. So, we made plans. I proposed. Then she announced that it was a false alarm. But we got married anyway. Eventually, she did get pregnant of course. I got a job. It was a difficult time. Our babies came right away."

He gazed over at her. The room was very dark, faint starlight coming through the open windows, which had curtains drawn back to allow cool night air to enter. "I was never happy in Madrid," he told her. "First I had a warehouse job during the day and was a dishwasher at night. I use to fantasize about the girls, which made me feel guilty and ashamed. I became a bartender. Then one night, Gertrude came in. She was an American student. I was a whole different person with her, much more sure of myself. When she left for California, I went to visit her and I never got back to Spain."

"Do you want to go back?" she asked him.

"I've often thought about it. With all the babies coming so close together, it was impossible back then."

When he stopped speaking, Bethy waited for a moment. In the darkness, she began, "Henry bought me a drink in the hotel bar in Honolulu. I was vacationing with my girlfriend and he was traveling on business. He sort of swept me off my feet. I thought I'd found Mr. Wonderful." She paused. "It was my mistake. I turned over control of my life and I'm never going to do that again."

"I never really had a plan," he confessed. "I stumbled into living with my Madrid German girlfriend. I then fell into marrying her." He paused. "There were many times when I was younger that I thought about leaving her. But I knew I lacked confidence with women. I feared that I could only be intimate with Gertrude."

"Are you afraid of me?" she asked him.

"No," he said, turning his head to her. Then, staring up again, he confessed. "Yes, I am. I mean you're only here in bed because Bert wants to stay with Caitlin."

"Do you want me to leave? I can sleep downstairs."

"No, that's not what I meant," he stated, then got out of bed, wearing only boxer shorts. "I have to go use the bathroom. Will you leave when I'm gone?"

"I don't know if you're afraid of me leaving or if you want me to."

"I'm glad you're here," he told her as he stood by the door from where he could barely see her face with only the white sheet reflecting the starlight. "Yes, I want you to stay."

When he came back several minutes later, she was lying on her stomach already sleeping. Quietly shutting the door, Carlos rounded the bed and carefully climbed in without waking her. Gazing out the window at the stars, he soon shut his eyes, hoping to soon be asleep himself, no longer thinking about the thirty-year-old dark-haired woman breathing next to him, her t-shirt lightly against his side, her hip tight to his hip. Finally he just tried to focus on the stars, twinkling with a nocturnal mountain clarity that he envied.

—

Meanwhile, in the other secondary bedroom across the hall, Caitlin spoke, waking Bert, "I can't sleep."

"What?" he asked drowsily, lying on his stomach.

"I'm worried about the ride tomorrow."

"No problem," he assured her. "We'll be fine."

"I've been thinking about making love," she said in the darkness.

"What? Are you sure?"

"No, I'm not sure, or at least, I'm not sure about tonight," she began. "Actually, I am sure about tonight. I want to make love tomorrow night after the ride."

"Not tonight?" he questioned, unclear of what she was saying.

"I don't want anything to interfere with our ride tomorrow," she said. "I want all our focus on doing all five passes."

"Fine," he murmured softly, letting his momentary excitement pass.

She paused. "Do you love me, Bert?" she asked, then quickly added, "Don't answer that. I was just thinking out loud and I don't want to know. Good night, Bert," she concluded and rolled over on her side.

Now he was the one who couldn't sleep.

—

Katherine got into bed first. Lying there, she thought about their little episode in the Carson Pass parking lot earlier in the afternoon. Late as it was now, she prompted herself to be agreeable in case Boston wanted some play before sleeping. However, she decided to wait on his mood. Tomorrow, just a few hours away, was the day for which he had trained all this year.

Getting into bed, Boston gave no indication that he was interested in sex. In the dark of the room, he spoke, "I don't know if I'll definitely make all five passes. My only concern now is to not oversleep and wind up getting a late start. The mountains might beat me, ok, but I don't want the clock to."

It was difficult for her to feel the same amount of drama regarding the bike ride. After all, it was only one day. The news he had given her about his company being sold was much more important. But she recalled how her second husband Mark used to tense the day before a century ride. She appreciated that men manufactured these tests. That Boston focused on it was enough for her to not interfere with her perspective. "Did you set your alarm?" she asked.

He reported that he had and thanked her. She was sure he would do well tomorrow. Regardless of how much he fretted, Mark always seemed to triumph on his long rides and Boston had proven himself just as capable. It was what was going to happen after the ride that held her attention. Helping him get restarted was where she could offer real support, if he were open to accepting it.

A short time later, Katherine woke Boston, asking about noises coming from the living room. Getting out of bed, Boston opened the bedroom door to see Raymond and Lina carrying their bags into the house. Walking out in his underwear, he greeted them.

"Hi," said Raymond, seeing him while putting down his gear. "We got a late start and then had car trouble."

"You guys eat?" Boston asked.

"Yeah," Lina replied. "There was still some spaghetti at registration. We just made it." She set down her stuff next to her husband's.

"I'm afraid there's no more bedrooms," Boston said.

"That's okay," Raymond said, looking around the room. "I brought our sleeping bags." He returned to their Pathfinder.

Meanwhile, Katherine came out the bedroom door, wearing a short nightshirt and boxers. "Welcome. What time is it?"

"About 11," Lina answered. "Sorry to wake you."

"No problem," Katherine replied, pushing her hair away from her face. "I get to sleep in tomorrow. You're the ones who'll have to get up in a few hours."

"With a two year old, I'm use to it," Lina told her. Katherine went into the bedroom and came back with a couple extra pillows and blankets that she and Boston weren't using.

Raymond entered, putting down the bags as he said hello to Katherine. Boston informed him that they were all getting up at 4 am and leaving at 5. Katherine apologized for not having a bed available for them.

"First come, first serve, we understand, no problem," Raymond stated. The four chatted a little longer, then Lina announced she was exhausted. Boston and Katherine excused themselves and went back into their bedroom. Raymond and Lina debated each sleeping on a couch but finally opted for the floor, spreading out their sleeping bags side by side. Soon they were stretched out on the floor, quickly falling asleep with lights out.

Back in bed, Boston lay wide awake while Katherine quickly dozed off. Having already fallen asleep once envisioning asphalt and bike wheels, he now thought about the closing of his engineering company. At least his daughter Serina's last year of college was funded by savings he had long ago set aside. He would soon be working for someone else and, after a couple of very low income years, a steady paycheck would be very welcome. As Katherine began lightly snoring, he thought of her and how successful she was in her own well-paying business. He admired her for that and wondered how whatever new arrangement he found would affect their five-year-old marriage.

—

By 2 am, Erik was alert after lightly sleeping for a couple hours, worrying about his food, how much liquid to take and also how or even if his shirt scheme would function. Then he began to fret about if he would soon fall asleep again and, if not, what that would do to his performance in the ride. Irina awoke, sensing something was wrong and asked him what was the matter. He admitted to being anxious about everything involved with the ride.

"I've never seen you like this, not even when you're starting a new house design."

"I would never start a house this early in the morning," he replied.

"I know. What's wrong?"

"Nothing's wrong," he assured her before adding, "I've never been a team guy, never did team sports. Even as an architect, I work solo and I used to bike solo as well."

"So?" she asked, listening with eyes shut.

"So now I'm part of this group and I don't want to let the group down by doing poorly."

"I thought this wasn't a race."

"It's not," he emphasized. "If I went out by myself and things weren't going right, I could just quit and nobody would be the wiser. Tomorrow, if I quit, everyone will know."

"So what if you have a bad day? Everyone does, don't they? Anyway, they'll likely be having just as hard a time."

It'll matter, he thought. If I fail and they don't, it will be because I wasn't as strong mentally and that I gave up. Icelanders don't give up, he told himself, visualizing his stepfather instructing him when, as a young boy, he listened intently as his stepfather had intricate preparations for whatever he did. Now, the middle-aged adult, Erik considered once more all his planning: the bike, the training, the food, the dried energy powder, the open shirt, repeating the various elements over and over, seeking where he might have overlooked something, anything that might knock him out of the ride while the others continued. Meanwhile, he became aware that his wife was once again asleep.

At 3 am, he decided to finally get out of bed without waking Irina. Going downstairs, he flicked on a light in the entry hall below. Once in the living room, he saw two bodies under blankets sleeping in the living room, revealed by the light that he now turned off. Quietly, he went to the kitchen, once again turning on lights as he slowly began getting a breakfast of oatmeal ready.

—

Carlos woke a little before 4 am. He left the dark bedroom for the darker hallway in order to use the bathroom. However, the door was shut with light shining underneath. He stood there for a moment and then the door opened and a topless Caitlin appeared. "Oops, hi Carlos," she said, covering her chest with her arms as she returned to the other bedroom.

When Carlos returned to the bedroom, Bethy was awake with the light still off. Flipping up the switch, he went over to his bike clothes. Off came his boxers and on went the bike shorts. Bethy sleepily asked "What time is it?"

"Four o'clock," he told her, putting on his jersey. From across the hall, they heard an alarm go off in the other bedroom.

As Carlos sat in a chair to put on his socks, Bethy slowly got out of bed. The night had passed without any activity between them. It occurred to her that maybe that just being underneath the same sheet for one night would be all she would ever get with him.

Yawning, she then took off her t-shirt and bottoms, her bare backside facing him. Picking up her shorts, she turned to him. "Do we really have to do this?" she smiled.

"Com'on," he told her. "That's why we're here."

"And I was so happy sleeping," she said, putting on the shorts, then finding her sports bra. "Hope I don't disappoint you on the ride."

"You'll make it no problem."

"Yeah, sure," she said, fitting into her top.

—

Across the hall, Bert watched Caitlin also getting dressed into her biking clothes. "You better start getting ready," she told him, zipping up her jersey.

"I will," he said. "How'd you sleep?"

"Sex would have helped," she smiled. "Get dressed, will you?"

She went downstairs where the kitchen light was on. Erik was eating a banana next to an empty bowl of oatmeal, sitting across from Boston and Carlos who were both eating cereal. Katherine was also there, in a sweater over her short nightgown, making coffee. As Caitlin said hi to them, Raymond wandered into the kitchen, dressed in his bike shorts and a sweater. "You made it," Caitlin happily greeted him.

Raymond replied that they had started very late and arrived well past 11. Erik offered his chair and left the kitchen, going back upstairs, passing Bert coming down. Bethy soon followed. Lina was the last one into the kitchen. She had her biking shorts on but still wore the red t-shirt she slept in. For the next several minutes, the early morning household was busy with individuals eating, filling water bottles, going to the various bathrooms, all passing each other up and down the stairs. Meanwhile, the house clocks kept moving toward 5 am.

Finally, they assembled in the bright light of the garage almost right at 5 am. Erik had a video camera with which he wanted to document the group. Although, Boston was eager to push the group out onto the road, he conceded to the filming, seeing that at least it was one way of getting everyone organized to go out. Erik stood in the doorway, holding up the camera, asking everyone to approach rolling their bikes, announce themselves and their age. "Why our age?" Carlos asked.

"Because years from now, we're going to want to know," Erik replied.

"Let's just do it," Boston said. He got his bike and approached the camera. "Boston Reed, 46," he said, adding, "and this is my Trek."

One by one they followed:

"Bert Leunberger, 51, Cervelo."

"Caitlin Carter, 26, Mercyx."

"Carlos Cordova, 45, Colnago."

"Bethy Kono, 31, but I'm getting divorced. LeMond."

Erik put down the camera. "Where are the others?" Standing at the garage-house door, Katherine went to get them. Raymond and Lina soon appeared, fully dressed in biking clothes, followed by Irina, in her robe. Erik told the two what he wanted and began filming again.

"Raymond Delzio, 33, BMC."

"Lina Delzio, 32, Specialized. Mother of Zack."

"Hey, over here," Caitlin said. Erik swung the camera around as she rolled her bike back into the garage light. "I'm also the mother of Mandy," she stated.

"What about you?" Katherine asked.

Erik turned the camera towards her and Irina standing alongside. "And here is our support team." The two women said nothing. "Go ahead," he told them. "Name and age."

Katherine went first. "Katherine Kirk, wife of Boston Reed."

"Age?"

"47."

"Irina, your turn."

"I just woke up," she said, "Don't film me."

"Thank you, Irina Ivanova Erikksson, 42," Erik announced.

"43," she corrected him, "Here, let me film you."

Erik handed the camera to her before getting his bike. "Erik Erikksson, 44, Cannondale."

"Ok," said Boston, checking his watch. "Let's go. It's already 5:15 and getting lighter all the time." Raymond remembered he still had water bottles to fill. "Turn right at Markeeville," Boston called out. As he started, Katherine ran forward and kissed him.

Irina continued filming the departure, stopping the camera only to kiss Erik as most of the group took off. With the eastern sky already beginning to lighten, Irina filmed the dawn horizon. Turning on Pleasant Valley Road, at last they were finally on the bikes as their months long anticipated Death Ride had begun.

Boston marveled that this was what he had set out to do back in October when he suggested doing the ride. He didn't need be group leader anymore but instead was caught in the same current drawing the group toward Markleeville and the high mountain passes beyond. His business troubles were left behind, along with the cabin and his wife.

Chapter 26

Monitor Pass

Monitor Pass lies on the southernmost segment of Highway 89 as it connects from Highway 4 in Alpine County to Highway 395 in Mono County, crossing county lines. The town of Monitor was located at a dirt road turnout located at the first junction up from Highway 4. It was named in 1863 that the Union ship Monitor drove the Confederate Merrimac from their battle waters.

Southern sympathizers named several features in the area after Civil War references, including Jeff Davis Peak near Highway 88 and Bull Run Peak close to Highway 4. Fredericksburg off Highway 88 in Nevada, named in 1864, may reflect the Confederate victory, or a local sawmill operator, or both.

Monitor flourished as a mining district, having a post office from its inception to 1888, with a population high in between of 2,000. By 1893, the settlement was deserted. Five years later, the ghost town was revamped by Dr. Loope, naming it after himself. Now only a dirt road is left, leading to the Morningstar Mine.

Monitor Pass Road was not built into Mono County until the 1950s and the pass itself was not officially named until a 1956 United States Geological Survey map was printed. As a continuation of Highway 89 which begins off Interstate 5 near Mt. Shasta City, hundreds of miles to the north, the highway's most southern segment, Monitor Road, follows the narrow ravine of Monitor Creek to a reservoir named Heenan Lake, named for a miner killed in the nearby Leviathan Mine in the 1860's.

A 37-foot tall dam built in 1914 augmented the lake into which Heenan Creek flows. At the reservoir, the road turns left and dips down through Sagehen Flat, passing the Leviathan Mine dirt road, before it bears right, resuming the climb to the large flat where Monitor Pass, elevation 8340 feet, is located. Nearby rounded Leviathan Peak is 8963 feet tall, the highest point in the pass.

Quickly the road descends into Mono County, with a series of sharp turns until it hugs the mountain side, with a view of elongated Slinkard Valley to the right, named for a former Nevada county official, who had constructed a road up the main creek of the valley. Eastward on the road are views of Antelope Valley and the elusive White Mountains in the distance. In the foreground are the Sweetwater Mountains, through which the road winds in a narrow canyon.

At the junction with Highway 395 is a California state road sign that reads: "Highway 4 18/Markleeville 22/Lake Tahoe 51." 18 miles describes the return route from Highway 395 to Highway 4, which is approximately 9 miles up, one mile across the saddle through Monitor Pass again and 8 miles down to Ebbetts Pass Road, under which Monitor Creek flows into the Carson River.

Saturday, part 1

The cold predawn air chilled the group of riders descending gradually on Hot Springs Road to Markleeville. They stayed together, right-turning the corner at the Wolf Creek Restaurant and Bar, careful to avoid the stream of riders smoothing out level in town from their freezing downhill from Turtle Rock Park. Having entered from the side street, the group merged instantly into the ride proper.

Crossing Markleeville Creek found the coldest air of all. In the dark, with other riders joining alongside and everyone in jackets, it was hard for the group to track each other. Boston noticed Bert and Caitlin pulling ahead on the short uphill. Erik kept next to him for a while, then drafted a small group near the crest and descended with the faster riders. Dropping past the river bridge, the road trended slightly uphill past Carson River Resort on the left with the swirling river itself on the right.

The riders Boston encountered, either being passed or passing him, sped along full of adrenaline, anticipating the difficult effort that was approaching ahead. This part of the route, even with some climbing, was easy though the tension permeated the pack of riders.

Farther behind, Carlos rode with Bethy, riding side by side as big swarms of bikers went by. She finally told him to go at his own pace, adding that she was surrounded by all kinds of support. Raymond passed by, having finally caught up and rolling as fast as anyone, not recognizing the two. Carlos turned again to Bethy. "Go!" she yelled, making sure he heard.

Speeding up, Carlos caught up with Raymond just before making the sharp left turn at Monitor Pass Road. Already the dawn was much lighter than just minutes before. Ahead, in the flat portion, they saw Boston stopped, taking off his windbreaker even with temperatures still low. Pulling alongside, they did the same.

Before they restarted, Bethy arrived with now Lina alongside, both also stopping to remove their jackets. The five of them shared a so-far-so-good conversation, drinking nervously from the water bottles in the early morning chill.

Starting out, Raymond pulled away while Boston and Carlos stayed together, talking back and forth, commenting on the steep ravine on their right, the bottom of which rose steadily parallel with their increasingly pitched climb.

Narrow Monitor Creek seemed to continue forever in front of them, rising in a tight v-shape on the uphill horizon miles away. Finally, the creek rose up to the road, which turned left into a little valley containing a small but broad lake and a welcome, temporary break in grade.

Out of the initial canyon, they met the first rays of dawn sunlight. Although the grade had eased, they could see the string of riders hugging the mountainside ahead, climbing out of the valley.

Slightly weary, Boston was pleased to have Carlos nearby. They had not ridden alongside much since the group had expanded, especially with Carlos always falling back with Bethy. So much had happened over the past six months that Boston felt their normal pattern of conversation was now outdated. He asked, "Are you having a good trip?"

"We had sex if that's what you mean," Carlos replied as they pedaled amongst a group of other riders. Boston was shocked at this unusual frankness and was unsure of whether Carlos was referring to the restaurant hostess or to Bethy, either one of which would have surprised him. Carlos continued, "Imagine coming to Nevada to finally being intimate with a Spanish woman, albeit a Basque. And all because of this Death Ride." Boston told Carlos that this was quite a revelation. "Sometimes I think too much about everything," Carlos responded with a smile. "It wears me down."

With such long stretches of climb visible at a time, progress uphill seemed very slow and they spoke little, appreciating each other's company in silence. Finally, the route wove into a little grove of white aspens, with the sun disappearing once again below the southeast ridge top, and then up a little pitch. Cresting, they saw a broad valley with a welcome rest stop occupying the right-hand field below while the highway stretched out straight and level for what looked like at least a mile.

At the rest stop below the crest were stationed volunteers, attaching a sticker to the paper registration number pinned onto each rider, thus officially certifying completion of the west side of Monitor Pass, the first pass on the Death Ride course. While other riders halted for the food and water tables, the two restarted, rolling out across the flat plain.

Ahead was a little cluster of trees, containing a monument commemorating Monitor Pass. The two stopped as had several riders. Some were putting on jackets, eating gel packets or even taking a picture of each other with the sign in the background, while others were ducking into the trees. Boston and Carlos stared at the elevation sign that showed the road at 8314 feet. "One down," Boston commented.

Putting on windbreakers, they headed east toward the bright, risen sun as the road gently sloped away from the broad valley's subtle high point. Rolling past rounded hilltops on either side, the grade began to steepen, getting faster with riders tucking lower as the pavement curved around to the right, soon facing south away from the sun's glare. Always the faster downhiller, Carlos turned to him, gave a wink and then pedaled off toward the sun. Going well past 30 miles per hour, Boston hung on. In front, Carlos pulled away at a startling speed.

Soon the route was making switchbacks down the mountainside with Carlos now out of sight. Straight sections led to sharp turns. Through another grove of threes, the road remained tucked into the slope and got very fast. Looking down, Boston saw his speedometer registering over 50 mph. Even at that, riders roared past him, jackets rippling in the windstream. Curves ahead required a slight touching of brakes plus now the first few riders were coming uphill, hugging the far shoulder, working hard in contrast to the effortless high speed descent. When sections briefly straightened, Boston quickly glanced right, seeing what appeared to be a beautiful, green valley to the south before his concentration had to focus on the next bend.

Swiftly the road soon bottomed out toward a narrow canyon. Boston rapidly pedaled alongside the pack of riders around him, entering the canyon slot where the air temperature plummeted. In a matter of moments, he was through and quickly coming upon the next rest stop with its own set of volunteers putting on stickers in full sunshine.

As he halted, a beaming Bert called over to him, "Wasn't that great?" Boston agreed as he saw Bert and Raymond both beginning the ascent back to Monitor Pass, some three thousand feet above where they were now. Carlos stood nearby, standing over his bicycle, catching his breath. Boston motioned to the food tables but Carlos stated he was waiting where he was for Bethy.

Laying down his bike, he met up with Erik and Caitlin, still at the food tables. Underneath umbrellas, there was all kinds of things to eat: melons, watermelons, bread, peanut butter, energy bars, gel packets, grapes, even cookies, all being offered by friendly volunteers. Big yellow water coolers were marked separately as water, electrolyte drink and lemonade.

Getting a peanut buttered bread and piece of watermelon, Boston sought out a place in the dirt to sit, soon joined by Caitlin. While they watched, a young woman approach a van, parked a distance away. Screened by the van's side from all the other activity, she glanced their way and then furtively dropped her shorts, apparently unwilling to wait in the long portapotty lines, at least as long as her privacy was only compromised by being within the view of just two others.

"There's your kind of girl," Caitlin commented, eating her sandwich.

"You know, that so called piss-rule was all Bert's idea."

She laughed, "I know. It was all Bert's bullshit."

"How'd you know?"

"Com'on, rules about where to piss? But, hey, it's part of the fun of riding with you guys. Plus it made life easier."

Boston chuckled, looking into her blue eyes for the first time, realizing that despite all the biking time together, he had not really faced the twenty-six-year-old blonde woman, or was she now twenty-seven? She could have been eighteen for how she appeared to him. "So, how do you feel today?"

"Real good. Bert and I were together until Raymond came by and then Bert took off with him. Too fast for me. How're you doing?"

"I feel good," he responded. "The climb out of here won't be easy."

"I'm so glad we started so early," she added. "It feels like it might get really warm today."

No doubt about that, Boston thought, seeing that Lina had arrived and was talking with Erik. Near the volunteers applying stickers, Carlos still searched up the road. Shortly, Bethy appeared, getting her second pass tag while Carlos helped take her bike.

The two came over when Boston called to them. Bethy was upset and angry with the descent. "God, I've never been so frightened," she began. "I was so slow. Guys were yelling at me."

"Me, too," Lina agreed. "They get going too fast for crowded conditions. I'm surprised there weren't any collisions."

Erik joined in, "Some flew by me like I was standing still and I was doing 55."

"It wasn't fun," Bethy emphasized

Carlos spoke, "I should have stayed with to you."

"Why? You're a great downhiller. I just don't enjoy it and I know I sound like a big baby," Bethy said, voice shaking.

Caitlin came forward and gave her a hug. "There are some of the best, craziest road bikers around out there who just eat this mountain up."

Bethy tried a smile, "Maybe I just need some food." She looked past the rest stop to the junction, level with Highway 395. "I don't suppose we can take that way back."

"It'll be safer going back up," Carlos offered. "All the downhillers will be going the other direction."

"Until the other side," she said. "Then they'll shoot by me again."

"We better hurry and get something to eat," warned Lina. "We're losing time."

She and Bethy went toward the food tables while Erik, Caitlin and Boston took off their jackets as they got ready to start back up the canyon. Boston asked Carlos if he was coming, too, but Carlos replied he was going to wait for Bethy. "Riding with her will cost you time," Boston warned him.

"I think I hit 60," Carlos replied, looking a little shocked at himself. "It might be good for me to take it easy for awhile. Plus, she seems a little upset."

"Well, you shouldn't have any trouble making up any lost time once you hit the downhill," Boston responded. Carlos nodded. Boston, Erik and Caitlin left without him as they slowly ascended into the canyon, joining with churning uphill riders while downhill bikers were bleeding off speed on the other side of the yellow line as they arrived at the bottom.

They biked together for what seemed a long time, heating up in the growing morning sun, around 8 am. After biking and biking, they passed an elevation 6000 FT sign. "How high do we go?" Erik asked Boston.

"8300 feet."

"That's what I was afraid of."

Boston looked upslope to his right, seeing bikers way uphill on a switchback. It was going to be a long climb, he realized, settling in to a rhythm, wanting to stay with Erik and Caitlin, both going slower than on any Bay Area ride. They came to a water stop where boys wearing their high school football jerseys and shorts were collecting water bottles on the fly, then racing ahead a short distance up the road to large coolers and handing back full bottles just in time to their owners pedaling by.

Turning the corner in the trees, Erik began to slowly pull out ahead but Caitlin stayed with him. "Feels like we've been on this hill forever," she admitted, as they broke out onto the sunlit slope again.

Boston agreed, then looked south to the same long valley he had seen on the descent, only now he had plenty of time to take it in. The green valley tilted away from them in a broad plain flanked by rounded slopes. Caitlin commented it was beautiful.

Having Caitlin alongside helped to distract him from the monotonous pedaling. She was working hard, dripping sweat, but otherwise handling the climb. Boston pushed himself and was able to keep up with her, figuring either she was saving herself or else the increasing heat and altitude had slowed down her usual pace. It was definitely taking a toll on him. Turning to his left, he saw more switchbacks extending uphill, again with lines of bikers, who once more appeared so small.

Finally the road slightly crested, but then it seemed to take forever to curve around to the large valley on top with the small group of trees containing the summit sign. In the high mountain air, the distant rest stop looked closer than it must have been but, methodically pedaling and with the benefit of a slight downhill, they soon arrived.

Stiff-legged, the two approached the food and water tables. It was now quite warm and they were beat. Boston had not planned to stop but he plopped down along with Caitlin, in bright sunlight, next to Erik, sitting down with his small russet potatoes that he offered to share with them. Too tired at the moment to walk over to the food tables, Boston and Caitlin both ate a couple of the small russets. "Any other ride day, the ride so far would be enough and we'd go home figuring we'd accomplished something," Boston stated.

"I think we'll feel better again downhill," Caitlin said, eating away. "Anybody have some ibuprofen?"

Boston gave her two. After refilling water bottles, the three were soon off again with Erik shooting far ahead. Bit by bit, Caitlin pulled away from Boston, handling the curves with more slightly more speed than he wanted. Passing the lake, he raced to catch her but, as they rounded alongside the Monitor Creek ravine, she sped away once more as he checked on some of the curves.

Finally, the road began to flatten. Reaching the intersection with Highway 4, Boston turned left, seeing Erik and Caitlin waiting for him just up the road. Having made the descent, his legs felt better as did his breathing from not having to climb for the last ten minutes of downhill. As they continued alongside the river, his mood also felt better now that he was at a lower altitude on a fairly level road next to a rushing Sierra stream in all its whitewater glory. Other riders headed in their direction were celebratory with both Monitor climbs behind them.

At least I've done two passes, Boston considered. During the night in his half-asleep state, he had tried to convince himself that doing the whole ride didn't matter. But he didn't believe it. Ahead lay Ebbetts Pass, the longest and highest pass on the ride.

Chapter 27

Monitor Creek

Monitor Creek drains out of Heenan Lake and into the East Fork of the Carson River on the other side of the road where Highway 4 from Ebbetts Pass meets Highway 89 from Monitor Pass.

Highway 4 from Angels Camp to Monitor Creek was taken over by the State in 1911 and named Alpine State Highway. In 1925, it was renamed as the Ebbetts Pass Highway and designated as forest highway 35 under the Federal Highway System. State renumbering eventually took over in the mid-1960s.

Highway 4 begins just west of Interstate 80 at San Pablo Avenue, once State Highway 40, opposite San Pablo Bay, in the town named for the Hercules Gunpowder Company and continues as the John Muir Parkway and past Muir's former residence and across the breadth of California to its eastern termination at Monitor Creek.

The area's first gold and silver mine, Targish Mine, was up Monitor Creek, founded in 1857, a year before the Silver King Mountain silver strike, which changed everything. (The Targish Mountains are part of the Sahara region).

Saturday, part 2

Lina, Bethy and Carlos started the climb up the east side of Monitor Pass together. As they proceeded, the amount of bikers approaching downhill began to thin out, indicating the tail end of the ride. Most of the five-passers had already made the turnaround and were part of the extended migration uphill of the three.

When Lina started edging ahead, Carlos pulled alongside Bethy, talking to her, trying to give her a boost. "Carlos," she gasped. "I can't make conversation."

He paused, seeking a topic to distract her. "Can I tell you more about my daughters?"

"I know all about your daughters already," she said, breathing heavily. "Tell me about growing up in Spain. Anything, everything. Just don't make me have to talk."

He got the message, telling her about growing up in his village, close to Oviedo; how his father was a plant foreman for a tool factory; how his family never traveled and considered going to the ocean to be an epic trip even though it was only less than twenty miles away. He did not mention the fights he used to get into, thereby avoiding discussing the one that sent him to Madrid.

When they got to the water stop with the boys running in football jerseys, she received her bottle, biked around the bend and pulled off the road in the shade to drink. They both were sweating in the heat, she more than he was. "I don't know, Carlos," she said in exasperation. "This is not for me." He didn't know quite what to do. A few moments later, gathering her resolve, she stated, "Ok, onto Madrid. You were young and studly, I presume."

"That wasn't the case," he said solemnly, beginning to talk about Madrid as they continued, grinding up long switchbacks. He told her how he worked menial jobs and lived alone, basically intimidated by women. It was a different side of him than she had imagined, so unlike her philandering husband Henry. Side by side, Carlos was so much stronger than she was, breathing more easily and able to tell her many things about himself.

When they finally reached the rest stop on top, Bethy worried that he was losing too much time with her and should hurry on. But Carlos stayed at her side as they went to the food tables. Sitting in the shade of a van to eat, she again repeated her concern for him and again Carlos refused to leave her.

They departed the Monitor rest stop around 11 am, descending alongside other riders, most of whom didn't seem like five-pass candidates to begin with. At the bottom, they turned left, following the highway alongside the Carson River towards Ebbetts Pass.

The Wolf Creek Road lunch stop at Centerville Flat was still being set up across the road for the eventual arrival of the downhill riders as the two came upon it. They were pedaling moderately fast on the fairly level road when Bethy veered at the fork over to the stop. One of the volunteers told her that they weren't quite ready yet. Drawing a deep breath, she let Carlos know she was done and was going to head back to Markleeville.

"I'll go back with you," Carlos told her. He gazed into her face. She was tired, sweaty, serene, dark-haired, brown-eyed, vulnerable, resolute and beautiful.

"No, you've done enough already. I don't have any problem getting back. It's mostly downhill," she pleaded. It didn't matter, he insisted and he refused to go on. "Are you trying to make me feel so guilty that I continue? Remember, I'm the psychoanalyst here."

"I've had a good day already and don't need all five passes to make it complete. I'd much rather be with you."

"Until just now, I didn't think you've been even glad that I was along."

"I thought about you all night long," Carlos told her. "When we were sleeping, the ride barely crossed my mind."

"And that restaurant woman?"

Carlos peered over her head at the pine trees and then gazed into her eyes. "That was something left over from Spain."

Not quite convinced of anything except that she was too beat to go on, Bethy turned around and headed back toward Markleeville with Carlos behind her, as they followed the river downstream to Hangman's Bridge, then over the ridge into town. Turning at the Wolf Creek Restaurant and Bar, they casually rode to the house, quiet and welcoming in the midday sun.

No one was home and Boston's car was gone, used by Katherine to drive with Irina to Carson City. "That hot tub might feel good," Bethy hinted. For once they were alone, in a neutral house, and, she thought importantly for Carlos, he had chosen to now be with her rather than be assigned.

Taking off their helmets and shoes, they both went upstairs to the room they had just shared. "Just think," Bethy began, standing as she took off her socks, "seven hours ago, we both got into our biking clothes, not knowing what we'd run into. Are you sure you're ok with not riding?" He replied that he was as he sat on the bed, studying her as she unzipped and pulled off her jersey and her bra. "You have to get undressed," she told him. He quickly yanked off his jersey but nothing else. "Are we even going to the hot tub?" she asked.

"We'll see."

She pulled down her biking shorts, standing there naked while he eased back onto the bed until his head. "Let me help you," she said, taking hold of his shorts and tugging them off. He moved to the side, allowing space for her.

Alongside him, she thought, "Out of all mornings and places, we are here in bed, in Markleeville on a day that was supposed to have been wholly devoted to agonizing bike riding."

When she put her hand on his chest, he suddenly got up, surprising her as he walked over to his things to take from his trousers a little cellophane square that he tore open, then brought back to the bed. Without having to ask, she wondered if he had acquired the protection before or after Gardnerville, but ultimately she didn't care. What she didn't know was that he taken a couple extra from Carla. He said nothing about it, nor did she, knowing that it saved her from having to take from her purse what she had brought along as well, just in case.

From then on, Bethy turned over the control to Carlos. For a moment, she appreciated that there had been someone else in between herself and his ex-wife. Then she no longer thought anything about it as his body took over.

—

Carlos later woke to the sound of Irina coming upstairs and going next door into the master bedroom. With Bethy stretched out asleep, he left the bedroom and went downstairs bare-chested in his shorts, finding Katherine in the kitchen. "What, are you done already?" she asked, surprised. "What happened?"

Carlos explained that he quit early after doing both sides of Monitor Pass. When Katherine expressed surprise, he told her, "This way, Ebbetts and Carson are still out there for me." She replied that she still didn't get it. "In the town where I grew up," Carlos continued, "the coast was only twenty miles away. My father didn't like to travel, not even that short distance, so we hardly ever went but when we did, it was this big production. The family would plan for months. I think Hannibal had a less trouble crossing the Alps. Whenever we got there, which wasn't often, it never quite measured up to our preparations."

"But Carlos, all that training and no finish?"

Before he could answer, Irina popped into the kitchen stating that someone was in the hall shower before she noticed Carlos. Seeing him, she correctly guessed out loud that the other person in the house was Bethy. "Carlos," Katherine began, turning to him, "you didn't say that Bethy also quit early. Now I think I understand." Carlos said nothing while Irina only smiled.

Katherine paused, tilting her head at him. "So, Carlos, we were going into town to cheer on the rest of our group coming through. You guys want to join us? I'll drive."

"I'll go ask Bethy." Leaving the room, he bounded upstairs. Knocking on the bathroom door without reply, he entered the steamy room where Bethy was still showering.

"Are you joining me?" she asked.

"Katherine and Irina are here. They're going to watch the riders going through town and asked if we wanted to go along."

She pulled back the shower curtain just enough to stick out her head. "Can you stand seeing everyone riding by?"

"No problem."

"Are you sure? Did you give up too much for just a roll in the hay?"

"What's a 'roll in the hay' mean?"

She laughed. "Are you teasing me, Carlos?" He shook his head no. "Okay, let's go but first get in here with me." Dropping his shorts, he climbed into the narrow shower.

Downstairs, Katherine and Irina conversed over what they presumed had happened. "Can you believe the only sex around here is between the unmarried couples?" Irina asked.

"What else is new?" Katherine smirked.

Chapter 28

Ebbetts Pass

Ebbetts Pass is the highest point on Highway 4, which begins near San Francisco Bay, winds through the Sacramento River Delta into Stockton, then across the Central Valley, through the Gold Country foothills into the Sierra, past the Bear Valley ski area where it narrows beside Lake Alpine until it finally breaches the crest at 8730 feet before descending along Silver Creek to its terminal at the Highway 89 junction to Monitor Pass to the south and Markleeville to the northeast.

Major John Ebbetts led a group of gold rush prospectors along an Indian trail over an eastern Sierra pass in the April of 1850. With little snow that year, he kept the pass in mind as he later hoped to promote a transcontinental railroad route and was hired by the Atlantic and Pacific Railroad Company to gather a survey crew to scout the route. In 1854, before he could accomplish the survey, the self-proclaimed major was killed in a boiler explosion while on board during a highly touted steamboat race on San Pablo Bay. It is probable that Ebbetts did not even go over the pass that now bears his name but rather crossed over what was called Border Ruffians Pass north of Hermit Valley on the western flank of Jeff Davis Peak. The pass was once the main route from South Lake Tahoe and Carson River Valley through Hope Valley to Hermit Valley and west to Murphys, Angels Camp and finally Stockton.

The Border Ruffians were pro-slavers from Missouri who terrorized neighboring residents favoring a "Free State" during the Bloody Kansas violence of the mid-1850s, culminating in the destruction of Lawrence and the retaliation brought by abolitionist John Brown.

A wagon road was not even built to Hermit Valley over the pass named by the Missouri-sympathizers into Hope Valley until two years after Ebbetts' death. The road was financed by merchants from Murphys in order to accelerate commerce with the Carson River Valley on the eastern side of the Sierra. A stopover called Holden Station was built in Hermit Valley. The discovery of silver at Silver Creek in 1858 led to miners creating their own trail over what is now called Ebbetts Pass, which eventually had a road completed with State funds in 1866. Tolls were collected in Hermit Valley as Holden Station became a hotel serving a settlement of 400 voters and its own post office.

Ebbetts' name was not associated with his namesake pass until the United States Geologic Survey published a map in 1893, at which time Border Ruffian Pass had long been supplanted by a more direct route to the booming silver mines surrounding Silver City. Major Ebbetts was remembered as having once endorsing a mountain pass crossing in the area and so it was named.

Two miles westward on Ebbetts Pass Road from the Highway 89 turn to Monitor Pass, Wolf Creek Road enters from the left. The river along the road is actually the East Fork of the Carson River, with Wolf Creek being a tributary. The level area here was once the site of Centerville, located in the former heart of the Silver Creek Mining District, with Silver Hill nearby. Alpine County once had 15,000 people living in Centerville and Silver Mountain City, which was further uphill along now Highway 4 following Silver Creek.

In another three miles on the right are several buildings and a sign posted as Scossa's Cow Camp, named for a homesteader Joseph Scossa. Just west on the left is a marker identifying the former site of the town of Silver Mountain City, originally named Kongsberg, by a group of Norwegian prospectors around 1860 after a town in the home country, famous for its silver mines. Silver Mountain City was renamed was elected in 1864 by residents as the first county seat of Alpine County. When the United States quit the silver standard in 1873, the silver boom abruptly died. The Silver Mountain City post office, once served by Snowshoe Thomson, closed shortly thereafter and the county seat moved to Markleeville in 1875.

Thompson's "snowshoes" were actually long skis. The local Norwegians use to stage ski-jumping contests in town. While living in Silver Mountain City, Thomson served on the Alpine County Board of Supervisors from 1868 to 1872. He died from pneumonia following appendicitis at age 49 in 1876.

Originally hired in 1867 by London investors who formed a mining company, Lewis Chalmers purchased the Isabella Mine, built himself a mansion and wound up marrying his housekeeper. Adjusting to his good life, he became known locally as Lord Chamlers. A last ditch attempt to find more ore at his mine failed in 1885 and he returned to London, seeking more financing but died still overseas, leaving wife and baby daughter forced to abandon their home. By 1886, Silver Mountain City was completely deserted. The tall, isolated chimney alongside the former Chalmer mansion is what's left of his mine's stamp mill

Locked in the mountains, Alpine County remains the least populated county in the state, with a population around 1200. The county seat was moved to Markleeville to be more accessible from both Lake Tahoe and Nevada's Carson River Valley while the town became a Mecca for fishermen and hunters on the east side of the Sierra. The county's largest real estate development, Bear Valley, lies across the range's summit and is cut-off every winter by snow, which can even blanket the town during heavy years.

To the south is Silver Peak, at 10,774 feet, highly visible from the Monitor Pass and Markleeville area. Highland Peak to the west is a little higher at 10,934 feet. The peaks on the north side of Highway 4 are somewhat lower, including the volcanic knob called Ebbetts Peak at 9160 feet, overlooking the highway.

Going west from the Silver Mountain City site, the highway climbs abruptly and then passes a campground on the right with a snow gate just beyond. From here the road has sharp turns and beautiful views of the Silver Peak and Highland Peak as well as the Silver Creek Valley. Amidst a steep section, a bridge crosses Upper Cascade Creek, before entering a section of aspens with a break in grade. Ahead is Kinney Reservoir, named for a former resident of Silver Mountain City. Climbing to the left of the shining lake, the highway winds past the Pacific Crest Trail parking lot, with brown-rock Ebbetts Peak visible, and begins a final steep pitch as the top of Ebbetts Pass at 8630 feet is reached.

From there the road descends six miles to Hermit Valley, just over a thousand feet lower. The valley is a large flat around 7000 feet, with a campground scattered amongst the pines on one side of the highway and, on the other side, a gentle stream that later becomes the North Fork of the Mokelumne River.

The Death Ride route turns around in Hermit Valley to return 1200 feet up Ebbetts Pass, the shortest and fourth climb of the ride.

Saturday, part 3

Bert was surprised to see a rest stop along the lower section of Ebbetts Pass Road and would have not minded halting there. Being still early in the mid-morning, the stop was not yet well attended by bikers. However, in front, Raymond barreled past it. Staying with Raymond since the top of the first morning climb up Monitor Pass, Bert had kept up with his heady pace. On the return trip up the back of Monitor, they had halted at the top for only just a minute, long enough to fill their water bottles and grab a piece of fruit.

That second Monitor climb having drained him, Bert knew that he could have rested at the stop longer. At least he partially recovered on the fast descent with its cool breeze and drop in altitude. Rejuvenated by the time the two reached the turn onto Ebbetts Pass Road, Bert continued at top speed on the gradual grade alongside the river, side by side with Raymond, as they neared the rustic buildings of Scossa's, where the two passed up the water and food stop.

Past by a tall chimney ruin, the road suddenly steepened, requiring most bikers to stand in the pedals. Pushing hard up the long incline, Bert felt his knees cramp for the first time ever, causing him to sit on the bike's saddle and grind his way up. The steep section quickly crested out and he recovered as they neared the entrance to a campground with a few spectators by the road. Still, he worried about the surprised cramping.

Just beyond the campground was a sharp right hand turn requiring them both to stand again. As soon as Bert did, his knees cramped up again and he was forced to sit back down a second time. Raymond edged slightly ahead but remained close by. The road leveled slightly at a concrete road bridge marked as crossing Upper Cascade Creek. It was sunny and hot. Starting across the bridge, Bert called out to Raymond that he was stopping and halted in the middle of the short span. Raymond also got off his bike.

Bert explained that he had never had this happen to him before. Both men took big drinks of water. Starting once again, the climb resumed just as steep on the other side of the bridge but then the road dipped down for a short section for a temporary recovery. Ahead, someone shouted "rider" just before a bicyclist zipped by going the other way, downhill in the shadow of the cliff.

As the road continued its constant ascent, rounding the hillside, holding tight against a cliff, Raymond began to get farther and farther ahead on the relentless climb. Bert could only watch him go. It could not be much further to the top, he figured, but he was exhausted, realizing he had gone too fast on too little water and food, normally not a problem for him but he did not usually ride at 8000 feet.

Stopping by a large reservoir to take another drink from a now almost empty water bottle, Bert took off once more for the top, climbing past the lake, passing the Pacific Crest Trail parking lot on the left as he now faced at an uphill wall of roadway. He wasn't going to stand but then he had to, going slower than usual. His knee muscles held firm for a while but then they knotted, forcing him to sit and struggle with the last grade, seeing the crest just ahead, barely close enough for him to struggle up it.

The top was very crowded, mostly with bikers headed west to Hermit Valley but now also with several coming up the summit from the other side. A young girl placed a third pass sticker on the number sheet pinned to this back. Hot and exhausted, Bert felt that staying at altitude would make him feel worse. The descent was fast, which was ominous for the return trip, but at least he could coast down. At the bottom, the road continued to roll out with no stop in sight.

Finally he coasted into the rest stop where another set of volunteers applied fourth pass stickers. The only way out of Hermit Valley to Markleeville was back up Ebbetts Pass

Feeling the day's heat on the small valley floor, Bert left his bike on the shoulder and found the shade of a pine tree. Sitting for a moment, he then laid on his back, breathing hard, resting. Raymond soon found him and sat alongside, offering Bert a slice of watermelon.

Accepting it, Bert sighed, "I think I've used everything up already."

"You'll get a second wind," Raymond told him.

"I sure as hell hope so."

Raymond sat beside him for a while then took off on his bike to meet with Lina, whom he figured must be coming up the front of Ebbetts by now.

Bert felt recovered enough to get something to eat from the food tables, where he downed some fruit and a Coke. As he returned toward his pine tree, he saw Erik, Caitlin and Boston arrive. After he called to them, they walked their bikes over his way and parked them on the ground. Caitlin's cheeks were bright red but she didn't look as tired as he felt.

"I got my pine tree over there," he said, pointing to his spot in the shade.

"Raymond called out to us going the other way," Boston told him. "He seemed strong."

"We rode together up until the top of Ebbetts. Then I started cramping," Bert announced, glancing at Caitlin for her reaction.

"That doesn't sound like you," she frowned.

"It's gotten much hotter since Monitor," Erik added, his open shirt dangling from his shoulders. "My system's working perfectly."

Erik and Boston headed toward the food tables. "Will you wait?" Caitlin asked as she began to follow Boston. Bert answered yes and went back to his tree.

While he and Erik were sitting in the shade, a male biker approached them. "Hey, remember me?" he asked, taking off his sunglasses. "Erwin from Chicago. We met at dinner. How's it going?"

It took a moment for Bert to recognize him. He then explained to the 60-year-old Midwesterner about his difficulties. Erwin empathized with him, adding, "I'll say one thing. Biking in Chicago heat got me prepared for the weather here today even if there aren't any hills back home. The hookers are about the same, though. That bartender really set me up well last night. Lyud-whatever her name is was worth every penny."

Ignoring the hooker story, Bert laid back, his head resting on his helmet. My life's come down to this, he thought, fifty-years-old, totally beat with only a bike to get me out of this god-forsaken Hermit Valley. How am I ever going to bike back out of here?

"Lyudmila," Erik said. "That's the name of the Ukrainian at the Pigeon Coop."

"She flew the Coop last night, buddy," Erwin chuckled. "Tonight, too, if I survive this damn ride."

Meanwhile, Caitlin loaded up a plate of watermelon slices for Bert. "Is he going to make it?" she asked Boston, who was getting his own rinds.

Boston was no longer sure of anything. "We've all trained for this," he said. Looking around, he saw all types of bikers, most of them pretty well exhausted but still of good spirit. "It's a big ride and Bert's a big dog," was all he added.

—

Descending from Ebbetts Pass, Raymond intercepted Lina on her uphill a short distance above the Upper Cascade Creek bridge. She admitted struggling in the heat but said she was determined to keep going. He told her that she wasn't too far behind the others, but also added that she could also ride down with him if she wanted to turn back. "I might regret it, but I'll keep going. I want to make the top of Ebbetts at least once," she told him. He told her not to push herself too hard while she, in turn, urged him to stay strong.

When Lina reached the summit, she immediately started down the back without stopping for refreshments. About a mile from the top, she heard her name called. Noticing a group of four plodding uphill, she recognized Caitlin amongst three male riders and shouted back. Speeding downhill to the bottom, she got her fourth pass sticker and something to eat. She knew she would have to leave shortly to keep on track to beat the time cut-offs.

When Raymond got to Centerville Flat, the lunch stop was just getting crowded, mostly by two and three-pass riders. The afternoon heat sapped the air even in the shade. He grabbed some food at the tables, quickly reaching in between people lined up, and then took off for Markleeville. In a moment, he had pedaled into a hot headwind blowing upstream in the river valley, which offset the road's downhill trend. Still, he felt strong and overtook all other riders he saw on the road, usually drafting for about a few seconds just to get a respite from the wind before passing.

Meanwhile, the backside return up Ebbetts for Boston's group was slow with hardly any shade on the southerly facing slope. Erik gained distance on Boston as Caitlin and Bert slipped even further back. Wilting in the heat, whenever he tried to stand, Bert's knees cramped again. He finally had to stop for a breather, something Caitlin had never seen him do before. When they reached the Ebbetts top once more, both being woozy in the heat and elevation, they decided to descend right away.

Erik and Boston had earlier paused briefly on the Ebbetts Pass crest, with the second crossing counting as the fourth pass, though to Boston it didn't feel as if they were four-fifths of the way through the ride. He had also lost energy coming up the backside but was relieved the worst of Ebbetts was over. So far the ride had been all that he had expected and hoped he had some reserves left.

Starting down from Ebbetts, Erik felt amazingly energized, anticipating a thrilling descent. He told himself that he was no longer the French musketeer d'Artagnan but was now a full-fledged Viking with his bike as his battle-axe. Amongst a steady flow of downhill bikers, he was one of the fastest, choosing strategic sections where to pass. Coming to the sharp curve just before the campground, he braked hard and heard a snap as his front wheel began to wobble. Frantically trying to keep control, he slowed down enough to guide the bike off the pavement into the gritty shoulder. Balancing the twisting bike, he was able to stay in control without falling. Once stopped, taking a deep breath, he saw that his front wheel was crumpled, bent so that it could no longer go through the brake pads and that one of his spokes was completely sheared off.

That meant his ride was over and he was stranded in place on Ebbetts Pass Road. He carried his bike across the road to where some ride spectators were sitting in lawn chairs, having observed his near spill with concern. Passing by just as Erik was moving off the road, Boston barely got a glimpse of the Icelander before he could slow down and turn around.

Returning uphill, Boston examined the trashed wheel and agreed that it was ruined. One of the men in the chairs said he would like to give Erik a ride but the road was closed to cars until 3 pm. Another male biker slowed to a stop. Erik explained that he was ok but his bike was done. The biker said he would tell the crew at Scossa's to send up an official support vehicle to pick him up.

Bert and Caitlin soon came by, rounding the sharp curve as they spotted Erik and Boston. Stopping to find out what was wrong, they crossed the road. Bert looked beat. Erik explained about his wheel and told them that an official vehicle was mostly likely soon coming for him. "Take my bike," Bert told him. "I'm suffering." He swung his leg over the frame and leaned over the seat, seeming totally defeated.

"I can't do that," Erik said. "You'll recover on the downhill."

"You'll feel better," Caitlin assured him. "You've never let me quit."

"Yes I did. Around Calaveras Reservoir, you sat there while I went for the car."

"That's because I had heat stroke," she argued. "I was puking. We have a nice long downhill back to Markleeville. You'll be ok."

Bert straightened up and took a deep breath. "I'm too wasted to argue about it. Fine," he told her as he got his water bottle. "I guess you're snake bit today, Icelander."

"Not your fault, don't worry about it," Erik returned.

"We should wait until your ride gets here," Caitlin hesitated. "Have you seen Bethy or Carlos?" They both shook their heads no.

Boston had figured to see Carlos along with Bethy shortly after Lina passed by going down to Hermit Valley. But for now, he was more concerned about Bert's condition. With Erik breaking down, Carlos missing and Bert weakening, Boston sensed the group's defeat, something he had not expected.

Knowing that the hard climbs were over for a while, Boston led Caitlin and Bert as they left Erik by the side of the road. As they descended, a support motorcycle soon arrived. Placing one hand around the motorcyclist and one holding onto his bike, Erik hopped on.

The motorcycle passed by Bert, Caitlin and Boston and dropped off Erik at the lunch stop. Soon all four of them were together again. After searching Bethy and Carlos, Caitlin expressed worry at not having passed them anywhere on Ebbetts Pass Road. Boston guessed that the two could have been off the highway at one of the other stops. As Bert seemed somewhat recovered due to the shaded, easy downhill grade, Boston indicated they should keep moving to stay on schedule. Reluctantly, they abandoned Erik once more.

The motorcyclist had returned to Scossa's, leaving Erik to seek out somebody else to take him into Markleeville. Finally, he was told that the driver of a GMC Yukon support vehicle was coming down the hill and could take him soon. Getting out the remaining russet potato from his jersey pocket, Erik sat off to the side, watching riders pour into the stop. He felt that the fates had worked to knock him off the team. His food and water intake had been working as had his open shirt system of heat control. It was as if something from the long Icelandic wintry nights had reached out and caught him.

He had never expected his Cannondale to fail, but it was the wheel, not the frame, that had broken down. In any case, his group had departed and he was left by himself, off the team. The Yukon soon arrived. A handful of volunteers from Scossa's got out and Erik put his damaged bike on the rack in back before climbing into the front passenger seat for his helpless lift back to Markleeville.

Chapter 29

Markleeville

In 1861, five months to the day after the start of the Civil War on the East Coast at Ft. Sumter, Jacob Marklee settled in what he thought was Douglas County, Nevada jurisdiction on land near the booming Silver and Monitor mining districts. He built his cabin on a rise adjacent to a deep Sierra creek. A year later, he filed a claim for 160 acres only to have the survey reveal that his property was in California. Building a bridge over his creek, he created a toll road that was used mainly by miners going back and forth from Lake Tahoe and Nevada to the silver rush area along Silver Creek, a tributary of the East Fork of the Carson River several miles to the south.

Marklee was killed in a gunfight in 1863. His assailant was found not guilty for reasons of self-defense. A settlement formed at his vacant property. Although never as populated as Silver Mountain City, the new village got less snow and was more accessible than the larger mining town in the pine trees. With lumber and agriculture providing the local economy instead of the crashed silver market, Markleeville replaced Silver Mountain as the county seat in 1875. The county courthouse was built where Marklee's cabin had been. Both the town and little creek below were given his name as well.

During another murder trial years later, the county judge ruled that the town was so prejudiced due to all the eyewitnesses that the defendant would have to be taken to neighboring Mono County for impartiality. Fearing that the cost of sponsoring a trial so far away would bankrupt the county, a group chased after the prisoner being escorted out of town, catching up with him near the Carson River Bridge where they hung him, apparently validating the judge's basis for approving the change of venue motion.

Saturday, part 4

Sitting in a tree-shade on the green courthouse lawn, Katherine, Irina, Bethy and Carlos all watched the Death Ride bicyclists streaming by on Markleeville's main street. It was around 1 pm and frying pan hot without breeze in the little pocket of town. Eating sandwiches, they watched for the remaining biking members of their group.

They didn't recognize Raymond but he spotted them, giving a big wave and stopping. Setting his bike aside, Raymond was surprised to see Carlos and Bethy there, rested and changed out of their bike clothes. Carlos explained that after they had completed both Monitor climbs, they simply decided not to bike the rest of the way.

Katherine offered Raymond a cold sports drink from the ice chest Carlos had carried over. "How's Lina doing?" she asked.

"She was going up Ebbetts while I was going down," Raymond said, sipping from the plastic bottle. "Ebbetts was tough. Not as hot as it is here, though. What is it, about a hundred?"

"Ninety-something," Katherine answered. "And Boston?"

Raymond mentioned that he saw Boston with Erik, Bert and Caitlin going down the backside of Ebbetts Pass for about two seconds as he was going up. Bert, Raymond continued, had seemed a little exhausted after their hard push this morning. But, he added, the worst was pretty much over and he expected Bert to recover on the run in back to Markleeville.

Downing the cold drink, Raymond said he would meet everyone at the Turtle Rock Park finish and rejoined the flow going northward on Highway 89 toward Woodfords.

—

No one else of the group biked by for the next hour. A large Yukon pulled up alongside the courthouse blocking the view of the spectators of the riders. From the passenger's seat, Erik called out to the four on the hill. The vehicle then pulled forward to a better parking spot as Irina got up and ran over to Erik, who was getting out. He appeared unhurt and healthy as he retrieved his bike from the van's rear.

After letting Irina know he was fine, Erik thanked the driver and hoisted his disabled bike over his shoulder, following her to the group on the lawn. Carlos inquired about the damaged wheel. As Erik explained, he suddenly wondered what Carlos was doing there.

After going through again why he and Bethy had quit early and why stopping did not matter to him, Carlos then offered the use of his bike to Erik. The Icelander refused, stating he had quit the ride.

"Did you officially quit?" Carlos asked. Erik shook his head no. Carlos continued, "Have you missed any passes?" Again, Erik shook his head.

Getting up, Carlos checked out the number slip on Erik's back. "You have four stickers. Why not finish the ride? My bike is just sitting there back at the cabin."

Irina interrupted. "Maybe the broken wheel was some kind of sign that it's not your day. Don't temp fate, Erik."

Carlos disagreed. "No need to let a mechanical failure stop you. We've all trained so hard for this."

"It's true that nobody's given me a ride uphill," Erik added. "I could still do the fifth pass in good conscience."

"Your bike is broken. We have the whole rest of the afternoon together," Irina argued. "Quit this thing. Lake Tahoe's not very far away. We could get a nice supper on the lake."

Erik looked at her. "I really feel like riding. It's what we all set out to do."

"Carlos had the sense to stop," Irina said sternly, pointing to the Spaniard. "He's spending the day with Bethy and they've not been married for twenty years like we've been."

Erik shook his head no. "I want to ride. Carlos, I accept your offer."

Carlos turned to Katherine who tossed him the keys to her Expedition, thereby earning Irina's glare. Without looking at her, Katherine shrugged as she knew that Irina's argument had been made and lost. Carlos asked Bethy if she wanted to ride along but Bethy declined, staying in case Caitlin arrived.

When Carlos returned, he announced that Erik was already on the road, which made Irina even madder that her husband had not come back by, undoubtedly because she was still upset at his continuing the ride.

Slightly past 2:30 pm, Caitlin arrived along with Boston following and Bert last. Bethy rushed down to roadside to greet them. Getting off their bikes, all three looked much sweatier and redder than Raymond had been an hour and half earlier. They dragged themselves up the courthouse slope and flopped onto the grass.

Boston asked Carlos what had happened. "It was always your ride, Boston," Carlos said. "Bethy and I don't need to do all five passes."

"Missed you out there," Bert told him, flopping onto the lawn. "We needed the Spanish Armada to give us a draft."

Caitlin also sat down on the grass, holding her sports drink. 'It's just so damn hot."

Katherine handed her husband a cold bottle, seeing him taking deep breaths. "Are you all right?"

"Yes," Boston said, still standing.

"I'm not," Bert mumbled, also taking a sports drink from Katherine. "I'm fried," he muttered, staring up at the sky, weary.

"No, Bert," Caitlin pleaded. "You've got lots left, more than you think. Rough and Ready, right?"

"Boiled and plucked," he responded trying to kid, face still hidden.

"Where's Erik?" Boston asked, looking around.

"I gave him my bike," Carlos stated. "At least my bike might do Carson."

"How're we doing on time?" Caitlin asked Boston.

"We have a little over a hour to get to Woodfords. It's only seven miles away."

"Ok, Bert, you can do it," Caitlin said, offering her cold sports drink.

Bert was even too tired to take a sip so she placed the cold plastic against his forehead. "I'm done," he told her. "You have to go without me. It was all I could do to bike up past the bridge and that was nothing. I'll never even make the three-mile uphill to Turtle Rock." Slowly sitting up, he finally took a long drink.

"You're all crazy," Irina told him. "You'll all kill yourselves."

Ignoring her, Bert looked to Caitlin. "You better get going soon. I just pushed myself too hard and now I feel like shit. I can't even take a deep breath. Go do it for both of us."

"Com'on, buddy," Boston began. "Aren't you supposed to be Doc Holliday to my Wyatt Earp?"

Bert smiled wanly, "Remember how Doc begged Wyatt to leaved from his death bed?" Suddenly he got on his side and vomited. Katherine handed him napkins when he was done. For a moment, it seemed like he might just fall face first into his own mess. Wiping his mouth, he kept his head lowered. "Actually I feel better now," he joked softly.

"Good enough to ride?" Caitlin asked.

"You don't quit, that's good. You and Boston go."

Caitlin turned to Bethy, "Take care of him. I hate going on like this."

"It's too hot," Bethy answered.

Katherine suddenly spoke up, "You should all just stop right now. We can go pick up Erik and have a good dinner tonight knowing everybody's safe." When Boston gazed at her, she knew that such good sense would be unheeded. "Why push your luck?" she continued. "Bethy's the smartest one of the whole lot. Six months from now you won't even remember this damn ride."

Boston scooted over next to her and put his arm around her. "Don't say anything," she told him as her eyes began to get weepy.

"You better get going," Bert softly reminded Caitlin.

Caitlin stood up, walked over and kissed him on the forehead. "I'd give you a real kiss but you still have stuff on your lips."

"True love?" he grinned.

She bent down and kissed him, then wiped her mouth. "Yuck. True love."

Taking off his yellow Lance Armstrong wristband, he handed it to her. "Take this up Carson for me. See you at Turtle Rock with your five pass pin." Reluctantly, Caitlin took it as she headed down the grassy slope to her bike.

Boston stood while Katherine stayed seated. "If you get overheated, you can stop," she told him.

"Don't worry." He bent down and kissed her. Then he looked to the other two guys.

"You can do it," Carlos told him. "Just one more."

"Go get 'em, Wyatt," Bert waved, grinning and giving Caitlin a wink as well.

It wasn't supposed to be like this, thought Boston. These were the two men with whom he had ridden for years. The big dogs are gone, he told himself. Meanwhile, out there somewhere, Raymond and now Erik, both much better uphillers than he was, were still pursuing the course. Weary but rehydrated, he got on his bike and rejoined the ride once more, trailed by the young, former UCLA women's team rider.

Katherine watched him leave while both furious at him and worried. Irina meanwhile sat fuming. Nudged by Bethy, Carlos got up to get soft drinks from the close by store.

"True love," Bert silently mouthed to Carlos as the Spaniard left.

Spotting him miming the words, Katherine sat next to him. "Making fun of love, Bert?" she quietly accused him.

"I can't believe she took me up on it and kissed me," he briefly grinned then changed tone seeing Katherine's seriousness.

"Do your kids know you're dating a twenty year old?" Katherine asked him. Bert started to say "twenty-six" but didn't as Irina got up from the lawn and left. Katherine went with her as both women set off walking along the highway edge toward no particular destination.

Past the edge of town, Boston stopped to call his partner while he still had cell phone service. Only getting Larry's voice mail, Boston left another message, wondering once more about the status of the sale.

As Carlos was still at the Markleeville store, Bethy sat with Bert on the lawn, watching the riders passing by, figuring that Lina should be coming by soon.

"You know, about a month ago my daughter Jackie called me from New York," started Bert, speaking to Bethy sitting alongside. "She's twenty-four, hardly ever discusses her boyfriends with me. But this time she told me that she was starting to date a guy who was forty and asked me what I thought. Her brother Michael, who's only a year older than she is, was dead set against it."

"So what did you tell her?" Bethy asked.

"First I asked if she knew for sure if he was married or not and she said not."

"Did you tell her about you and Caitlin?"

"No. I simply said it was probably ok."

"You're not only hypocritical but you're also withholding, you know?"

"You're not the only psychoanalyst here, don't forget," Bert reminded her.

"You know my girlfriend, your biking girlfriend, has already had her heart broken and by her child's father no less."

"She may still love him for all I know," Bert offered, gazing out over the constant line of riders being cheered on by the spectators aligning Markleeville's main street. Then he admitted, "She asked me if I loved her. Before I could say anything, she told me not to answer."

Bethy paused, then asked, "Did you cramp up on purpose just to send her on her way?"

Bert fell back on the grass, laying his forearm across his closed eyes. "That's a professional question, I presume."

"Is that your professional answer? When this ride's over, then what?" She asked but he just lay there, silent and still. Keeping it to herself, she also wondered the same about her relationship with Carlos.

—

Meanwhile, slowly and patiently, Lina had made the six-mile return climb out of Hermit Valley, then hurried over the top, knowing she was running late. Prepared to blow past the Centerville Flat lunch stop, she halted anyway, out of fuel and out of energy, surrounded by riders mostly resigned to abandoning after four passes, eighty mile into the ride with another ten left to get to Turtle Rock. Eating something but to not much effect, she then left the pine trees for the open road, pedaling wearily alongside the hot and windy river canyon, alone without any other riders within sight, making arduous progress.

She realized all the others were ahead, except for Bethy and Carlos, whom she last saw going up Monitor and assumed had quit since she hadn't seen them after the turnaround. Her thoughts scrambled around, anything for a distraction. The scenery was nice enough but it passed so slowly. Anyway, she had signed herself and Raymond up not for the view but to prove she was the same woman as before giving birth. Her elastic waistband tugged at the scar tissue left from the caesarean, the spandex stretched over the extra fifteen pounds she still carried.

None of her biking mattered to her family. Her two sisters had succumbed to significant weight increases from having birthed multiple babies each. Her mother had refused to hear about anything having to do with biking in streets, much less something called the Death Ride. Having been raised in a generation and culture where women were not athletic, her father thought of her as a tomboy. Certainly Raymond was supportive but he was so strong on the bike that she constantly worried she was holding him back. All the previous suitors in her life had possessed less strength and will than she did, except for the college English professor, whom her family liked but never really got. Having registered for this ride to whip herself into shape, she wondered where her husband was, realizing that he must be miles and hours ahead.

Alone, she thought of her son Zack, having dedicated the day's effort in an attempt to him and his birth although she never actually experienced any of the childbirth, except for the surgical healing afterwards. She also realized that her three-year-old son had no awareness or interest if she did the ride or not. Exhausted, she felt she belonged at home with her son instead of on the desiccated highways of Alpine County.

Crossing the sign identifying Hangman's Bridge over the Carson River, she barely made it up the slope curving around the ridge. Once over the shaded bridge spanning Markleeville Creek, she heard people on the courthouse lawn calling to her and then spotting a group of three. Stopping, she took a deep breath. Without a watch, Lina still knew she must be very short on time for making it to Woodfords. Her butt hurt, her crotch was sore, and her arms ached from supporting her upper body while standing in the pedals. If she got off her bike, she felt that she might not get back on it.

Scanning the lawn, she was surprised to see Carlos and Bethy dressed in regular clothes but she noticed Bert in biking clothes lying on his back, his head resting on his helmet, taken off and used as a pillow. Reluctantly, she got off the bike but did not feel like even pushing it up the hill. Bethy came down the hill, bringing her a cold soft drink.

Lina briefly thanked her and said that she had better get going. Sitting up, Bert called out, "It's late. It's 3:45."

"I can still make Woodfords by 4," Lina stated.

"No you can't. It's seven miles and three are uphill."

"It's a state highway. They can't stop me."

"Then it's five miles, all uphill to Picketts Junction."

"I'll still be under the 5:15 cut-off," she said.

"No you won't," Bert replied. "From there, it's nine miles to the top of Carson. The rest stop will be closed with nobody handing out fifth past stickers. Then it's twenty miles in the dusk back to Turtle Rock."

Looking to Bert, Lina's eyes began to well up. Why did it have to be him telling her this? "It's my goal," she said in a hushed voice. "After having Zack, I told myself I could do this."

"You pretty much did," Bethy softly answered her.

"This was my one thing I did for myself. I don't even work anymore," she was weeping. "I'm sorry I'm crying."

Wet-eyed, Bethy gave Lina a big hug. "You did have to choose the toughest ride. You got twice as far as I did."

"It's no problem for Raymond," she sobbed on Bethy's shoulder.

"He didn't have a caesarean either," Bethy responded.

Bert slowly got up, walked down the lawn and stood alongside her. "You got as far as I did. You only ran out of time. I ran out of energy."

Lina sipped from the drink, tears receding. "Tell you the truth, so have I. But I don't want to quit."

Bert then suggested that they ride up to the finish at Turtle Rock Park, only three miles away. He stated that he was feeling a little better, at least well enough to make it and, after all, it would give Lina a chance to ride into the finish, even without doing the fifth pass.

Lina looked up the road. All those miles spent training dissipated before her in the sweltering afternoon, thinking that of all people, it would have to be Bert willing to accompany her to the end, unlike how he wormed out of their relationship. She was too tired to be angry with him and picturing her three-year-old son Zack did not help overcome her fatigue. Just the thought of restarting deflated her. "I guess it'll be as close to finishing as I'll get."

Bert put his helmet and gloves back on. He asked Carlos to drive his Silverado to Turtle Rock Park. Stiffly, he got on the bike and started out of town with Lina behind him. Motioning for her to pass him, he followed her along the dry gulch the led up toward Turtle Rock. Coming in with Lina was not how he expected to finish today's ride either, especially with Caitlin out there somewhere.

Wanting her husband to successfully complete the ride, Lina wished he were here with her for this last stretch. Zack was home, Raymond was far up ahead and she was disconnected in the middle of this boiling town. Nothing to do now but focus on Bert's wheel and the pavement in front of her. Trudging along, Lina asked, "Where's Caitlin?"

"Ahead," Bert sighed back over his shoulder.

Walking back to the lawn, Katherine and Irina had been surprised to see Bert riding by once more, then followed by Lina. Returning to the lawn, the two women gathered up Bethy and Carlos for the return drive to the cabin.

Back at the rental unit, while Carlos went to find the keys to Bert's truck. Katherine took Bethy aside and told her that she and Irina were going to spend the night at Lake Tahoe. When Bethy asked why, Katherine explained at they both had cabin fever, that Irina had never seen the lake and that everybody was going to be all exciting talking about the ride tonight, which was driving both of them crazy.

Bethy felt obligated to talk her into changing her mind. "Look," Katherine told her. "You did it the right way. A little tough riding and then taking it easy with Carlos. He really cares for you."

"Boston really cares for you, too," Bethy told her.

"I know," Katherine answered. "I know he does. Tell him, I'll be back in the morning. Please tell Erik, too, that Irina is also spending the night at the lake."

Carlos meanwhile found the keys and went out to the Silverado. He was surprised to see Irina coming through the garage with her suitcase, which she put in the Expedition, followed shortly by Katherine also putting her luggage inside. Last out of the house, Bethy got in next to Carlos. Without knowing what was happening and unwilling to ask, the Spaniard started up his vehicle as did Katherine. They caravanned away from the cabin and eventually out to the highway, the shoulders of which now consisted of bikers straggling back to Turtle Rock Park, having surrendered any hopes of completing all five passes.

Chapter 30

Picketts Junction

Picketts Junction is at the T-intersection of Highway 89, connecting to South Lake Tahoe, and Highway 88 running past from Carson Pass into Nevada. There was once a stage stop there called Pickett Place owned by Edward Pickett. South of the highway is a 9118-foot mountain named Pickett Peak.

The junction lies in the large basin called Hope Valley, named in 1848 by Mormons returning to Salt Lake City. Nearby Faith and Charity Valleys were named by surveyors in 1855 in keeping with the theme.

The original Pony Express route was rerouted at the junction to South Lake Tahoe through Luther Pass, which had been identified in 1852 by Ira Luther, recently arrived in California two years previously. Wagons first made it over the pass in 1854. For several years, the Death Ride used a Luther Pass climb up and back as the fourth pass.

The narrow canyon of the West Fork of the Carson River pretty much allows only one route between the Carson River Valley in Nevada and the Hope Valley where the Carson Pass and Luther Pass roads converge.

Saturday, part 5

The ride out of Markleeville southward to Turtle Rock Park was a hot metronomic rolling of the pedals. Boston led out Caitlin not for drafting purposes—it being too slow for that—but to take her mind off the heat and fatigue, giving her nothing to concentrate on but following. As the road rose out of town, he was soon drafting others, finding a string of riders going just a little slower than he had been, but fast enough.

The road finally leveled as it neared Turtle Rock Park. With cars parked on both shoulders along the highway, they were suddenly opposite the entrance, which was lined with supporters cheering the steady flow going north to Woodfords while they also noisily greeted the first individuals completing the ride coming from the other direction.

Whether it was encouraged by seeing the finish that was in their future or cresting out at the top of the climb by the park or both, Caitlin revived and passed Boston with a smile as they started on a long, straight downhill. Tucking into an aerodynamic position, Boston soon overtook her. The rest of the run toward Woodfords was mostly downhill and they rolled swiftly along.

Boston focused on a rider climbing up the other direction, admiring that the rider was almost at the park finish, separated from them by about thirty feet of asphalt and thirty miles in distance to be covered. He seemed fit and determined, as Boston expected from an early finisher. As they approached Highway 88, two more riders appeared. Halting at the highway stop sign, they could see more descending from the west.

Across the highway, a carnival mood was in full celebration at the Woodfords rest stop, located next to the store in a shaded bypass road called Old Pony Express Way, fronting some cabins and a fire station. The riders here were exclusively those chasing after all five-passes. It was about 3:30, almost ten hours since most riders had left early in the morning. Boston and Caitlin stopped briefly to grab from the snack table providing melon slices, pretzels, cookies and the like. Both also topped out a single water bottle, just enough additional weight to cover five miles until the next stop at Picketts.

Caitlin motioned that she wanted to go without any more delay and he agreed, feeling somewhat revived from the recent downhill. In front of the fire station was a mist tent for bikers, through which they both rode, getting doused with a fine spray. Leaving the little street and its pine-tree shade, they rejoined the highway, breaking back into sunlight and a hot, dry headwind from their direction to the west. The benefits of the mist didn't last long as they cut into the breeze.

The pitch of the highway actually dipped for a short distance, allowing them to mentally reset for the climb to come. On both sides were the steep sides of the tree-lined canyon. To the left was another road named Crystal Springs that snaked into a grove of pine trees shading several cabins. Comparing it to the hot highway, Boston was tempted to detour to it but was unsure of its course. Instead, he continued as the highway climbed slightly up the mountain sideslope. Soon the other end of Crystal Springs Road came into view, which meant that they could have detoured only through a quarter mile of shade.

More and more riders began appearing on the other, downhill side of the road, so much so that Boston quit paying attention to them. Instead, he focused ahead as the road pitched upwards. Suddenly from the other side, he heard a yell. Quickly turning his head, he saw a speeding rider briefly make a short wave before getting his hand back on the bar. Caitlin asked him who it was and he guessed Raymond, headed back after doing Carson Pass.

As they started the serious climbing, Boston never thought that he could be forced to go so slowly on something that did not look all that tough. It was so hot with the wind squeezed between the canyon slopes. Looking back over his shoulder, he saw that Caitlin was still right behind him.

Ahead on the right, he noticed a side road dipping through the trees. As he neared, he saw a narrow bridge over the river. Too cotton-mouthed to say anything, he signaled to Caitlin that he was veering off. He turned down the paved side road, seemingly a former stretch of highway, with a sign stating it was a dead end. Caitlin followed him, stopping as he did in the shade of the trees at one side of the bridge while Boston bent over his handlebars with a big gasp.

"I'm burning up," Caitlin told him. Removing her helmet, she ran a hand through her soaking hair.

"Me, too," he replied, taking a big sip of water.

"Give me your shirt," she told him.

Too tired to even ask why, he took off his helmet and handed her his jersey. Parking her bike against the bridge railing, she took his jersey and slid down the dirt and rock bank to the side of the stream. As Boston watched from above, she took off her own jersey and, now bare-chested, soaked them both in the water. Holding them up, she squeezed water down upon her head, splashing over her topless upper body. Then she soaked them again. Upstream, Boston noticed two teenage boys stopping their fly-fishing. With both shirts in one hand, Caitlin climbed back up the tall bank and handed Boston his shirt.

Putting on the freezing cold shirt startled him but it felt great, especially on his aching muscles. "Good idea," he complimented her. "You missed a couple boys fishing who also enjoyed it."

Caitlin squealed as she put hers on. "No, I didn't," she smiled. "Let's go."

Dripping wet, they restarted. The road continued climbing, passing the Kit Carson Campground, while the upper canyon finally appeared to be opening. The highway curved steeply to the left around a rocky slope before crossing another river bridge, over which they both stood to pedal. As the road leveled on the other side, there was a little store on the left with a small crowd cheering them on. With the road still climbing, but less than before, they passed the charming cabins of Sorenson's Resort, also on the left and also with people rooting them on.

The whole world seemed to open up now with a high, wide valley on their right. The wind was less constrained now, making it less forceful. Their previously soaked shirts were now barely moist. Ahead, they could finally see the rest stop tents with volunteers and bikers milling around.

—

Raymond had spotted Boston and Caitlin toiling uphill where he had been two hours ago. Going too fast to take a hand off his bars to wave, he had merely yelled and wasn't sure if they had recognized him. Focusing back on the road ahead, he instantly saw a car turning left from the highway onto the side road, directly in front of him. Without much time to brake, he shouted while directly staring into an driver's face, seeing the old man's eyelids open wide

—

Driving Bert's truck with Bethy, Carlos turned into Turtle Rock Park while Katherine and Irina continued north, now with bikers on both sides of the road.

When Lina and Bert arrived by bike at Turtle Rock Park, talk was circulating already about a bicyclist critically injured in the Highway 88 canyon above Woodfords. Not thinking much of it as she searched the finish area for Raymond, Lina heard her name being paged. Reporting to the race office, she was told about there had been a car accident involving her husband and that he had been taken by ambulance to Carson-Tahoe Hospital in Carson City, some 35 miles awake. He was conscious, the race director said, and had no apparent head injuries but had broken his arm, his collarbone and several ribs.

Lina desperately wanted to get to Carson City as soon as possible. With her car back at Markleeville, Lina turned to Bert, who agreed to accompany her if they could get a ride. As they went with a ride volunteer to the parking lot, they met Bethy and Carlos, who had just arrived. A distraught Lina told them what had happened and Carlos tossed Bert the keys to the Silverado. Bethy stayed at the park in case the others showed while Carlos rode in the back seat so he could return with the truck.

A few minutes later, with two bikes on the truck's bike rack, the Silverado sped back to the cabin where they quickly loaded Raymond and Lina's luggage and sleeping bags into the Pathfinder. Lina could have cared less about her bike, which Carlos unloaded along with Bert's. Waiting until they were ready to leave, the Spaniard followed in the Silverado until Turtle Rock Park, where he turned left. Bert and Lina continued in the Pathfinder to Woodfords, passing riders on both sides of the highway until turning right, away from the Death Ride and toward Carson City.

Around a half mile in the opposite direction to the left was the scene of the accident, with the smashed car pulled off the main highway along with the crumpled bicycle. Earlier, Katherine and Irina had driven past it on their way to South Lake Tahoe.

"That's another reason to avoid this biking," Irina stated at the time, shaking her head, and pulling out her cell phone.

"Who're you calling?" Katherine asked.

"Dennis," she replied.

Katherine started to say something but thought she would wait until the end of the phone call. By that time, Lina had already invited Dennis to come join them in South Lake Tahoe, wherever they might wind up.

Before Katherine could comment on that, she noticed Boston and Caitlin pulling into the last rest stop, located a little ways before the right hand turn onto Highway 89 toward Tahoe. Without even honking, she just kept driving.

Seeing the Expedition go by, Boston assumed that this wife was headed up to Carson Pass to see his arrival of the fifth and last pass.

—

Volunteers at Picketts Junction offered to take their bikes, which Boston and Caitlin numbly surrendered. The last rest stop had all the feeling of an emergency aid station, with several lawn chairs strung out underneath a canvas tent canopy. Boston got himself and Caitlin each a Coke. Grabbing a couple cookies, he found an empty chair. His mouth, even after taking a swing, was too dry to swallow the cookie and he tossed it over his shoulder into the grassland. Sitting next to him, Caitlin brought him a slice of watermelon, which he could down.

Though the volunteers were chatty, the tired bikers were not. It was a little past 4:30, less than forty-five minutes before the time cutoff. "I feel like burying my head in that ice chest," Caitlin told him, rolling her eyes. "That wet jersey really helped me. I was getting light headed."

A middle-aged female volunteer asked Boston if he wanted her to fill his water bottle. He told her sure but the water came back lukewarm. Still, he drank it but didn't know how much it could hydrate him at this stage. At least the Coke had sugar and caffeine to kick in.

"I can't believe I'm here and Bert's not," Caitlin said to him. "The heat's not my thing and he usually has no problem."

"All we have is one more pass," Boston said. "Eight or nine more miles."

"Nine," said the male biker slumped in the chair next to him. "And I'm still not convinced I can make it." He appeared to be in his mid-forties, like Boston, balding with his remaining hair plastered down by sweat.

"I didn't come this far not to finish," Caitlin told him. Looking to the west, still with sun high, she commented that it did not look so steep ahead.

"It's not," the biker informed her, adding, "At least not for a while."

—

"I appreciate this," Lina told Bert, breaking the silence as the car cruised past the Carson Valley pastures, now in the early evening shadows of the tall Sierra escarpment. Bert replied that he was happy to help. Lina continued, "I mean, I was really pissed at you and I moved on. But then you came back in my life and now are driving me in our car. How do you explain that?"

"I was an asshole," he admitted. "Now, I'm doing a good thing. That's pretty much how my life has gone. Most of the time, I'm a strong biker, today I sucked."

"And today my husband smacks into a car," Lina responded, staring out the window in sudden dismay.

Bert could tell that she was weeping. He stayed quiet, not having driven Lina Rodriguez anywhere since the night he took her back to his place and they had sex. That moment long ago was always on his mind ever since he had met her again, even now. He did not know what they would find at the hospital and if were just broken bones, as they had been told, then everyone could count their blessings. He wanted Raymond to be all right, Lina to be happy and himself get back to Caitlin, whom he decided, driving in the middle of Carson Valley, that he did truly love.

—

Putting away her cell phone, Irina told Katherine that Dennis was coming up. "I guess we'll need a room," she commented.

"Are we staying the night?" Katherine asked, driving up the short incline to Luther Pass.

"Well, I don't expect Dennis to drive four hours just for a cocktail."

"Have you really thought this out? When you don't return tonight, what's Erik going to say?"

"I think it's too late for him to say anything," Irina answered. "What's Boston going to say?"

"I'm not the one staying with my lover."

"Your ex-lover of not too long ago, don't forget."

Katherine certainly had not forgotten. She anticipated having a nice dinner, some nice wine, then returning to a worried husband.

"I brought the massage oil," Irina stated. "Maybe Dennis can do us both? Massage I mean."

"You are some crazy Cossack," Katherine smiled.

"It's what Erik use to love about me," Irina responded.

Chapter 31

Carson Pass

In February, 1844, scout Kit Carson guided US Army lieutenant John C. Fremont and his expedition south from eastern Oregon into the what later was named for him as the Carson River Valley, keeping now the great Eastern Sierra escarpment on the right or western side. It was now mid-winter and cold with snow on the grasslands they rode horses through with snow capping the impassible mountains. The Indian villages they met along the way were settled in for the long season with barely enough food based on generations of experience to see them through. Fremont, age 31, judged that their only chance of survival was to push through he mountains into the Sacramento Valley due west.

Christopher Carson was 33 years old. Some thirteen years before, he had been the young kid on an exploration that came and went through Southern California, making it up to San Francisco Bay as far as Mission San Jose, now located in the city named Fremont. Grown into an experienced, tough mountain man, he and the Army lieutenant listened to Indians telling them that a winter crossing of the mountains was impossible. But to stay where they were or continue wandering south was out of the question. They decided to follow the river upstream into the mountains, on the same route now traced by Highway 88. It was not so difficult at first. Dealing with a narrow canyon, they broke out into the broad span of what is now Hope Valley. Continuing west, Carson led them up to the Sierra crest and carved his name and year into a pine tree on top: Kit Carson 1844.

Eager to get his bearings, Fremont wanted to climb on the nearby peaks. Accompanying him, Carson spotted far to the west the prominent rise of twin-peaked Mt. Diablo, which he easily recognized from his time over a decade ago in the East Bay. From their lookout, Fremont also saw a huge lake to the north.

They had climbed up to the divide of the Truckee River, which they had crossed near what is now Reno, and the lake below was later named Tahoe.

Not without extreme hardship, the expedition made it through the mountains and to Sutter's Fort in the Sacramento Valley. Fremont and his party left California later in the year but he and Carson returned in 1845, again in force, as both were factors in the revolt that created the Bear Flag Republic and then in the subsequent conflict between the United States and local Mexican forces.

Both Fremont and Carson were Union generals during the Civil War, with Carson also being made the Military Governor of New Mexico. Carson City, the capital of Nevada, is located beside the river bearing his name along the route he scouted leading up the pass he pioneered.

Saturday, part 6

Erik Erikksson biked up to a rock cliff that finally shielded him from the steady headwind. Curving to the left, the road reached the cliff's shadow, providing relief from the high altitude sun. Just now, he finally allowed himself to accept that he was going to complete the fifth pass climb.

An hour earlier, sitting at the Picketts Junction rest stop, he had not been sure he could reach the top, even though there was only nine miles left. Food and drink didn't replace the energy used in the Woodfords Canyon climb. But, passing the Highway 89 turn-off to South Lake Tahoe, the road continued forgivingly flat into the distance. He knew he could spin out level miles, even into the headwind. When two strong thirty-year-old males passed him, Erik sped up and caught them, latching onto their draft. Feeling better after being protected, he even took a turn at the front, which they seemed to appreciate as he matched their pace.

At a turn-off to Blue Lakes to the left, the road steepened. The two younger riders gradually pulled away from him. Shirt flapping open, Erik was not in a hurry and let them go, settling into a stroke-by-stroke repetition which carried him up the inevitable slopes toward a daunting rock-wall cliff.

Rounding past that cliff, he broke once again into bright sunshine and strong westward breeze. Riders who had already turned around, descended on the other side of the road called out encouragement, shouting to the cresting bikers that they were almost there. Passing an elevation sign and an official ride photographer taking photos, Erik could see the crowded rest stop ahead.

Gliding downhill, he slowly gained the fifth pass finish area, approaching along with spectators congratulating the weary pedalers. Soon a woman was placing a sticker on his back, telling him what a good job he had done while someone else offered to take his bike but he held onto it, walking alongside it, not wanting to release that which had faithfully carried him to the top. Putting it down in the open parking lot next to other bikes, he sat, sipping the warm fluid inside his water bottle. A seven-year-old girl took an Eskimo Pie out of a box and held it out for him. Taking it, he unwrapped it and put his dry mouth over the cold chocolate. The taste rippled inside him.

To the east, Boston and Caitlin were once more on their bikes, passing the Highway 89 intersection, pointed into the wind with Boston leading. Caitlin appreciated having his larger body to tuck behind. Individual riders and groups of riders occasionally passed them, but she didn't feel she could go faster and was happy with Boston's pace. Her concentration was solely focused on his back wheel. Peripherally, she allowed herself glances right and left but it all seemed to be mountains and more mountains. She just wanted to get through this.

Boston would have liked to draft someone, but the riders he overtook on his right were too slow and the ones passing him on the left were too fast. The sublime grade stayed consistent until the left-side Blue Lakes turn off, at which point the highway tipped upwards. The increase in grade sucked out what was left in his legs. In his lowest gear, following Caitlin, he crawled up the hill.

Each pedal stroke seemed a chore to him now, his body drained of any re-energizing fluid while his legs kept repeating the constant piston action. He knew the top would arrive if he just kept at it but the simple motion of pedaling was becoming the hardest physical thing he had ever done. His concentration narrowed on Caitlin's tight bottom that swayed back and forth with each leg extension as her back bent forward, presenting him with a view of tight spandex cheeks which he used to disassociate from the revolving monotony.

When the road leveled off, he thought he would pass her but she stayed ahead. There were more inclines, a sign on the left to Red Lake, and then a large sweeping curve to the left with a long guard rail on the right traversing openly to the northern mountain slope, exposing them to a warm crosswind sweeping into the valley on their right.

The road was surprisingly steep at this guardrail bend and he felt his legs slowing. Ahead were two bikers stopped at a small dirt drive-off area just beyond the end of the rail where the road turned left once again. With a last bit of energy, he sped up to pull alongside Caitlin. "Want to take a break there?" he asked.

"If I stop, I'll never get started again," she replied.

He felt he had to halt before his legs quit on him and so pulled over, standing over his bike as we watched her continue around the turn. Other bicyclists passed by and Caitlin became another rider in the long line rolling toward the rock cliff.

Getting off his bike, he noticed a tall man and a smaller woman standing farther off the road, next to their bikes on the ground. The woman, with long red-hair in a pony tail, looked at him for a moment, then turned and disappeared into the group of big fir trees. Meanwhile, the tall man came over to him, speaking in a thick Italian accent, and asked him in broken English how far it was to the top.

Turning toward the cliff to the west, Boston told him it was just around the corner. Then, he asked him where he was from. "Milano," the rider answered.

Boston nodded with a grin, then got off his bike to have one more gel packet, his last one. As he sat on the ground, the woman came back out of the trees. "That's better," she said, very American. "Ready to go, Carlo?"

"We're close," he said, pointing to the rock-wall. The man appeared to be about mid-thirties while the woman was maybe fifty.

"Cool," she said, picking up her bike as he picked up his and they were gone.

As Boston watched them leave, coming downhill, Erik suddenly crossed over the road and came over to him. "Hey," the Icelander called out, stopping, "no sitting down on the job."

Boston smiled, looking up at him, and congratulated him on doing all five passes. Ecstatic, Erik then mentioned that he noticed Caitlin walking ahead but that he was going too fast to stop. Standing, Boston said he would see him at Turtle Rock, then got on his bike as the Icelander crossed back over the road and resumed his downhill glide around the right-hand curve.

Revived with his rest, Boston started out with a little burst, but soon the relentless uphill brought him back to his drudging pace. Ahead, he could see Caitlin walking on the shoulder. While passing, the redheaded woman appeared to say something to her, but Caitlin waived her on. Soon, Boston was beside her. "Hey," he called, "what's up?"

"Hi," she said, hot, flustered. "I got a flat and I'm whipped. I wanted to cool off before fixing it."

She stopped as Boston got off his bike. They were almost at the shade of the cliff where the road turned left. He offered to take care of it, which she appreciated and accepted. They walked together to the turn's wide shoulder. Getting her front wheel off, he sat in the dirt with his plastic tire irons and patch kit. Sitting down next to him, she sipped from her water bottle watching him. "I hate fixing flats. I'm so glad you're here." She paused. "How could I make it this far and not Bert?" Boston continued working on the tire. "Think I should stay with him? You do know we've been sleeping together, don't you?"

Boston was applying the patch now. "Don't tell me any secrets."

"Doesn't Bert talk about me?"

"Bert's very discrete."

"Bert?" she asked. "You're kidding. Well, maybe I'm not that big a thing for him. Why should I be? He's fifty for God's sake. A son and a daughter about my age."

Boston was holding the patch tightly, letting the glue apply. "He hasn't talked about you to me but anybody can see you two are close. That hasn't changed from that first hot tub in the rain."

"I love the hot tub and I love everyone being naked."

"Like I said, don't give away any secrets."

"What secrets?" she smiled.

Nodding distractedly, Boston stood up and took the wheel over to her bike. "He did ask once if I thought you were still in love with your daughter's father."

Caitlin gasped. "When was that? What did you tell him?"

"It was months ago and I never got the chance to answer. It's none of my business."

"He's never asked me that," she continued. "I've never talked about Mandy's father with him either. I should." Seeing Boston was done with her tire, she stood. "The top of Carson Pass might have been a good place to sort it out, if he had made it."

Having taken several minutes to deal with the flats, they started out again, both feeling better than they had been before the stop. Boston began leading Caitlin but then he waved for her to pass him. Happily, she zipped by, leading with the rock-wall on their right.

He realized that making the fifth pass was beyond doubt now, knowing from his previous drive that it was around the cliff as long as he simply kept pedaling. Though the official Turtle Rock ending was twenty miles back the way they had come, Carson was the real finish, the fifth and last pass. The standard question put to any rider admitting to doing the Death Ride was, "Did you do all five?"

Out of the shade rounding the cliff, he watched Caitlin bike ahead past the summit's elevation sign and the official ride photographer, to whom he gave a big smile as they started the gradual descent to the welcome party at the Carson Pass rest stop. I did the Death Ride, he told himself, suddenly elated. I did the Death Ride. I did the Death Ride, over and over again.

Turning into the parking lot, Boston expected to see Katherine cheering for him. As the fifth pass stickers were applied, he didn't spot her or Irina. Putting down his bike, he took off his helmet.

Caitlin appeared with two Eskimo Pies and handed him one. "I don't see Bert up here," she told him. "I guess we have to congratulate each other." Then she leaned forward, wrapped her arm around his shoulders and gave him a kiss on the lips. "And then there were two," she commented.

Boston gazed about the Carson Pass mountains, seeing the shadows starting to lengthen. "After this ice cream, we should head back," he told her.

She slowly did a 360, taking in the complete scene. "We did it," she told him. "You got me up here."

Nodding in agreement, he studied her. What began as the Four Horsemen was now just this twenty-six-year old woman and himself.

Soon, they were back on their bikes, rounding the rock-wall corner and gaining speed on the descent in the shadow of the cliff, bikes wobbling on the rough pavement. The surrounding peaks still caught the sunlight. As Caitlin zoomed ahead, Boston maintained a moderate speed, observing a lake down low on his right that he had either not noticed or forgotten on the long climb up.

"I did the Death Ride," he exclaimed out loud for the first time.

—

Boston caught up with Caitlin over the level grade before the Highway 89 turn and the ensuing steep bobsled run through the canyon to Woodfords, now completely in shadows. She took off faster again but this time he stayed close behind her, duplicating her moves. With his heavier weight, he easily overtook her near the bottom, seeing a few burned out flares where Raymond's accident had been but no other indication of the collision.

As the two of them raced by, they missed seeing the damaged BMC bike leaning against a pine tree, a short distance from the road, left there for the owner to retrieve on another day.

Headlights were on by the time the two make the turn toward Turtle Rock Park. Elated with their success, they overtook other riders wearily pedaling back to the finish. Caitlin kept repeating how amazed she was that she completed all five passes, recounting her demise months ago on the Mt. Hamilton climb.

Listening, happy for her and tremendously pleased with his own effort, Boston kept waiting for the Expedition to return from wherever Katherine had taken it earlier in the afternoon. Cars now were driving with their lights on as the two began the last hill climb to the park's entrance, around 7:30 pm, closing in on the end of a long day.

Chapter 32

Turtle Rock

Turtle Rock is the name of the campground at the Death Ride registration, start and finish site. It is a name symbolic of the Native American way of life. Turtle Island is a synonym for North America, as it existed prior to the arrival of Europeans, of which one, Amerigo Vespucci, added his name to the bottom of a map, guiding the way, however imprecisely, for an inter-continental wave of migration.

Saturday, part 7

Bethy was waiting for the two as Caitlin and Boston turned into the Turtle Rock Park entrance. Appearing unexpectedly grim, she explained what had happened to Raymond. She went on to repeat what Bert phoned to her from the hospital. Raymond was awake off and on, and was pretty groggy from painkillers. Lina was at his side and planned to check into a motel but was too exhausted for any visitors tonight, maybe tomorrow, Bethy continued.

When Boston asked where Katherine was, Bethy explained that she and Irina had gone to Lake Tahoe, adding that she had also informed Erik, who was inside eating spaghetti inside. She suggesting that if they wanted a quick bite, then she and Carlos would drive everyone to the cabin before going to Carson City to get Bert. With their mood subdued, Caitlin and Boston followed Bethy, walking their bikes up to the finish area where they picked up their five-pass pins before entering the cafeteria.

Getting their plates of spaghetti and salad, the two sat next to Erik, Carlos and Bethy. Any enthusiasm they might have shared about completing the five passes was gone. Erik mentioned arriving on top of Carson Pass just as Raymond was leaving. "He didn't seem even that winded," Erik noted. "Definitely the strongest rider in our group."

"Are accidents destiny or bad luck?" Carlos questioned. "I'm never sure which."

"I figure bad luck," Boston answered, "Whatever went wrong, probably five seconds either way could have avoided it."

"That's exactly why I think it might be destiny," Carlos replied.

"Doing the Death Ride might be destiny," Erik joined in. "What happens during the ride is whatever happens. I get a broken wheel, bad luck, but I don't crash. Raymond on a perfectly good bike gets hit by a car, also bad luck, terribly bad luck."

Bethy spoke up, "I don't believe in either. I think terms like destiny or luck means that you just didn't see it coming." She was going to say like her marriage to Henry but let it pass.

"Wasn't it lucky that Bert could drive her there?" Caitlin piped up. "I mean, pretty amazing isn't it that her old boyfriend was available to be her hero?" Caitlin's face had a slight frown, accentuated by all the road grime and sunscreen for the day's ordeal.

"Now that would be good luck," Erik responded. Nobody else said anything, waiting to see if he was being sarcastic but apparently not.

Erwin, the sixty-year-old from Chicago, came over to their table with his own plate of food. Asking first to sit with them, he let out a sigh. "What a day. How did everyone do?" Boston explained that their friend got hit by a car on the descent from Carson Pass. Erwin said that he had heard about the accident and inquired about the extent of the injuries. They told him that it seemed that just broken bones were involved. "Knock on wood, I guess any one of us could have wound up like your friend at any time," he stated. "You guys going down to the Wolf Creek tonight? I'd like to buy you a round." No one in the group expressed an interest. "Actually," he confessed, "I need a ride. I'm staying at the Toll Station."

"I think Bert's truck can take four bikes," Carlos spoke up. Erwin thanked him as he quickly finished his meal so as to not hold them up.

As they waited, Boston's phone rang. Expecting it to be Katherine, he saw Larry's name on his cell phone screen.

—

Though there was a faint purplish glow in the west, the night sky was lit with stars as Bert's Silverado, driven by Carlos, dropped off Erik, Caitlin and Boston, along with their bikes, at the cabin after first letting Erwin off in town. With Bethy alongside, Carlos then headed off toward Carson City, some forty-five minutes away.

Alone with just Erik and Boston, Caitlin said that she had been thinking about the hot tub all day. Erik declined, stating that he was going to take a quick shower and then go have a drink with Erwin back in Markleeville.

Caitlin remained at the bottom of the stairs, stating that she was going to rinse off before dipping into hot tub. She welcomed Boston to join her and if so, would he please get a bottle and glasses for both of them, after his shower of course. Then she turned and went upstairs, much more slowly than Erik, who had preceded her.

At this point, Boston realized that he could either ride with Erik the few miles into town for a round of drinks, which he didn't really need, or lie down with a glass of wine waiting for Katherine to return, if she was returning tonight; or, third option, enjoy a soak with Caitlin, with whom he had partnered four out of the five climbs, including the all important concluding one up Carson Pass. He chose the latter and ducked into his downstairs shower for a quick rinse.

While showering, he dwelled on the phone call he had received. His partner Larry had told him that all the details were now concluded. The new owners would close the office and pay all the debts. From the office staff, they were only interested in one of the young engineers. The survey crew would be cut loose. Everyone let go would be given two weeks pay. Finally, they had decided not to hire Boston for a month. In essence, the two partners would close their business on Monday and spend the rest of the week preparing all files to be transferred to the new owners. As worn as he was from the ride, the news had drained what remaining energy he had left. He could have stayed an hour in the shower had not the even more relaxing hot tub been waiting.

Dressed in just a towel, he went to the kitchen as Erik came down the stairs, said goodbye and took Highlander toward town. Boston got a chilled bottle of white wine from the refrigerator, two glasses from the cabinets, and was in the hot tub a few moments before Caitlin appeared. With the towel wrapped only around her waist, backlit by the house lights, she walked out onto the deck area. Draping the towel over the back of a chair, she carefully entered the steaming water, slowly settling in until the water reached just below her neck. "I see Erik took off already. I guess it's just you and me, Wyatt," she told him.

"I guess so," he replied, pouring her a glass of wine.

Crossing the tub to receive the wine, she then sat next to him, her hip touching his in the narrow seat. "Here's to Carson Pass," she cheered, waiting with her glass for him to tap with his, which he was still pouring. When they finally toasted each other and had a sip, she put down her glass on the side of the tub. Then she took his glass and placed it aside as well.

"I don't think my little kiss on Carson Pass was sufficient thanks for all you did today," she murmured to him. Before he could say anything, she lifted her arms over his shoulders and leaned forward. Pressing her breasts against his chest, she began her kiss, which included the tip of her tongue parting his lips.

As the kiss ended, she broke away, turned to get her wine and said to the sky, "I can't believe that I did the Death Ride." Then she took a big sip of wine. "Of course, I'm sorry for Raymond but I'm so happy. You and I can celebrate, can't we? We accomplished so much today. Let's talk about the ride, pass by pass." As she started recounting the day, her hand rested on this thigh, which she continued to squeeze during her reverie.

Listening to her, Boston marveled that out of a full house this morning, the evening has just distilled down to the two of them. Of all that had occurred today, he remembered most her standing topless in the cold mountain stream, an indefatigable smile on her face as the sunlight shone on her small breasts. As she went back to her wine, he said, "I think you soaking my shirt in the stream saved me." It was a flirtatious line and he knew it.

"I know we don't belong together," she noted. "But I am so pleased that I just have to share it. Unfortunately or fortunately, you're the only one here, team leader." Putting down her glass again, she put one arm around his shoulder and kissed him again, taking his hand and placing it on her nipple.

Touching her naked chest above the waterline, he was enthralled with her and debated whether or not to share his other news. After all, there was no one else to tell.

"My company was sold today."

"Two reasons to celebrate," she grinned and draped her leg over his. Opening her leg, she added, "Does doing the Death Ride give us a free pass?" Leaning her head back, she kissed him again. Underwater, his hand drifted. She touched his face.

With his other hand, he took up his glass, staring at the night sky.

—

From a bar atop the Harrah's Casino overlooking the cobalt-blue lake, Katherine and Irina watched the sun set over the snow-topped mountain peaks to the west. "It's so beautiful," Irina said. "Why hasn't Erik ever taken me here, I wonder."

"Do you think Dennis is going to take you to Lake Tahoe ever?" Katherine asked.

"Don't be a wet blanket. He's coming here tonight, isn't he?"

"Is he?"

"Of course, he is," Irina replied. "And to tell you the truth, I'm also surprised. It's a long way. Maybe he really does like me."

Katherine was not really surprised but for other reasons. She knew how Dennis could be very accommodating in the early part of a relationship. After all, he had built a whole lap pool for her, although it also wound up as an attraction for the self-named Crowe's Nest. "I just don't want you to make a big mistake."

"I'm through making mistakes," Irina responded, finishing the last of her martini. "Let's get some wine and find a motel where we can wait for him." Putting down some cash, Irina paid the bar bill as Katherine left behind some of her drink.

They purchased a bottle of wine before pulled into the 7 Seas Inn, one block off Stateline Boulevard, where Irina ordered one room with twin queen beds. They had not discussed the sleeping arrangements but Katherine had no intention of staying in the same room with Irina and Dennis bedded alongside. Irina signed for the room. Leaving the luggage in the Expedition for now, they took in just the bottle. Taking the shrink-wrap off two plastic cups, Irina filled them with wine. Katherine was reminded of their very recent night in Stockton, beginning the same way only the wine was drunk while they were both in bed naked under the covers.

Now sitting in a dingy room holding a plastic cup with Dennis most likely on the way, this night just felt different to her. "I'm thinking about going back to Markleeville," she announced. "You can always come with me. Let Dennis stay by himself. He'll survive."

"I don't know if I will," Irina smiled, sipping her wine. "Are you serious? Won't you be getting your own room?" Katherine did not commit but did not drink any more wine either. She did not try to talk Irina into leaving and Irina did not attempt to convince her to stay. Instead, the two women sat across from each other and, for lack of any other topic, discussed ongoing and upcoming projects.

Irina was on her second glass when Dennis knocked on the door. She gave him a kiss whereas Katherine just said hi. After telling them how cozy they looked and obviously noticing the two beds, Dennis said he was starving. Irina responded that Harrah's was within walking distance for dinner. That sounded good to him.

At that point, Katherine said she was heading back to Markleeville. Unable to convince her to stay, they both expressed disappointment in her leaving and walked her out into the parking lot. Her Expedition was parked next to a new Ford Freestyle. When Katherine turned to Dennis, he gave her a sheepish shrug.

As she drove to the main boulevard, she looked east toward all the bright neon of the Nevada casinos, then turned right and to the west, passing the No Vacancy signs of the California motels. With each increasing distance from the state line itself, she was glad to be getting away. Once past the end of the cobalt-blue lake and cruising alongside thickets of pine trees, she felt as if she could wind up anywhere as she stared out at snow-topped mountains to the west.

Out there was any number of towns, so she wondered why she now thought of Stockton and Boston's ex-wife Shannon, who had met them for breakfast, so sweet and settled in her new life. Turning south onto Highway 89, the ride was beautiful, past a few cabins until the scenery was all dark, except for occasional meadows reflecting the night sky. She knew she was going back to Markleeville, her choice.

—

Carlos and Bethy found Bert in the waiting room, still in his bike clothes and reading a magazine. He took them to Raymond's hospital room where they met Lina, also still in her biking outfit, watching her husband who was asleep with a tube stuck in his arm, draining a clear solution. He was propped up against several pillows and had his arm in a cast and sling with a thick wrap over this collarbone.

Seeing the group, Lina gave a smile and then her eyes began welling up. Outside the door, she began to sob. Nearest to her, Carlos put his arm around her. "I feel like such a fool," Lina cried. "I wanted to do this ride for my son Zack and," she hesitated, losing her voice mid-sentence, then continued, "and Raymond almost gets killed."

"These things happen," Carlos told her. "Luckily, he'll be okay."

"He was just doing it for me," she lifted her head, then lowered it on his shoulder.

Carlos began to speak again but Bethy just shook her head for him not to. Let her cry, she thought. What can we tell her that she doesn't know already?

When the crying began to abate, Bethy said, "Thank goodness he's going to be all right."

Withdrawing from Carlos and wiping her eyes, Lina replied, "I'm so grateful that he's okay."

"Raymond last seemed in pretty good spirits actually," Bert stated. "He joked it was all that Eskimo Pie's fault. If he hadn't eaten it on top of Carson, he would have been further downhill when that old man pulled out." Lina smiled, confirming that Raymond's comment, on morphine of course.

Though she told him it wasn't necessary, Bert drove her to the nearest motel where he helped her check in and then all three escorted her to her room. Thanking them, she said that they were welcome to come by tomorrow but she would understand if they drove straight home instead. Each of the three expressed coming by.

As Carlos and Bethy returned to Bert's Silverado, she took Bert aside. "Thank you so much," she told him, adding, "As far as I'm concerned, the slate's clean."

"Just clean?" he asked with a wink.

"No," she smiled. "The slate's in good shape. You better get back home to that pretty little blonde."

Handing her the car keys to the Pathfinder, he blew her a kiss and then hurried off to his truck where he hopped in the driver's seat.

—

After Caitlin was gone, still in the hot tub, Boston stared up at the sky, seeing a bright star directly overhead that he recognized as Vega, a familiar object from his backpacking evenings. Out of college, he had hiked through the Sierra alone for several summers before meeting Shannon. They had once spent such a night at a remote hot springs somewhere, sipping wine, staring at the sky, their campsite close by.

That had been a wonderful time for both of them. He was beginning his career where he met the also young, also married civil engineer. Caitlin reminded him of her and yet not quite the same. Boston loved the other woman for several years and had sex with her for just one time before she was gone, evaporated into the Arizona deserts. The thought of having known her made it easy for him to watch Caitlin go back into the house. That time in his life was passed, replaced by something much more tangible. Shannon had given him Serina and Katherine was giving him the rest of his life.

In the late evening silence, he heard a car drive up. The kitchen screen door opened and Katherine walked through it. "Good," she said, "you're still up." She began to undress on the deck. "So, did you make the fifth pass?" Then she caught herself. "Why am I even asking? Of course, you did." He nodded in agreement.

Taking off the last of her clothes, she climbed into the tub. "Did Caitlin make it, too?" she asked, then again stopped him. "Of course, she did also. We passed both of you while you were on the way. Did you see my car?"

"I thought you were going up to Carson."

"We went to South Lake instead. Irina's still there." Boston waited but she did not elaborate. "Where are all the other cars?"

Boston told her of the accident and how everyone went to Carson City, except Erik was having a drink at the Wolf Creek. Katherine responded that she didn't remember seeing his Highlander parked there, but then she wasn't looking for it either.

"That's a shame about Raymond."

"There's something else," he began. Katherine got a sinking feeling. "Larry sold the company. I'm out of a job."

Her chest heaved with relief. "Thank goodness it's over. Are you ok?"

"I guess."

She draped her arms around his neck. "I don't think I've ever seen you so relaxed."

"I've never done the Death Ride before."

Katherine then noticed the bottle of wine and two glasses, one half full and one empty. "I don't suppose you brought out that glass for me."

"It's Caitlin's."

"Oh. Is she inside waiting for you?"

"No," he smiled. "She's inside but probably sound asleep by now."

Taking the bottle, Katherine filled the empty glass and took a big drink. "Are you upset at me for not being here, I mean, not being here earlier to celebrate?" Before he could answer, she continued, "You know I dreaded this whole thing. Thank goodness you survived it."

"Thank you for coming back."

"Of course I came back." She kissed him, not exactly as Caitlin had done, but in her own way. His hands gripped her waist as she moved to sit on his lap, facing him. Her hand reached underwater.

He felt no need to tell her that it was his second erection of the evening. She did not bother to disclose that she had finally put her ex-lover behind her after meeting him yet again in a motel room, although somebody else's this time. Instead, they silently made out under the stars, each touching the other with an easy freedom.

When the bottle was finished, they moved inside to the bedroom to conclude what had been interrupted while they were parked on Carson Pass the day before. Boston discovered that he was not too tired while Katherine was pleased to be in her own bed, at least the one she warmly shared with her husband in the rented cabin.

Upstairs, Caitlin dozed away. She had left the hot tub as she had entered, with only a towel draped over her shoulder. She had tried to stay awake for Bert's arrival but the combination of drinking wine and soaking in warm water didn't take long to put her out. In her last moments of being half-awake, she was glad to at least have had someone's hands all over her. Doing the Death Ride deserved some kind of physical release. Bert could do the rest later and hopefully as soon as possible.

—

Entering the bar at the Wolf Creek Restaurant, Erik found Lyudmila but no Erwin, whom they had dropped off at the Toll Station less than a half hour earlier. Tanya introduced Lyudmila as her friend and also Ukrainian, which of course Erik already knew. Another couple was also in the bar along with a young man and older woman, who judging by their sunburnt faces, had also done the ride.

Erik's attention was on Lyudmila, however. She wore dark eyeshadow and very red lipstick. Her eyes were kept on the door, waiting for her Chicago date. Almost done with her beer, Erik bought her another as well as one for himself. He was eager to learn about her profession but did not know how to approach asking her. Instead, he began telling her about Iceland, which he thought was dumb on his part. However, she didn't seem to mind what he was saying. In a heavy Russian accent, she commented enough for him to know she was listening, at least to some of it. In between serving drinks, Tanya kept an ear on their conversation. She mentioned that Erik had finished this huge bike race but Lyudmila was not really interested.

Finally, Erwin appeared and her expression brightened. Erik bought him a beer and then listened to Erwin tell Lyudmila, and Tanya, when she was close by, all about his ride and how difficult the last pass was. His face was very red with dark circles under his eyes. He drained his beer while recounting the ride and then asked Lyudmila to step outside for a private word. The Ukrainian took her purse along.

A few minutes later she returned with a dejected expression on her face and without Erwin. When Tanya came by, they conversed in Russian. Then Lyudmila just sat there, staring glumly at the wall. Leaning over to quietly explain, Tanya told him that the gentleman informed her friend that he was too tired for a date tonight. He paid her something for her time, but she had taken a cab over tonight and now would have to wait for Tanya to get off work for a ride home.

Erik started to ask where she lived but then he remembered Tanya had said they had an apartment in Carson City. He offered to drive her back and Lyudmila accepted. Done with their beers anyway, they both left in Erik's Toyota Highlander. It occurred to Erik that most young women might have refused a ride from a stranger, but then again, wasn't she a prostitute?

Erik also figured that it might not be good if he were pulled over with such a passenger, although Lyudmila hardly appeared like a common streetwalker, instead being dressed reasonably enough for the Wolf Creek. Once past the traffic commotion at Turtle Rock, his paranoia decreased. Turning on Highway 88 toward Carson City, his was the only car on the road.

Feeling awkward speaking to her about his interest in her profession, he reminded himself that he had just completed the Death Ride and therefore should not be afraid of anything. He remembered his Reykjavik uncle's philosophy that women were all the same woman, just in different forms. The Ukrainian woman was, sitting in the same seat, buckled in the same seat belt that his Russian wife usually occupied. His uncle would have appreciated the juxtaposition. "I actually tried to look you up at the Pigeon Coop," he told her, then immediately worried if that sounded too much like stalking.

"That place is a dump," she replied in her accent, emphasizing *dump*. Erik mentioned that he had only been in two brothels in his life, "Let me guess," she said, smiling, "Iceland." She pronounced it as if it were a description and not just a country, accenting *Ice-Land*.

"I was only fourteen," he told her. "Scared out of my mind. I guess that's the European way."

"That's the way everywhere," she told him. "Of course, not at the Coop. Their license won't allow it."

From that point on, they spoke freely back and forth. When Erik mentioned that his wife was from Moscow, Lyudmila made a face. As he was chuckling, he pulled up to the stoplight intersection where Highway 88 terminated at Highway 35. While waiting, he saw Bert's Silverado go by in the other direction. Then Erik remembered the hospital visit, realizing that Bert and his passengers were returning from visiting Raymond. At first he felt guilty about not going with them, even though Lina had said no visitors, but then feeling more strange about having a Nevada prostitute in the front seat. Perhaps they didn't see him, he thought, but if they did, at least he had done nothing to be guilty about.

Soon they were on the highway rise just above the state capitol, which was still lit up. As he drove into town, Lyudmila directed him to park in the lot of a restaurant, where a few cars remained scattered about. "So," Lyudmila began, "you've come this far. Would you like to do a little business?"

"Business?"

"I've been warned not to have any more men come to my apartment," she told him. "We could go to a motel if you wanted to pay for a room. But you have a nice car here. We could go to the back seat." Saying that, she looked over the seat and then at him. Erik sat there in silence. "You like me, don't you?" she asked him, sliding her miniskirt up a little, her legs opened a little too immodestly.

"This is our family car," he stated.

"And you are a family man, I can tell. What work do you do?"

"I'm a gynecologist."

Her knees immediately pressed closer together. She paused, waiting for a punch line that never came. "Well, doing it in cars is not my first choice anyway. The night is still young in my business. Would you mind taking me out to the Coop? It sounds like you already know the way."

With Irina apparently gone for the night as he was told by Bethy, Erik felt no obligation and no urge to return right away to Markleeville. The drive out of the capital would not be far and for the moment at least, he enjoyed the starry evening with his Nevada Ukrainian prostitute in the front seat, something he would have to undoubtedly keep to himself.

When he finally pulled into the Coop parking lot, she asked him if he wanted to visit a girl. It wouldn't necessarily even have to be her if she wasn't his type, she told him. He said the she definitely was his type but he was going to pass. Under some other circumstances, he would have liked knowing her better. "Well, I don't know what those circumstances would be. I'm a working girl. Thanks for the ride," she said and left the Highlander.

Erik turned his vehicle around, toward Highway 395. He assumed Irina and Katherine had driven to Lake Tahoe. After such a glorious day of bike riding, his felt his evening fizzling out. Considering getting a cup of coffee at a 24-hour convenience store, he instead headed back to Markleeville, sore and tired, avoiding the headlights of the night trucks flowing into Nevada.

Coming upon the intersection to Genoa, he thought about the Lake Tahoe pass that he had biked past earlier in the week. Wanting to see if it was as steep as it looked, he turned right, heading toward the steep mountainside whose rocky slopes shimmered in the pale light of the moon riding across the starlit sky.

Chapter 33

Daggett Pass

Daggett Pass is the name of the Nevada state route that connects between Kingsbury on the Lake Tahoe side and Genoa on the Carson Valley. The pass was named for Charles D. Daggett, an attorney and doctor, who resided in a log cabin at the base of the roadway in a few miles south of Mormon Station, renamed Genoa. Born in Vermont, he moved west in 1851 at age 45, sharing the cabin in Mormon Station. In 1855, he was named Prosecuting Attorney, County Assessor and Tax Collector for Carson City by Judge Orson Hyde, one of the leading Mormons in the area, who also gave Genoa its name. Hyde was also the owner of the first sawmill in the Tahoe basin.

Daggett was Nevada's first resident attorney and also the first tax collector, which is one of the reasons Judge Hyde appointed him and which also distinguished him from the predominantly Mormon citizenry that issued several threats on his life as the Carson Valley residents had never paid taxes before.

In December of that same year, he doctored to health Judge Hyde who had stumbled upon his cabin, exhausted and frostbitten from crossing the pass in the snow. It was the first medical treatment in the state.

Daggett's cabin was at the base of Haines Canyon, now the bottom of the Old Emigrant Road, but then was a pathway known as Georgetown Trail. In 1860, David Denman Kingsbury and John McDonald completed two years of constructing a wagon road from the Lake Tahoe side for which they acquired a territorial franchise a year later. The road cut off 15 miles from Sacramento to Virginia City, due east of Carson City. The Tahoe portion of the road is still called the Kingsbury Grade.

Daggett was one of the forces to help bring statehood to the Nevada portion of the Utah Territory. Nevada was made its own territory in 1861, helping to *ensure that its gold and silver would remain in Union possession. Statehood was achieved on Halloween in 1864 as the Civil War was winding down.*

In the winter of 1968-69, Daggett Pass received 34 feet of snow with a record 14 ½ feet on the ground, both records for Nevada. The top is 7315 feet. The road, Nevada State Route 207, was rerouted a few miles south of the old route to Mottsville, founded by Hiram Motts and his son Israel in 1851.

Daggett Pass was one of the original five Death Ride passes in 1982, along with Luther, Carson, Monitor and Ebbetts. It was closed to the ride in 1984 due to roadwork but returned the next year. Eventually, it was bumped for the second Monitor Climb, although it returned to the ride in 1995 due to a slide closing Ebbetts Pass Road.

Saturday, part 8

As Erik Erikksson drove slowly up the steep grade, he had the sensation of being in an airplane taking off from the flat valley to his right, with his Pathfinder right on the edge of the largely unguarded shoulder. The grassy pastures seemed to spread forever in the late night starlight. The sheer vertical drop to the valley floor increased rapidly. Biking it would be as formidable as the other passes. He wished he had actually taken the time to bike it last Thursday.

He wondered if he could talk Irina into staying one more day, perhaps joining her at wherever she was staying in South Lake Tahoe. Tired as he was, he felt he might try to bike one more pass tomorrow. He remembered Boston's comment that all mountains were part of the same mountain.

After a few switchbacks, the road skated the edge of forests. Erik drove to the summit, located at a junction of roadside businesses closed for the night and adjoining condos. Rather than continue to the developed and well lit lakeside, he chose to turn around and enjoy the midnight glory of the descent. Once the valley came into view, he pulled off onto the shoulder to examine the nocturnal scene stretched before him. Leaving the car running, he walked out onto the road's edge. A slight glow came from Carson City to the north but the pasture land before him was dim and serene.

—

The phone call came in the morning. That Sunday, the group all drove to Carson City. Bert drove Caitlin, Bethy and Carlos in his Silverado truck while Boston and Katherine traveled in their Expedition to the Carson-Tahoe Hospital where Lina was already at Raymond's bedside. Relief about Raymond's improving condition was overwhelmed by the news of Erik's fatal accident as delivered by Irina to Katherine from her South Lake Tahoe motel room.

Boston and Katherine met Irina at the coroner's office in the hospital morgue. Dennis Crowe was with her, having driven her over Daggett Pass in his new car. Told about his visit by Katherine, Boston was not surprised to see him although he was still somewhat unsure about why he was there.

Irina appeared stoic, shocked but not in shock. "He must have been coming to see me," she told Katherine. "How could he even hope to find me?"

"His car was pointed back to Carson City," Katherine reminded her. Upon hearing the news, she and Boston had discussed the evening thoroughly, at least Erik's portion of it. They stopped at Erwin's room at the J Marklee Toll Station. Erwin only told them what he knew, which was he had left Erik with the Ukrainian bartender and her girlfriend before going straight to bed. Erik had made no mention about later going to Lake Tahoe or anywhere else.

The coroner had told Irina that his vehicle had been parked on an outside curve. Another car headed downhill toward Carson City rammed the Pathfinder into a ravine where it slammed into a tree. The victim had actually been outside the car and was thrown down the hillside where his head struck a rock. At first they couldn't figure where the Pathfinder's driver was, as they assumed he'd been in the car when it was struck. But no body was found inside the wreck.

It took a while for Irina to grasp that the Pathfinder had been parked pointed downhill, away from Lake Tahoe. Understanding that, she wondered to Katherine if maybe Erik had discovered her eating dinner with Dennis in South Lake Tahoe, maybe even seen her going back to the motel with him. Katherine dismissed that possibility as well.

Dennis Crowe stayed off to the side, out of the conversations but tacitly agreed that her husband was dead for reasons that nothing to do with either himself or Irina. His focus always returned to Irina Ivanova Erikksson. They had spent a quiet evening together, more peaceful than he had known in a long time. She had seemed reconciled to her marriage breaking up. He had no idea what her husband was doing on that road but he kept reminding himself that Irina had called himself to come to Tahoe and not the other way around.

Early in the morning, she had been woken by a call to her cell phone from her eldest son telling her to contact the Nevada county sheriff's office. Dennis remained in the bed they had shared while, covered with a blanket, she sat in a chair and called first the sheriff's office and then back home, calmly telling her sons about the fatality. On the drive to Carson City, she had not shown any attempt to blame herself. "We never know why these things happen," she told Dennis as he drove.

Debris was still on the road as they had passed by the accident location. Dennis noticed it but said nothing to Irina. Being Sunday, the coroner's officer, a young Native American male, wanted to know if Irina could stay into Monday to complete all the paperwork details. Seeing her abhorrence at spending anymore time there than necessary, Dennis stepped up and asked if they could to the rest by phone. The young officer said certainly and had her sign several papers.

Taking Dennis off to the side, the officer told him that the other driver had been a nineteen-year-old driving a couple buddies into Carson City late at night for probably some fooling around. They were all banged up but not seriously injured. The driver would most likely face charges but did not appear so far to have been under the influence. Dennis thanked him for the information and said that he would pass it on later.

After listening to Katherine, Irina also discounted the idea that Erik would have searched for her in South Lake Tahoe. She asked Boston if Erik had completed the ride. Replying that he had, Boston also recollected that Erik had been fascinated earlier with Daggett Pass. She nodded. "That sounds like Erik to have driven up to explore it. He must have been very happy and proud to have done the Death Ride and was not quite ready to end the day." Then she added, "He could just have easily been killed on the freeway near home." Saying no more except to extend her wishes to Raymond for a recovery, she immediately left for home with Dennis.

Back in the hotel room, the women stayed at Raymond's bedside while the three men went out in the hallway. Once by themselves, Bert spoke to Boston about seeing Erik with the Ukrainian prostitute. "She was the same one whom that Chicago fellow had taken to dinner Friday night. You know, with that bright red hair." Boston commented that it hardly sounded like Erik. "Remember all his talk about brothels," Bert reminded him.

"Maybe he was upset his wife had run off with another man," Carlos added, expressing a dislike of Dennis.

Boston shook his head. "Irina called Dennis while on her way to Tahoe, according to Katherine. As far as Erik knew, Irina was with my wife. That's even what I thought. In fact, she was, at least she was earlier in the evening. Dennis didn't show up until late."

"Should we tell Irina that Erik was not alone?" Bert asked. "Carlos said that he had also seen Erik and the prostitute, as Bethy must have but Carlos told me that she's never mentioned it to him."

Boston summarized, "You both saw him driving a woman, a prostitute. Erwin from Chicago told me that he had cancelled her services for the night and had paid her off. Obviously, she didn't have a car and needed to get back to town somehow. Erik had been curious about her anyway, but not for sex. My thought is that, after giving her a ride, Erik just went up that mountain for the pleasure of doing one more pass, even if it was by car."

"And, between us, what about the Pigeon Coop?" Bert questioned.

"I think his brothel days ended in Iceland. I don't even care to find out."

Katherine came into the hallway with Caitlin, Bethy and Lina. "We're all going out for coffee," she told Boston. "Why don't you guys go give Raymond some male company? He wants to talk about what happened to himself and also to Erik."

Boston nodded. "Ok, but first listen to this. Bert said that he passed Erik near Minden that night, going the other way into Carson City. So, he must not have driven through South Lake Tahoe. I'm staying with my theory that Erik went up Daggett Pass from the Nevada side just for the hell of it and had gotten out of the car for a view."

"Irina accepts that. Should have been the safest place around," Katherine commented.

Chapter 34

Peters Creek

Devils Canyon Creek off Skyline Boulevard was renamed Peters Creek in the 1860s in honor of Jean Peters, a homesteader who lived near headwaters of the creek below the ridge.

October

Three months since completing the Death Ride and Boston felt like most of his extra conditioning was gone already as he reached the top of Page Mill Road on his bike along with Bert and Caitlin. This was his first time up to Skyline Boulevard since the Markleeville ride last July, as it was for the other two.

The three of them turned left on Skyline, descending through the cool October shadows south toward Portola Heights Road. After a couple climbs in sunlight, on the highway they entered through the private gate and began the steep climb to the Pomponio Ridge Road turn to Crowe's.

Bert groaned about the hard work, prompting Caitlin to encourage him with a "Com'on, old man." All three struggled to make the ascent but were then rewarded with a beautiful downhill through the thick forest, glimpsing views of the splendid Devils Canyon on their right. Caitlin was impressed, having never been to Dennis Crowe's before.

Stirring his barbeque as they arrived on his gravel driveway, Dennis greeted the threesome as they dismounted their bikes, leaning them against the shed garage. It was the first time he and Boston had seen each other since meeting at the hospital. He then introduced himself to Caitlin, whom he had not met at the hospital that Sunday morning in July. "Welcome. Got the pool heated up and I just started the fire. You can jump in the water or have a seat by the fire. Soon I'll put the sausages on. I got elk mostly, although also some wild pig plus a little bear. It's all from my Wyoming trip."

"Dennis is a hunter," Boston told her, "as if you couldn't tell."

"I just get away for one trip a year. You want some wine," he asked them, turning toward the house. "Make yourself at home. Hop in the pool if you want. I'll be right down."

As he left, Caitlin began to undress. "You know me," she told the two men. "Never saw a hot tub I could pass up." She headed toward the pool, quickly took off her bike clothes and dipped into the water.

"Excuse me for saying this," Boston said to Bert as they stayed at the barbeque pit, "but it looks like Caitlin tossed her razor away."

Bert laughed. "Still shaves under her arms, but you're right. The funny thing is that she quit shaving right after the Death Ride. I've not asked her about it."

"You're the psychoanalyst. Can't you tell why?"

"I'm not sure. You know what? She wants to move to Southern California to be closer to her daughter, who's turned three."

"What's does that do for your relationship?"

"I'm thinking about moving there with her."

"You're kidding."

"Nope. What's keeping me here anyway? My son and daughter live far away. I have my practice but I also know of a few other psychoanalysts who tell me that there's plenty of business. She's been searching teaching jobs around LA."

Dennis brought down a bottle of wine and a box of glasses. He then returned to his seat by the fire and began pouring.

"Bert's thinking about moving to LA," Boston stated as Dennis handed him a glass.

"I couldn't imagine living there," Dennis told him. "But then, I'm planted here like the trees. Sounds like you two are pretty serious." He lifted up two glasses to Bert. "Good for you. Here, have some wine." Turning toward the pool, he added, "She looks about twenty."

"Twenty-six but as a matter of fact, my kids aren't much younger," Bert replied, taking both glasses. "Anyway, as Boston knows, my daughter Jackie met her and they both took a liking to each other. My son Michael wants to know if she has any available friends."

"If I wasn't tied up at the moment," Dennis responded, "I'd want to know the same thing."

"Honestly, I've come to grips with her age just like I have with bonking on that Death Ride. Truth is, my whole perspective has changed," Bert stated. From the pool, Caitlin called out for her wine. Bert excused himself to join her.

Before anymore was said, Katherine arrived in her Ford Expedition, rolling down the driveway and parking on the edge. Greeting and being greeted in return, she brought out dessert from the car. After pouring her some wine, Dennis took her cake upstairs.

"That water looks pretty inviting, as usual," she said to Boston. "You going in?" Boston said sure and they both went over to the pool, soon undressing and joining Caitlin and Bert.

"Feels perfect," Katherine noted. Glancing at Caitlin, floating across from her, she stated, "Something's different."

"Yes," Caitlin confirmed, waving her hand over her lower belly. "I let it grow back out."

"Welcome to the women's club," Katherine smiled.

"I've had more contact with my daughter these last few months," Caitlin told them. "You know, I had dedicated the Death Ride to my two-year-old daughter Mandy. She's three now." She paused. "We got a card from Lina thanking Bert for taking her to the hospital that night."

"For an ex-bank robber, you're quite a guy," Boston kidded.

"I'm trying," Bert smiled. "Lina wrote that Raymond's back to teaching at Stanford. He's not a hundred-per-cent healed but he's getting around okay, although no biking yet."

Meanwhile, Dennis came back down the stairs, followed by Irina. He began unloading cooked sausages from the grill and slicing them onto a platter while she ventured to the pool. "Hi everyone, sorry I'm late to my own party but I was upstairs working on your plans, Katherine." Neither Bert nor Caitlin had seen her since that Sunday in July, but Boston had told them that she would be there, having heard so from Katherine. After a couple months of separation following the accident, the two had gotten back together.

With nothing on underneath, she took off her housedress and dropped down the ladder, joining the other five. "I never get tired of this pool," she stated.

Dennis brought over the platter of food, passing it to Boston while he began taking off his cowboy boots. "Where's the Spaniard?" he asked.

"In Spain, where else?" Boston said. "Vacationing with Bethy for a month. It's Carlos' first time there since before he was married."

"He's another cradle-robber, isn't he?" Dennis asked, yanking down his jeans.

"No," Bert answered. "She's an old lady of thirty-one." Then he gazed at Dennis. "Something's different about you," he told him. "I know. There's no cloud of smoke around your head."

Dennis entered the water, being the last one to do so. "I gave up pot," he responded. "You can say that I did it in honor of the Icelander. I hardly knew him, not like you guys. You all went to his memorial service. During that evening, I just sat here and decided to quit. One thing doesn't have anything to do with the other, I know, but it means something to me."

"Don't look at me," Irina told them. "For two months, I didn't even see him, didn't talk to him. As far as I knew, he was back with Ophelia."

"She stayed in Washington," Dennis stated. "She got a new teaching job and her grandchild's up there. We had more or less finished out our time together anyway." Taking the bottle of wine, he refilled everyone's glass. "So, what about this bank robbery business?" he asked Bert.

"Yeah," Caitlin perked up. "Are they still looking for you in Hawaii? What's the statute of limitations on that?"

"Five years. You'll have to ask me again next summer," Bert replied with a laugh. Not accepting that, she pleaded with him to elaborate. "Well, let me just say that when I moved there, I was in a bad place mentally and financially. Looking back on it, I can tell I was sort of a prick. Lina had it right. So did my ex-wife. But in the islands, I was also a prick running low on funds. Combine all that with being the adventuresome type and certain scenarios had crossed my mind. But no, I didn't rob any bank."

The group paused. Katherine finally spoke, "Bert, you may turn out ok yet."

Irina then began, "I found out about Erik's last day. As long as we're complementing Bert, he finally told me what he saw that night. I called that bartender Tanya. She called me back after speaking to her friend, the *prostitutka*. All Erik did was drop her off, according to her friend. That sounds like my husband, giving her a ride as if he was taking the babysitter home or something."

The others in the pool sat there, watching her. "You know, we were married a long time but there was much about Erik I really didn't know. Most of the time we were busy chasing after our sons, but also he was very closed up." She then nudged her shoulder toward Dennis. "I use to think this one was closed, too, but now I realize he was just stoned. Of course, I have no idea what really goes on in Wyoming."

She caught Dennis in a big gulp of wine. Wiping his mouth, he told her, "Well, in the old days, not that long ago, maybe even last year in fact, I wouldn't have dropped off any *prostitutka* in front of a cat house with paying first a little visit. Not that I'm proud of being a sporting kind of guy, but that's how it was. Now I'm just a hunter, a straight shooter, pardon the pun. Take my dope but leave me my Wyoming." He glanced around the group. "And my Russian," he added.

Katherine gazed at him. It seemed longer ago than it was that she was his woman on Pomponio Ridge. Irina had asked her a month ago how would feel if she, Irina, contacted Dennis once more. That place where Katherine kept Dennis, the always stoned, always sexy Dennis, was now stored somewhere, like a wedding dress boxed, sealed and never visited. This guy was her woodworker and better than ever at his craft.

Boston had formed a survey company, much smaller than his previous engineering firm but finally making money. He was happier at his work than before the sale while she was now busier than ever with her architecture. Their road ahead, she projected, would be a long one. She felt at ease with that, at least for now, soaking in the pool with friends.

"Boston, any more Death Rides?" Caitlin asked, then quickly turned to Irina. "I'm sorry."

"Don't be," the blonde Russian woman replied. "If Erik had to pick any day to be killed, I think he could not have chosen a better one. Maybe that's the Moscow fatalism in me."

All eyes then turned to Boston. "I thought about Erik while biking up, today. We all spoke at his service so I won't go repeat what we all said then."

"We don't have to bike back, do we?" Bert asked. "I mean, back down the hill? Remember, last year when you started our training right in the middle of our enjoying ourselves? This time, I'm perfectly happy to eat and drink for the rest of the afternoon."

"You softie," Caitlin nudged him. "Actually, I agree. I don't know if I could repeat last year if I wanted to. And don't even think about Bethy signing on again."

"No more biking today," Boston announced, looking around the group in the pool, all naked, standing in the clear water. For a moment, he saw them as strangers, even his own wife, to whom he had only been married now six years. "I don't know if I'll ever go back to Markleeville. I don't know if I'll ever leave Markleeville, either."

Taking Katherine's hand, he gazed over the heads opposite him to the forest beyond and the ocean to the west with its blue haze of horizon.